GOTHIC REFLECTIONS

GOTHIC REFLECTIONS

Narrative Force in Nineteenth-Century Fiction

PETER K. GARRETT

CORNELL UNIVERSITY PRESS

Ithaca and London

First published 2003 by Cornell University Press
First printing, Cornell Paperbacks, 2003

Printed in the United States of America

Library of Congress Cataloging-in-Publication Data

Garrett, Peter K.
  Gothic reflections : narrative force in nineteenth-century fiction / Peter K. Garrett.
      p.   cm.
Includes bibliographical references and index.
   ISBN 0-8014-4156-0 (cloth : alk. paper) — ISBN 0-8014-8888-5 (pbk. : alk paper)
   1. English fiction—19th century—History and criticism.   2. Horror tales, English—History and criticism.   3. Gothic revival (Literature)—Great Britain.   4. American fiction—19th century—History and criticism.   5. Horror tales, American—History and criticism.
6. Gothic revival (Literature)—United States.   7. Narration (Rhetoric)   I. Title.

   PR868.T3G37 2003
   823'.087290908—dc21
                                                                                        2003009978

Cornell University Press strives to use environmentally responsible suppliers and materials to the fullest extent possible in the publishing of its books. Such materials include vegetable-based, low-VOC inks and acid-free papers that are recycled, totally chlorine-free, or partly composed of nonwood fibers. For further information, visit our website at www.cornellpress .cornell.edu.

Cloth printing   10 9 8 7 6 5 4 3 2 1
Paperback printing   10 9 8 7 6 5 4 3 2 1

For Lillian
and for
Colin, Heather, Michael, and Carol

For Lillian
and for
Colin, Heather, Michael, and Carol

Contents

Preface

This book reads nineteenth-century Gothic fiction as a highly self-conscious mode whose writers and readers share an awareness of its stylized conventions and its expected effects of terror, horror, suspense, and other jointly desired disturbances. From its self-consciousness arise the more general reflections on narrative that are my main interest in all the chapters that follow; from its stress on effects I derive my focus on narrative force, not only affective, rhetorical, and ideological force but the dynamics of plotting and that active engagement of readers which makes every narrative a dialogical transaction. Reading Gothic for its reflections on narrative force as I propose should significantly change the current understanding of both Gothic and its place in the larger literary and cultural field of the nineteenth century. Pursuing that approach and exploring its implications will be my concern throughout the book; here I can offer only a preliminary outline of my argument.

After an introduction that uses James's "The Turn of the Screw" to exemplify Gothic self-consciousness and modern narrative theory to explicate conceptions of form and force, I turn to Poe's theory and practice of the Gothic tale as an exercise (or fantasy) of authorial power, imposing "the force of a frame" to concentrate and control the reader's response. I then go back to earlier Gothic, using Poe to frame readings that stress its reflexivity from its inception with Walpole through its later eighteenth-century development in Radcliffe and Lewis and the Romantic versions of Godwin, Maturin, and Hogg before returning to Poe and his reflexive use of doubling. In all these cases I am especially concerned with showing how Gothic fiction typically offers alternative versions of its stories that raise issues of narrative power and authority and how, for all its stress on isolated, often deviant individuals, it also explores their dialogical relations with others through its reflections on narrative as a social transaction.

The next section focuses on the most extreme and memorable cases of deviance, the great nineteenth-century monster stories: *Frankenstein, Dr. Jekyll and Mr. Hyde*, and *Dracula*. Again, narrative self-consciously links the extremity and isolation of these figures with the social groups they confront through the mirroring and antagonism of doubling. As we move from the nested triple narrative of *Frankenstein* to the shifting voices of *Dr. Jekyll and Mr. Hyde* to the assembly of a collective account in *Dracula*, I show how we also move from a Romantic concern with individual creation and responsibility to a Victorian stress on narrative integration that both affirms the value of social solidarity and reveals how much it may depend on the binding force of exclusionary violence.

The final section moves beyond the boundaries of what is usually considered Gothic fiction to show how Gothic infiltrates the more realistic social and psychological representation that predominates in mainstream Victorian fiction. One way I do this is by returning to the form of the Gothic tale, practiced not only by Poe but by Dickens, Eliot, and James, to whom it offered both release from realistic constraints and opportunities for narrative reflection through its formal drama of isolation and community, opportunities they also pursue in their novels. Another way is by investigating the narrative tropes of fate and destiny, Gothic figures that pose general questions about the force of narrative teleology and that play important roles in *Little Dorrit, Daniel Deronda,* and even a novel as far removed from the Gothic as *The Ambassadors*. I conclude by considering further how reading Gothic reflexively can also change our understanding of realism.

These reflections on nineteenth-century Gothic originally formed part of a larger study of narrative reflexivity from the eighteenth century onward. In the many years it has taken to produce this version I have benefited from a great deal of support, advice, and encouragement that I am pleased to be able to acknowledge now. Work on the earliest stages of this project was supported by a fellowship from the American Council of Learned Societies; the Research Board of the University of Illinois later provided crucial support by granting me released time. Several colleagues have read and generously responded to various parts and stages of the manuscript; I am grateful to Amanda Anderson, Nina Baym, David Hirsch, Simon Joyce, Deidre Lynch, Meaghan Morris, Armine Mortimer, Mary Ann O'Farrell, Robert Parker, and Joseph Valente for their comments and suggestions, as well as to the many students who have participated in a long running dialogue in my courses on narrative theory and Gothic fiction. For both incisive criticism and encouragement that led me to recast my earlier, unwieldy scheme in its present form, I am grateful to Willis Regier of the University of Illinois Press. Bernhard Kendler of Cornell University Press and Harry Shaw, who reviewed the manuscript, have both urged and helped me to make my arguments more accessible.

Part of chapter 1 originally appeared in *The Yearbook of English Studies* 26 (1996); part of chapter 5 originally appeared in *Dr. Jekyll and Mr. Hyde after One Hundred Years,* ed. William Veeder and Gordon Hirsch (Chicago: University of Chicago Press, 1988) © University of Chicago, all rights reserved. I am grateful to the publishers for permission to reprint, as well as to William Veeder and Nicola Bradbury for inviting me to contribute. Thanks also to Gillen Wood for helping me find the cover image.

GOTHIC REFLECTIONS

Introduction

From its beginnings Gothic fiction has taken an oppositional stance. "I wrote it in spite of rules, critics, and philosophers," Walpole said of *The Castle of Otranto;* "it seems to me the better for that." It was not, he claimed, written for the present age, "which wants only *cold reason.*"[1] In his preface to the second edition, he stresses his novel's resistance to the constraints of the ordinary, the norms of more realistic fiction in which "the great resources of fancy have been dammed up, by a strict adherence to common life" (7). Much of the appeal of Gothic and its many offshoots from Walpole's time to our own has come from such resistance, from its promise of release from the limitations of cold reason and the commonplace, "leaving the powers of fancy at liberty to expatiate through the boundless realms of invention" (7). Much of the recently increased critical attention to Gothic also dwells on its oppositional force, now given a more political valence. In these accounts its fantastic extremity opposes the middle-class ideology of the mainstream novel's domestic realism; its dark passions and nightmarish scenarios contest Enlightenment rationalism and optimism or destabilize the liberal humanist subject; "female Gothic," with its symbolization of women's oppression, exposes and undermines patriarchy.[2] Sometimes Gothic fiction is credited with deliberate subversion; sometimes it is read symptomatically for the ways its terrors betray

[1] Letter to Mme du Deffand, March 13, 1767, quoted in W. S. Lewis's introduction to Horace Walpole, *The Castle of Otranto: A Gothic Story* (New York: Oxford University Press, 1964), p. x. Subsequent parenthetical page references are to this edition.
[2] For an account that opposes Gothic to realism and the novelistic, see George E. Haggarty, *Gothic Fiction/Gothic Form* (University Park: Pennsylvania State University Press, 1989). For one that stresses Gothic irrationality, see Elizabeth MacAndrew, *The Gothic Tradition in Fic-*

cultural anxieties about sexuality and gender, the menace of alien races or the criminal classes—about whatever threatens the dominant social order or challenges its ideologies. As a mode defined by "excess and transgression," Gothic seems necessarily, essentially opposed to all norms and limits.[3]

Not that such accounts are entirely mistaken: Gothic clearly aims to disturb its readers, and the disturbance it produces can be cognitive or ideological as well as affective, but it is always accompanied by a strong concern for control. Concentrating on opposition can lead us to overlook the remarkable institutional stability of Gothic, its long history of repeating and reworking a restricted set of devices to reproduce similar effects. If this is subversion, it seems rather unthreatening, a well-rehearsed cultural drama that assures a safe experience of transgression. ("Gothic," we might imagine its promotional slogan, "over two centuries of subverting the established order.") Instead of seeking an intellectual equivalent for the thrill of vicarious transgression through still more of such adversarial readings (or reacting against them by asserting their conservative counterparts), we need to locate Gothic disturbance and control within the larger literary and cultural field. Walpole, we should recall, presents his invention as a hybrid, "an attempt to blend the two kinds of romance, the ancient and the modern" (7), which places the opposition of expansive imagination and realistic constraints within his "Gothic Story," not just between it and the prevailing mode. (And if he really believed his age wanted only cold reason, the warm reception of his book and of the imitators that soon followed

tion (New York: Columbia University Press, 1979). On Gothic and liberalism, see David Glover, *Vampires, Mummies, and Liberals: Bram Stoker and the Politics of Popular Fiction* (Durham: Duke University Press, 1996). The concept of "female Gothic" was introduced by Ellen Moers, *Literary Women: The Great Writers* (New York: Doubleday, 1976); it has been extensively developed since, for example in Kate Ferguson Ellis, *The Contested Castle: Gothic Novels and the Subversion of Domestic Ideology* (Urbana: University of Illinois Press, 1989).
[3] See "Introduction: Gothic Excess and Transgression," in Fred Botting, *Gothic* (New York: Routledge, 1996), pp. 1–20. For a recent corrective to the prevailing view of Gothic "subversion," see Chris Baldick and Robert Mighall, "Gothic Criticism," in *A Companion to the Gothic*, ed. David Punter (Oxford: Blackwell, 2000), pp. 209–28. Their alternative, however, is comparably simplified: instead of subverting bourgeois values Gothic fiction endorses them. "Gothic fiction is essentially *Whiggish*" (219), "tamely humanitarian" (227). Similarly, James Watt argues that "despite the aura of subversion that still surrounds the genre as a whole, nearly all the romances which actually called themselves 'Gothic' were unambiguously conservative." *Contesting the Gothic: Fiction, Genre and Cultural Conflict, 1764–1832* (Cambridge: Cambridge University Press, 1999), p. 8. For a survey of other recent participants in the ongoing (and probably irresolvable) debate between subversive and conservative interpretations, see Maggie Kilgour, *The Rise of the Gothic Novel* (London: Routledge, 1995), pp. 8–10.

proved him wrong.) We need to pay more attention to such inward oppositions and the cultural roles they can play.

This book is concerned with the roles Gothic played in the nineteenth century, when the novel became the dominant literary form, particularly with the ways it dramatizes solitary subjectivity under stress. Taking the exceptional figures of heroes, villains, and victims from their eighteenth-century predecessors, taking stories that turn on mysteries and secrets and the preternatural intrusions of ghosts and demons, writers from Godwin to James developed a mode especially suited for representing isolated individuals and extreme experiences. The most distinctive form of this development, from *Caleb Williams* to "The Turn of the Screw," is the first-person narrative: victims' accounts of their ordeals, criminals' confessions, madmen's monologues, whether standing alone in the form of the Gothic tale or embedded in longer narratives. These versions of the tale of terror intensify its inwardness and solicit our participation in their protagonists' experiences of mystery and dread, persecution and obsession, but they also allow and sometimes require us to adopt different, even opposing perspectives. When we question a Gothic narrator's account, suspect him or her of delusion, and try to construct a more probable alternative, we align ourselves with collective norms and consensual realities, enacting in our reading an opposition like those posited between Gothic and its rivals.

Here, as in many other ways we will be examining, Gothic opens an internal dialogue between perspectives, posing alternative versions. The greatest triumphs of nineteenth-century realism, supposedly antithetical, develop similar tensions, introducing Gothic figures and motifs into their panoramic social landscapes to render isolation and vulnerability or guilt. When Dickens introduces the motif of the Ghost's Walk in *Bleak House* and presents Lady Dedlock's suppressed past as a pursuing fate or the Chancery case of Jarndyce and Jarndyce as a family curse, he is drawing on Gothic in this way, as is George Eliot when she presents the nemesis that overtakes Bulstrode in *Middlemarch* or the nightmarish "dream-like strangeness" of Dorothea's honeymoon experience in Rome. In its darkened and monstrous images, Gothic reflects the central nineteenth-century preoccupation with the relation of self and society, which it shares with more realistic fiction, but reflects it in crisis and antagonism, where the self is estranged or abandoned, victimized or victimizing, absorbed in the self-enclosure of madness, the excess of passion, or the transgression of crime. What is more, and more important to stress because it is much less noticed, in allowing us more than one perspective on these extreme situations Gothic also enables self-conscious reflections on the form and function of narrative itself, the individual acts and social transactions through which fiction exerts its force. Developing this less familiar aspect of nine-teenth-century Gothic will be our main concern throughout the following pages, but we can begin with a brief reading of one of the best known ex-amples.

There is a moment in the early stages of James's "The Turn of the Screw" (1898) that raises many of the questions this book pursues. Shaken by her first encounter with the silent stranger she sees standing at the top of the house's tower ("An unknown man in a lonely place is a permitted object of fear to a young woman privately bred"), the governess invokes literary precedents in her first efforts at understanding. "Was there a 'secret' at Bly—a mystery of Udolpho or an insane, unmentionable relative kept in unsuspected confinement?"[4] Recalling *The Mysteries of Udolpho* (1794) and *Jane Eyre* (1847) here is a plausible response for this young woman lately come from the shelter of a Hampshire vicarage, where we may sup-pose reading has filled much of her time; it also develops and darkens her earlier view of Bly, with its "old machicolated square tower," as "a castle of romance . . . such a place as would . . . take all colour out of storybooks and fairy-tales" (645). But at the same time these allusions signal and prompt self-conscious reflections in James and his readers, indicating a ge-nealogy for his Gothic story that stretches back more than a century.

Those reflections can expand to include several aspects of Gothic as a narrative genre and mode, but before beginning to trace their extent I want to stress their characteristic presence. Nineteenth-century Gothic fiction of-ten includes such moments, and even when not explicitly marked, narra-tive self-consciousness regularly infiltrates Gothic writing just as Gothic infiltrates much of the fiction we usually oppose to it as realism. Often in-sinuating, sometimes insisting on such awareness, Gothic becomes the most distinctive way nineteenth-century fiction reflects on its forms and effects, foregrounds its status as fiction, makes us sense the forces of writing and reading that work through and between narratives.

Writing always stems from reading, fiction from earlier fiction, but Gothic makes that process particularly clear in its persistent repetition and reworking of a small set of devices. The motifs of the (possibly) haunted castle and the menaced maiden, for example, already appear in the first "Gothic Story," Walpole's *The Castle of Otranto* (1764), thirty years be-fore Emily St. Aubert's disturbing adventures, and they continue to the pres-ent. One effect of these iterations is to invite us to read the narratives they

[4] Henry James, "The Turn of the Screw," in *Complete Stories 1892–1898* (New York: Li-brary of America, 1996), pp. 653–55.

link as versions of a common story, their figures and situations echoing or reflecting one another. In the perspective opened by the governess's questions, Montoni, the brutal master of Udolpho, might be seen as a purely villainous version of the aggressive masculinity that becomes more complex and attractive (and eventually domesticable) in Rochester, the moody master of Thornfield. James's protagonist already seems to be drawing on the precedent of Brontë's governess story (or at least the Cinderella fantasy it rewrites) in her daydreams just before her disturbing encounter. She thinks that "it would be as charming as a charming story suddenly to meet someone," clearly the handsome, absent master of Bly, who "would appear there at the turn of the path and would stand before me and smile and approve" (652). When in the next moment a male figure does appear, her first shock comes with "the sense that my imagination had, in a flash, turned real. He did stand there!" (652–53). Her second, of course, comes with the realization that she has never seen him before, but the question whether this stranger has an independent reality or has indeed emerged from her imagination will continue to haunt her narrative.

With this apparition, soon identified as the ghost of Peter Quint, James's version of a familiar story takes an uncanny turn. Instead of the charming master we get "his own man," the sinister double dressed in his clothes who has played the villain's role in a different governess's story. Doubling, the production of alternative versions within as well as between narratives, is also prominent in Gothic fiction, another effect of the dynamics of repetition we have begun to trace. In the stories of the governess's predecessors, doubling is significantly linked with the "secrets" she cites. The mystery of the black veil in *Udolpho* is linked with the vanished Laurentini, a figure of uncontrolled female passion who stands as a warning to the heroine. The "insane . . . unmentionable relative kept in unsuspected confinement" in *Jane Eyre*, Bertha Mason Rochester, is a more graphic version whose relation to the heroine is more central and complex: a threatening rival, but also in her madness and rage a monstrous double to the demure governess who eventually takes her place.

Having his protagonist take the place of the threatening demonic other is also the way James marks the process of doubling between her and the ghosts who haunt Bly, again perceived as figures of foul passions. When Quint next appears, at the dining-room window, she rushes out to confront him and, finding him gone, takes his place at the window looking in. As the housekeeper Mrs. Grose enters the room, the governess has "the full image of a repetition of what had already occurred. She saw me as I had seen my own visitant; she pulled up short as I had done; I gave her something of the shock that I had received" (659). A similar switch occurs with the ghost of her "terrible, miserable" predecessor Miss Jessel, whom she has seen from above sitting on the steps, "her body half-bowed and her head, in an attitude of woe, in her hands" (686). Later, "tormented, in the hall, with difficulties and obstacles, I remember sinking down at the foot of the staircase—suddenly collapsing there on the lowest step and then, with a revulsion, recalling that it was exactly where more than a month before in the darkness of the night and just so bowed with evil things, I had seen the spectre of the most horrible of women" (704). Her revulsion and epithets betray an unacknowledged sense of their affinity, confirmed the next moment when she encounters her "vile predecessor" seated at her table in the schoolroom. Before she disappears, Miss Jessel "had looked at me long enough to appear to say that her right to sit at my table was as good as mine to sit at hers. While these instants lasted I had the extraordinary chill of a feeling that it was I who was the intruder" (705).

That chill, the disorienting effect of substitution and reversal, can also grip the reader who observes the doubling of the governess and her spectral antagonists and is left uncertain whether she is heroically opposed or becoming equivalent to them in attempting to "get hold" of the children. Like the tale's more notorious uncertainty about the reality of the ghosts, it arises from the typically Gothic multiplication of narrative versions, projecting rival readings that struggle for interpretive mastery.[5] The contentious reception of "The Turn of the Screw" has made its potential for provoking such struggles unusually clear, but they arise in most Gothic fiction as it deploys its narrative forces of disturbance and control. The disturbing, exciting mysteries of Udolpho, like those of Thornfield, eventually receive natural explanations, while in Otranto, as in many of its successors, they are assigned otherworldly origins. But in either case, as well as in narratives like James's that hesitate between these alternatives, something more than the reality of the preternatural is at stake.[6] As a post-Enlightenment genre, Gothic deploys mysteries and their possible explanations as plotting devices that allow it to explore relations between extremity and the ordinary, between "privately bred" isolated subjectivities and public

---

[5] Psychoanalytic readings that consider the ghosts as hysterical projections of the governess's unacknowledged desires can be seen to continue the process of doubling already at work in the tale's Gothic genealogy. For an extended discussion of how such interpretations engage in efforts to control meaning that double those of the governess, see Shoshana Felman, "Turning the Screw of Interpretation," in *Literature and Psychoanalysis: The Question of Reading: Otherwise* (Baltimore: Johns Hopkins University Press, 1982), pp. 94–207.

[6] In Tzvetan Todorov's analytic scheme, these three possibilities are "the uncanny," "the marvelous," and "the fantastic." See *The Fantastic: A Structural Approach to a Literary Genre*, trans. Richard Howard (Ithaca: Cornell University Press, 1975).

norms, engaging readers as well as characters in a drama of knowledge whose resolution is seldom complete.

To extend our sense of the range of possibilities that drama allows, we could add another text to the genealogy, another version of the repeated scenario that joins an inexperienced young woman with a mysterious old building. Austen's *Northanger Abbey* (1818) first stimulates and then disciplines Catherine Morland's imagination, as her infatuation with Gothic fiction leads her to suspect a dreadful "secret" at Northanger, the imprisonment or murder of Mrs. Tilney. Humiliated by Henry Tilney's reproaches ("Dearest Miss Morland, what ideas have you been admitting?"), she is "completely awakened" from "the visions of romance" and forced to recognize the disparity between fiction and reality. "Charming as were all Mrs. Radcliffe's works, and charming even as were the works of all her imitators, it was not in them perhaps that human nature, at least in the midland counties of England, was to be looked for."[7] Her transition from "the alarms of romance" to "the anxieties of common life" (203) assimilates her imagination to the norms of the probable and leads to her social assimilation in marriage.[8]

Against this effect of normalization, we could set the extraordinary final, undisclosed secret of *Jane Eyre*. Unlike the publicly exposed, naturally explained secret of Thornfield, the pivotal moment of telepathic communication between Jane and Rochester remains private and receives both natural and supernatural explanations. When she hears Rochester calling her, Jane rejects any preternatural account. "'Down superstition!' I commented. . . . 'This is not thy deception, nor thy witchcraft: it is the work of nature. She was roused and did—no miracle—but her best.'"[9] Later, however, when Rochester reveals that he did indeed call out to her and heard her reply, the moment takes on for her "the deeper shade of the supernatural" (472). At both points, this uncanny experience confers decisive power. Intervening when Jane is on the verge of yielding to St. John Rivers and sacrificing personal fulfillment to the claims of duty, it leads to a sharp reversal. "I broke from St John, who had followed, and would have detained me. It was *my* time to assume ascendancy. *My* powers were in play and in force. I told him

[7] Jane Austen, *Northanger Abbey* (Harmondsworth: Penguin, 1972), pp. 200–202.
[8] Henry's reproaches indicate the relation of realistic norms and social discipline. "Consult your own understanding, your own sense of the probable, your own observation of what is passing around you—Does our education prepare us for such atrocities? Do our laws connive at them? Could they be perpetrated without being known in a country like this, where social and literary intercourse is on such a footing; where every man is surrounded by a neighbourhood of voluntary spies, and where roads and newspapers lay everything open?" (200–201).
[9] Charlotte Brontë, *Jane Eyre* (Harmondsworth: Penguin, 1966), p. 445.

to forbear question or remark; I desired him to leave me: I must and would be alone. He obeyed at once" (445). It also marks her final ascendancy over Rochester, who has been punished for his earlier attempts to dominate her.[10] When he tells his version of their mysterious communication, she withholds hers. "I listened to Mr Rochester's narrative, but made no disclosure in return. The coincidence struck me as too awful and inexplicable to be communicated or discussed. If I told anything, my tale would be such as must necessarily make a profound impression on the mind of my hearer: and that mind, yet from its sufferings too prone to gloom, needed not the deeper shade of the supernatural. I kept these things, then, and pondered them in my heart" (472). Deciding between an enlarged conception of nature and a more orthodox supernaturalism is less important here than recognizing how both empower and sanction an exceptional private subjectivity, a position of narrative privilege we are invited to share: "Reader, it was on Monday night—near midnight—that I too received the mysterious summons."[11]

In the multiplying reflections that branch out from our starting point we can begin to recognize the psychosocial forces that work through Gothic mysteries and secrets. Although it often intensifies the extraordinary chill Gothic aims to produce, we do not need the deeper shade of the supernatural to register and participate in the impulses of incorporation and exclusion, exaltation and abjection that drive these narratives. As in its precursors, those impulses are densely interwoven in "The Turn of the Screw"; the possibilities for considering the governess "a remarkable young woman"[12] and those for considering her monstrous, a victim of the fate that threatens whoever fights monsters, are mutually dependent.[13] As nineteenth-century Gothic fiction repeatedly finds ways to remind us, these competing versions are themselves effects of narrative, the psychosocial

[10] "I did wrong: I would have sullied my innocent flower—breathed guilt on its purity: the Omnipotent snatched it from me. I, in my stiff-necked rebellion, almost cursed the dispensation: instead of bending to the decree, I defied it. Divine justice pursued its course" (471). Rochester's recognition of "the hand of God in my doom," his remorse, repentance, and tentative prayers appear in his narrative as the preconditions for his telepathic communication and reunion with Jane.

[11] Jane's identification with Mary, who "kept these things and pondered them in her heart" after the shepherds reported the angel's announcement of Christ's birth (Luke 2.19), intensifies her implied claim to uniquely exalted status.

[12] "I dare say I fancied myself, in short, a remarkable young woman and took comfort in the fact that this would more publicly appear. Well, I needed to be remarkable to offer a front to the remarkable things that presently gave their first sign" (652).

[13] "Whoever fights monsters should see to it that in the process he does not become a monster." Friedrich Nietzsche, *Beyond Good and Evil,* trans. Walter Kaufmann (New York: Vintage Books, 1966), p. 89.

transaction of telling and receiving stories. As the governess tells of her encounter with the stranger on the tower, she adds, "So I saw him as I see the
letters I form on this page" (654). Does this shift to the scene of writing, to
the moment of narration many years after the events of the story, suddenly
distance us just as the plot is beginning to thicken? Does it undercut the
representational claims of the narrative, exposing it as a written artifact and
so loosening its grasp on us? Few readers are likely to respond in such ways.
We may in retrospect feel uncertainty about whether the governess has
"formed" the apparition as well as the letters; we may even feel a chill in
recognizing the phantasmal presence shared by ghosts and fictions, but
these responses intensify rather than disrupt our fascinated involvement.[14]

Like the literary allusions the governess makes just a few lines later, this
reminder of her role as a writer not only evinces Gothic self-consciousness
but helps us understand what distinguishes it from more familiar kinds. Di-
verting attention to dramatized narrational performances, the typically
comic self-consciousness of metanarrative reflexivity, of Shandyism in either its eighteenth-century or its postmodern versions, defamiliarizes narrative with its playful disruptions of continuity and ironic subversions of
representation. Gothic reflections work differently, in part because the uncanny events and effects of Gothic already estrange us from the familiar;
their reflexivity is always linked with the problematic relations of subjectivity and the social, their self-consciousness always in tension with the
forces of the unconscious.[15] It is largely owing to the predominance of the
Shandean model that we have failed to recognize how Gothic offered nineteenth-century fiction an alternative mode of narrative reflection, and that
the nineteenth century has seemed to put "the self-conscious novel in
eclipse."[16]

[14] On affinities between ghosts, fictions, figuration, and other aspects of literariness in James,
see T. J. Lustig, *Henry James and the Ghostly* (Cambridge: Cambridge University Press, 1994).
For a more general discussion, see Julian Wolfreys, *Victorian Hauntings: Spectrality, Gothic,
the Uncanny, and Literature* (New York: Palgrave, 2002).
[15] Like other modal and generic oppositions this book considers, such as Gothic romance and
realism or the tale and the novel, the opposition between Shandean and Gothic self-consciousness begs to be deconstructed. As we shall have several occasions to see, Gothic can be
highly playful, and a complementary study of Shandyism could foreground the role of anxiety and dread. Consider, for instance, the thematic prominence and formal resonance of cas-
tration in Sterne's *Tristram Shandy*, Rushdie's *Midnight's Children*, and Barthes's *S/Z*. I return
to the relation between Shandean and Gothic reflexivity below.
[16] This is the title of the chapter on the nineteenth century in Robert Alter, *Partial Magic: The
Novel as a Self-Conscious Genre* (Berkeley: University of California Press, 1975). For Alter,
nineteenth-century realism interrupts the lineage that runs from Cervantes to Sterne and
Diderot until it is revived in modernism and postmodernism. The problem persists in a more
recent work, Jeffrey J. Williams, *Theory and the Novel: Reflexivity and the British Tradition*

What Gothic most often reflects on is the sense of narrative *force,* the force of the desire to disturb and to be disturbed that joins tellers and their audiences and the counterforces that seek to control disturbance, the force of destiny that overwhelms characters, the force of repetition that generates multiplying versions. Narrative force is the starting point for "The Turn of the Screw," the concern of its opening words: "The story had held us, round the fire, sufficiently breathless" (635). Like the frames of many other Gothic tales, James's opening situates its narrative as a social transaction, motivated here by the custom of offering "a strange tale" to fellow guests in an old house at Christmas. Proposed in competition with the one just completed, advertised as never told before and as being "beyond everything . . . for dreadful—dreadfulness! . . . for general uncanny ugliness and horror and pain" (636), the tale gains added power from its hearers' forced anticipation as they wait for the manuscript to arrive. These opening moves clearly aim at producing a similar anticipation in the reader, but they also open up reflections on the production, transmission, and consumption of "dreadful" narratives on a larger scale. The face-to-face exchange of such tales in a small, privileged social group is quite different from the actual reception of "The Turn of the Screw," either at the time of its publication, when it became James's most popular work since "Daisy Miller," or now, when it continues to be widely reprinted and recast in other media. As we have already seen, he locates his tale in a genre first made popular by Radcliffe and all her imitators in a vogue that, as we can recognize even more clearly after another century, was an important early moment in the commodification of affect that has since become a vast global industry.[17] Like several other writers of nineteenth-century Gothic fiction, James displays an uneasy sense of his relation to this popular form, fascinated by the power it offers but anxious to distinguish his from more debased versions.

Both the frame narrative and the governess's reflect this anxiety, which

---

(Cambridge: Cambridge University Press, 1998). In addition to instances of eighteenth-century comic self-consciousness (*Tristram Shandy* and *Joseph Andrews*), Williams also considers *Wuthering Heights,* "The Turn of the Screw," and *Heart of Darkness* but not as instances of nineteenth-century Gothic. Instead, his attention remains focused on the ways these texts foreground narration, while his account fluctuates between deconstruction and an ideological critique that assigns reflexivity the role of literary self-promotion.

[17] Austen, in her affectionately ironic account of Gothic fiction as a cultural commodity, acutely represents Catherine as a consumer, eagerly receiving reading recommendations from Isabella Thorpe ("But are they all horrid, are you sure they are all horrid?" [*Northanger Abbey,* p. 61]) and thoroughly enjoying the disturbing sensations such reading offers when she is "left to the luxury of a raised, restless, and frightened imagination over the pages of Udolpho" (72). It is this artificial "craving to be frightened" (201) that leads to her humiliating blunders at Northanger.

implicates readers as well as writers, in their accounts of seduction. When Mrs. Grose tells about Miss Jessel's degrading relations with Quint, who "did what he wished" with her, the governess replies, "It must have been also what *she* wished" (673). If this holds as well for the disturbing power of Gothic, does our yielding response subject us to something, like Quint, "so dreadfully below"? The exchanges in the frame between the first narrator and Douglas work to deflect this fear. When Douglas says he is sure the governess never told anyone before about her terrible experience at Bly, he adds, "You'll easily judge why when you hear."

> "Because the thing had been such a scare?"
> He continued to fix me. "You'll easily judge," he repeated: "*you* will."
> I fixed him too. "I see. She was in love."
> He laughed for the first time. "You *are* acute." (637)

A few lines later someone else asks, "Who was it that she was in love with?"

> "The story will tell," I took upon myself to reply.
> "Oh, I can't wait for the story."
> "The story *won't* tell," said Douglas; "not in any literal, vulgar way."
> "More's the pity, then. That's the only way I ever understand."

Inviting us to identify with the "acute" narrator and distance ourselves from those capable of only a "literal, vulgar" understanding of "love" prepares us for Douglas's "few words of prologue" about the governess's interview with the master. Struck by "such a figure as had never risen, save in a dream or old novel, before a fluttered, anxious girl out of a Hampshire vicarage" (639), she agrees to his demanding conditions, "she faced the music, she engaged."

> And Douglas, with this, made a pause that, for the benefit of the company, moved me to throw in—
> "The moral of which was of course the seduction exercised by the splendid young man. She succumbed to it."
> He got up and . . . stood a moment with his back to us. "She only saw him twice."
> "Yes, but that's just the beauty of her passion."
> A little to my surprise, on this, Douglas turned round to me. "It *was* the beauty of it." (641)

The beauty of this sublimated, self-sacrificing love separates it from grosser passions, just as James and his readers might wish to separate themselves from grosser forms of narrative seduction. But in seeking "the kind of emotion on which our hopes were fixed," joining the "hushed little circle," "subject to a common thrill," to which Douglas reads, "with immense effect," the governess's manuscript (638), we can recognize the affinities between acute and vulgar responses or elite and popular versions of Gothic, just as the unfolding story, though it may not "tell in any literal, vulgar way," will lead us to recognize the doubling between the seductions of the two governesses.[18]

We are close here to where we began. It is the governess's idealized passion, her fantasy of the master's smiling, approving face that sets the stage for the apparition of Quint and the questions about secrets that formed our starting point. The questions that moment raises in turn about Gothic reflections on narrative force could be extended further, but they also require us to draw on other contexts besides those "The Turn of the Screw" provides. The approach we have been following so far, drawing out issues and terms from a chosen narrative moment, will be important throughout the following chapters, but we also need to develop a more general understanding of the conception of narrative force that figures so prominently in nineteenth-century Gothic fiction. To do so will lead us away for a while from both Gothic and the nineteenth century, considering the more systematic reflections on narrative developed in modern theories. What is at stake there will inform all our readings of Gothic as a reflexive mode.

We can begin, however, by considering the relation between the first and last moments of James's tale, which both involve holding and being held. If the opening ("The story had held us . . . ") speaks of the way narrative can grasp its audience and of the audience's cooperating desire, the closing confronts us with an effort to grasp that overwhelms resistance yet fails, as Miles, frantic at being unable to see Quint, "uttered the cry of a creature hurled over an abyss, and the grasp with which I recovered him might have been that of catching him in his fall. I caught him, yes, I held him—it may be imagined with what a passion; but at the end of a minute I began to feel what it truly was that I held. We were alone with the quiet day, and his little heart, dispossessed, had stopped" (740). Shocking in its violent extremity, this abrupt conclusion leaves us also alone with its final image,

---

[18] The frame also offers an ironic slant on the tension between high and low as Douglas reports the master's account of the former governess, "a most respectable person," and the situation at Bly after "the great awkwardness" of her death, leaving Mrs. Grose in charge, with "a cook, a housemaid, a dairywoman, an old pony, an old groom, and an old gardener, all likewise thoroughly respectable." At this point someone asks, "And what did the former governess die of?—of so much respectability?" (640).

never returning to the framing scene of narration. We may find in it a reflection of our own baffled effort to grasp the tale, in which the struggle to master disturbance is itself disturbingly represented. The desire for complete possession ("What does he [Quint] matter now, my own?" the governess triumphantly exclaims to Miles. "*I* have you") is dispossessed of its object, its object dispossessed of life.

How should we understand the relation between these two versions of force? We might well stress their differences, contrasting a scene of interchange that despite all its tensions depends on mutual desire with one in which the will of one individual is violently imposed on another, setting up an opposition between seduction and rape. But recalling the equivocal sense that seduction has acquired, we might also begin to question this opposition, seeing a difference only between veiled and open forms of coercion. The final scene, unlike the first, is not openly concerned with narrative, but in the light of the tale's self-consciousness it raises troubling questions about the exercise of power by authors and readers, and by narrative itself.

Those questions, and the figures of grasping through which they are posed, return on a larger scale in modern theories of narrative form—return, indeed, to haunt them. The developments that began with James's Prefaces to the New York Edition and the work of the Russian Formalists culminated in the grand ambitions of structuralist narratology and its various continuations, whose theoretical models aim at a conceptual grasp of narrative as a universal structure. From the vantage of earlier reflections these developments can be seen not as an advance in our understanding of narrative but as a lapse, which is also how Derrida suggests structuralism may appear to later historians. "In the future it will be interpreted, perhaps, as a relaxation, if not a lapse, of the attention given to *force*. . . . *Form* fascinates when one no longer has the force to understand force from within itself."[19] We now inhabit that future, at least in the widespread deprecation of "formalism" and perhaps in a greater understanding of force.[20] But

[19] Jacques Derrida, "Force and Signification," in *Writing and Difference,* trans. Alan Bass (Chicago: University of Chicago Press, 1978), p. 4. Derrida's essay first appeared in 1963 as a response to Jean Rousset's *Forme et Signification.*

[20] Derrida's indictment reappears in Peter Brooks's preface to *Reading for the Plot: Design and Intention in Narrative* (New York: Knopf, 1984), p. xiv, where it signals Brooks's intention "to move beyond . . . the various formalisms that have dominated the study of narrative in recent decades." For Brooks, "narratological models are excessively static and limiting," neglecting the "temporal dynamics" and "play of desire" that drive narrative (xiii). His study represents a general reorientation that took place in the 1980s; another, exactly contemporary example is Ross Chambers's *Story and Situation: Narrative Seduction and the Power of Fiction* (Minneapolis: University of Minnesota Press, 1984), which stresses the inadequacy of

we should hesitate before accepting an exclusive opposition between "form" and "force," especially when deployed by Derrida, who has persistently taught us to question such hierarchical binaries. We should likewise question the commonplace polemical use of "formalism," which has for a long time distorted the history of narrative reflection.

Today as throughout its history in literary studies, "formalism" figures mainly as an accusation, an indictment of theory or practice for isolating texts from their contexts and neglecting their social or political functions, their cultural force. In such simplified versions, formalism and formalists serve as their critics' imaginary playmates, straw figures that, like the skeptic or the solipsist, offer easy targets for critique or refutation.[21] And like the skeptic or the solipsist, the formalist is marked not only by intellectual but by moral error, an irresponsible withdrawal into the self-enclosure of aesthetic states or objects, a failure to engage with the world, a refusal of history. Such charges may be aimed at imaginary opponents, but they gain their force from real anxieties, seeking a scapegoat for the threat of solipsism that attends any effort of the imagination. Gothic fiction, with its pervasive figures of confinement, exploits and struggles with those anxieties, as we shall see in a series of instances ranging from Poe's claustrophobic fantasies to the social panoramas of Victorian realism. We likewise need to think about formalism as an imaginative impulse, not a mistaken doctrine but a fascination with form, where the driving force is not fear but desire, the search for the intrinsic.

To trace the erratic course of that desire, and to see how it complicates the opposition of form and force, we need only look at one crucial early text in the history of modern Anglo-American narrative theory, Percy Lubbock's *The Craft of Fiction* (1921). Lubbock's influential codification of James's Prefaces has often been held responsible for reducing the diversity

---

"analysis of narratives in terms of their supposed internal relations alone" and maintains that "narrative is most appropriately described as a transactional phenomenon" (8). From the way the motifs of "seduction" and "power" have already figured in this book, it should be clear that I share these views. Whether Brooks, Chambers, or any of their successors (including myself) who also focus on narrative dynamics and transactions have actually moved "beyond formalism" is another question. For a more recent account of narrative force that locates its roots in Nietzsche's will to power and notes, in addition to Derrida, other poststructuralist versions in Deleuze and Lyotard, see Andrew Gibson, *Towards a Postmodern Theory of Narrative* (Edinburgh: Edinburgh University Press, 1996), pp. 32–68.

[21] On the role of "the relativist . . . the solipsist, the skeptic, and the moral nihilist" as "the Platonist or Kantian philosopher's imaginary playmates," see Richard Rorty, *Consequences of Pragmatism* (Minneapolis: University of Minnesota Press, 1982), p. 167. Traditionally, of course, it is the *anti*formalist who is accused of relativism and moral nihilism because of his denial of intrinsic meaning.

of Jamesian theory and practice to narrow prescriptions. For Wayne Booth, attempting forty years later to shift critical attention from restrictive conceptions of form to rhetorical and ethical force, Lubbock is the leading instance of this schematization, in which a wide range of issues are "reduced to the one thing needful: a novel should be made dramatic."[22] When we return to *The Craft of Fiction,* however, and read its first sentence, we find that what is for Booth a question of authority is for Lubbock a question of desire. "To grasp the shadowy and fantasmal form of a book, to hold it fast, to turn it over and survey it at leisure—that is the effort of a critic of books, and it is perpetually defeated."[23] With its figures of grasping and phantasms, Lubbock's opening is closer to the uncertainties of "The Turn of the Screw" than to any confidently prescriptive doctrine, and like James's governess he discovers that what he seeks to hold eludes him.

Lubbock's investigation of fictional craft offers its own strange narrative, a story of reading. It tells us that to be fascinated by form is to be engaged in a compelling but impossible project that leads to a troubling encounter with the figurative status of critical knowledge and a recognition that reading creates its own object. His initial problem is familiar: no matter how intently we read and reread, we can never grasp an extended narrative as a simultaneous whole. "Nothing, no power, will keep a book steady and motionless before us so that we may have time to examine its shape and design" (1). Already with these figures of holding and seeing, narrative is imagined as if it had an objective, spatial form, an intrinsic shape and design with sharply demarcated boundaries. Lubbock's account is remarkable for the way it both ignores and recognizes its dependence on figuration, both asserts and denies the possibility of grasping narrative form. He proclaims that "a novel is a picture, a portrait," possessing "form, design, composition" like "any other work of art" (9), yet a page later he will admit that "applied to the viewless art of literature" such notions are "only metaphors" (10–11). A "book" for Lubbock is not the physical volume

---

[22] Wayne C. Booth, *The Rhetoric of Fiction* (Chicago: University of Chicago Press, 1961), p. 24.

[23] Percy Lubbock, *The Craft of Fiction* (New York: Viking, 1957), p. 1. Lubbock seems to have received little attention after Booth's critique and the ascendance of structuralist narratology, but he reappears prominently in Dorothy J. Hale, *Social Formalism: The Novel in Theory from Henry James to the Present* (Stanford: Stanford University Press, 1998). Hale's conception of social formalism is capacious, including not only James and Lubbock as proponents of "the formalist vision of the novel" but also Booth, the structuralism of Genette and Barthes, Bakhtin's dialogism, and current identity studies. While her original and astute account of all these writers and schools continues the unexamined pejorative use of "formalism," she also effectively challenges the claims of several critics and theorists to have passed beyond it.

("the real book . . . is to the volume as the symphony is to the score" [2]); it is "an ideal shape, with no existence in space, only to be spoken of in figures and metaphors" (22). But he nevertheless affirms that when the critical reader's work is properly done, "we look back at the whole design," and "with the book in this condition of a defined shape, firm of outline, its form shows for what it is indeed . . . the book itself as the form of the statue is the statue itself" (24).

As the best hope for achieving this total grasp of form, Lubbock concentrates on the novelist's "craft," whose artistic materials are "the forms in which a story may be told" (20). This is the part of his story that has been best remembered, the systematic search through successive narrative techniques until he arrives at his climactic recognition. "The whole intricate question of method, in the craft of fiction, I take to be governed by the question of the point of view—the question of the relation in which the narrator stands to the story" (251). Here the figures and project of vision are transferred from the critical reader to the narrative itself; we envision the form of this "viewless art" by understanding narration as seeing, its various methods as visual modes: "panoramic," "scenic," or "pictorial." If Lubbock had simply claimed that these analytic terms enable us to grasp narrative form as a simultaneous whole, he would offer only a striking case of aesthetic hallucination. But the conclusion of his story instead returns to where he began: "And after all it is impossible—that is certain; the book vanishes as we lay hands on it" (273). The "shape," if not the design, of *The Craft of Fiction* emerges as a continual rhythm of forgetting and recalling that the very notion of narrative form is figurative, an imaginary object, as Lubbock alternates between dreams of ideal totality and rueful awareness that "the shadowy and fantasmal form" has vanished again.

This alternation, the perpetual renewal and defeat of the effort to grasp narrative form, is what remains interesting in Lubbock. His main project, like that of James, from whom he takes his spatializing visual figures, now seems remote and limited. Like James's artist, transforming the fluidity and excess of "life" through "the sublime economy of art," Lubbock's critical reader transforms the passive experience of narrative as "a moving stream of impressions" with its "lapse and flow" into something "existing in the condition of an immobile form, like a pile of sculpture" (14–15).[24] Both contribute to the modernist conversion of the novel from a popular to a

---

[24] For James's account of the artist as "the modern alchemist," see especially the preface to *The Spoils of Poynton,* in Henry James, *The Art of the Novel: Critical Prefaces* (New York: Scribner's, 1934), pp. 119–23. It is the close analogy between the artist's and the critic's transformations of experience that allows Lubbock to claim that "the reader of a novel—by which I mean the critical reader—is himself a novelist" (17).

high art form that demands sophisticated appreciation. Stressing technique and the transformation of evanescent experience into objectified, enduring value, they offer less a general theory of narrative than a rationale for a historically circumscribed fictional practice. What makes Lubbock's version of this aesthetic program particularly telling and compelling is his repeated reluctant recognition that it is impossible.

Lubbock plays the role of the Jamesian "form-lover," but he performs it in an instructively ironic mode of frustrated desire.[25] Insisting, in spite of his wishes, on the necessary failure of the effort to grasp form, he testifies to narrative force. The troubling refusal of a narrative to stay still in the mind is an instance of forces at work whenever we read, amplified in shifting and competing readings produced over time like the contending interpretations of "The Turn of the Screw" and leading us to sense the contingency of apparently intrinsic formal features, meanings, and values.[26] All of these are subject to the changes and chances of rereading, our own and others', to the retellings that multiply versions, the dialogical exchanges and negotiations that sustain the social and historical life of narratives. We should not, however, be too quick to affirm contingency and multiplicity as if they were themselves positive values, or disavow too easily the errors of formalism. To read a text as narrative, or fiction, or literature necessarily involves us in an effort to grasp phantasms (or an experience of being grasped by them), as if those terms denoted intrinsic properties, and in the case of narrative we can hardly read at all without granting a measure of objectivity to its represented content. The psychosocial forces that sustain narratives not only multiply and disperse but conserve and constrain them, so that to follow a story requires us to accept some of its features as fixed. We may never agree about the reality of the ghosts in "The Turn of the Screw," and some of the continuing force of the tale may depend on such irreducible

[25] See James's discussion of his method of "dramatic objectivity" in *The Awkward Age,* gained by renouncing the narrative privilege of "going behind." "Something in the very nature, in the fine rigour, of this special sacrifice (which is capable of affecting the form-lover, I think, as really more of a projected form than any other) lends it moreover a coercive charm; a charm that grows in proportion as the appeal to it tests and stretches and strains it, puts it powerfully to the touch." *Art of the Novel,* p. 111.

[26] A comparable effect appears in the development of Russian Formalism as it attempted to specify the intrinsic nature of literariness. "The paradox at the heart of the Formalists' endeavour was that the more they pursued this object, the more it receded from view. For they were forced, by the logic of their own researches, to call into question the assumption that there existed a fixed and stable body of texts which might be regarded as 'literature.' In Formalist parlance, the question as to whether a given text should be described as 'literary' could be resolved only with reference to the function it fulfilled. And that, so it turned out, obliged the Formalists to take account of considerations that were inescapably and radically historical." Tony Bennett, *Formalism and Marxism* (London: Methuen, 1979), p. 50.

ambiguities, but we can hardly question that Miles dies at the end. The moment in which the governess fails in imposing her grasp is also one where the narrative exerts its grasp on us.

Such restrictive force, which we can sense in the basic, defining capacity of narrative to represent determinate sequences of events, can provoke very different reflections from those we have just been considering. For an exemplary source of such reflections, an antagonist and double to Lubbock's form-lover, I want to turn briefly to Roland Barthes. Throughout his career, Barthes displays a resolute suspicion of narrative form that contains its own kind of fascination. Instead of focusing on the mediating techniques of narration, however, he is chiefly concerned with narrative linearity, which he consistently views as limiting and deceptive. This concern is evident in Barthes's earliest criticism, well before his involvement with structuralist narratology, and it persists long afterward. In his first book, *Writing Degree Zero* (1953), narrative causality and teleology are indicted for falsifying existence, violating the openness of temporality. "The Novel is a Death; it transforms life into destiny, a memory into a useful act, duration into an orientated and meaningful time."[27] His "Introduction to the Structural Analysis of Narratives" (1964) expands this challenge to the authority of all narrative sequences. "Everything suggests, indeed, that the mainspring of narrative is precisely the confusion of consecution and consequence, what comes *after* being read in narrative as what is *caused by*; in which case narrative would be a systematic application of the logical fallacy denounced by Scholasticism in the formula *post hoc, ergo propter hoc*—a good motto for Destiny, of which narrative all things considered is no more than the 'language.'"[28] By the time of his most ambitious study of narrative, *S/Z* (1970), the problem has been redefined in semiotic terms as he distinguishes the effects of the five codes that constitute the "classic text" of Balzac's "Sarrasine." Of these, the proairetic code of actions and the hermeneutic code of enigmas are strictly sequential and so more constrained than the others, whose elements do not follow any necessary order. Barthes stresses that "*it is precisely this constraint which reduces the*

27 Roland Barthes, *Writing Degree Zero,* trans. Annette Lavers and Colin Smith (Boston: Beacon Press, 1970), p. 32. Barthes's critique clearly draws on the authority of Sartrean existentialism. See, for example, Sartre's Roquentin on the specious effects of retrospective narrative significance: "Things happen one way and we tell about them in the opposite sense. You seem to start at the beginning: 'It was a fine autumn evening in 1922. I was a notary's clerk in Marommes.' And in reality you have started at the end. It was there, invisible and present, it is the one which gives to words the pomp and value of a beginning." Jean-Paul Sartre, *Nausea,* trans. Lloyd Alexander (Norfolk, Conn.: New Directions, 1959), p. 57.
28 Roland Barthes, "Introduction to the Structural Analysis of Narratives," in *Image, Music, Text,* trans. Stephen Heath (New York: Hill and Wang, 1977), p. 94.

plural of the classic text. . . . Of the five codes, only three establish permutable, reversible connections, outside the constraint of time (the semic, cultural, and symbolic codes); the other two impose their terms according to an irreversible order (the hermeneutic and proairetic codes)."[29]

For Barthes, "constraint" is a negative term in an evaluative scheme that favors plurality and considers restrictions of meaning as oppressive impositions. Meaning itself always aims at domination: "it is a force which attempts to subjugate other forces, other meanings, other languages" (*S/Z*, 154), and as Barthes works to expose and escape its effects, he makes explicit the ethical and political stakes in accounts of narrative form and force.[30] The linearity Barthes questions and resists involves more than the sequence of events in a story, as becomes clear in the programmatic declarations of "The Death of the Author." "We know now that a text is not a line of words releasing a single 'theological' meaning (the 'message' of the Author-God) but a multidimensional space in which a variety of writings, none of them original, blend and clash."[31] Opposing the linear transmission of meaning from univocal origin to final destination, the image of the text as a multidimensional space offers a way of imagining the ideal of an unconstrained plurality.

> Let us first posit the image of a triumphant plural, unimpoverished by any constraint of representation (of imitation). In this ideal text, the networks are many and interact, without any one of them being able to surpass the rest; this text is a galaxy of signifiers, not a structure of signifieds; it has no beginning; it is reversible; we gain access to it by several entrances, none of which can be authoritatively declared to be the main one; the codes it mobilizes extend *as far as the eye can reach,* they are indeterminable (meaning here is never subject to a principle of determination, unless by throwing dice); the systems of meaning can take over this absolutely plural text, but their number is never closed, based as it is on the infinity of language. (*S/Z*, 5–6)

Like Lubbock, Barthes opposes the commonplace sequential appeal of stories with a spatial image of an unrealizable ideal, just as he also wants to

---

[29] Roland Barthes, *S/Z*, trans. Richard Miller (New York: Hill and Wang, 1974), p. 30.

[30] "It is evident that the object of all his work is a morality of the sign." Roland Barthes, *Roland Barthes,* trans. Richard Howard (New York: Hill and Wang, 1977), p. 97.

[31] Barthes, *Image, Music, Text,* p. 146. Published in 1968, this well-known essay is closely linked with *S/Z*, opening with an example from "Sarrasine." Earlier, in his "Introduction to the Structural Analysis of Narratives," the image of this space is more abstract. To combat the systematic confusion of narrative consecution and consequence requires disclosing "an atemporal logic lying behind the temporality of narrative" (98). "Logic here has an emancipatory value" (124).

make reading active and creative: "the goal . . . is to make the reader no longer the consumer, but a producer of the text" (*S/Z*, 4). But Barthes's imaginary object is also the perfect antithesis of a graspable form; instead of a defined shape like a picture or statue he posits the image of networks without beginning or end, a texuality with no outside. If we can recognize our implication in Lubbock's impossible desire, we can also recognize the appeal of Barthes's utopian ideal and the suspicious resistance to all constraints it warrants.

Unlike theorists who treat narrative as a neutral medium, Lubbock and Barthes show how figures of narrative form become invested with feelings and values. Their opposed stances of desire and suspicion, for all their obvious differences, both focus on the problems of power and control that are also the concern of nineteenth-century Gothic reflections. The sense of mastery that Lubbock seeks through identification with the maker's craft becomes amplified in the dreams of total authorial control that recur in Romantic Gothic writers from Godwin to Poe, dreams whose inversion yields the nightmares of persecution and abject loss of control that fill their fiction. Barthes's sense of narrative linearity and closure as ideological constraints is echoed in Gothic figures of confinement, while his ironic view of narrative as the language of "Destiny" resonates with the thematization of fate in Victorian novelists from Dickens to James. In these and other Gothic reflections, the psychosocial forces implicit in modern theories of narrative form are dramatized in impulses of self-assertion and surrender, collaboration and resistance that involve writers and readers as much as the struggling fictional characters.

An additional assumption shared by this odd couple points toward the underlying logic that links twentieth-century theories with earlier narrative reflections. Both Lubbock's concern with types of narrational mediation and Barthes's concern with the linear ordering of events presuppose the possibility of distinguishing these elements as general aspects of narrative. Most narrative theories explicitly make such a distinction, beginning at least with the Russian Formalists' opposition between *fabula* and *sjužet*, a distinction between *what* is narrated ("story") and *how* it is narrated ("discourse"), though terminologies vary and further distinctions proliferate from one theorist to another. To differentiate between events and their subsequent presentation follows our commonsense understanding of narrative and seems a necessary first step in any analytical effort to grasp it, but this fundamental distinction breaks down under scrutiny. The breakdown follows two possible paths, the deconstructive and the dialogical, which each turn on terms that also figure prominently in Gothic reflections, "force" and "versions."

The deconstructive path has been laid out by Jonathan Culler, who argues that the story–discourse distinction is both "an indispensable premise of narratology" and fundamentally incoherent.[32] Its representational logic depends on a hierarchy in which the story is prior and determines discursive meaning, but by rehearsing a series of readings Culler shows how this hierarchy gets inverted at moments when crucial events appear to be determined by discursive requirements, the demands of meaning. Oedipus's murder of Laius, Daniel Deronda's Jewish origins, the primal scene in Freud's case history of the Wolfman—all display the "double logic" of reversible determination between story and discourse, events and their significance. In Culler's account, these texts "stage a confrontation . . . between a semiotics that aspires to produce a grammar of narrative and deconstructive interpretations, which in showing the work's opposition to its own logic suggest the impossibility of such a grammar,"[33] offering a theoretical demonstration of what Lubbock long ago recognized, the hopelessness of the effort to achieve a total grasp of narrative form.

Culler proposes no explanation for this inevitable failure, but we might develop one by considering the crucial role played in his argument by the notion of force. "Force" and other closely related terms are repeated so often in his essay as to produce an effect of incantation.[34] It is "the tragic force" of *Oedipus* that requires the hero to assume the guilt of his father's murder, even though conclusive evidence is never presented; "the power of Eliot's novel" depends on the double logic by which Deronda's identity is both freely chosen and determined by his birth; more generally, deconstructive readings foreground moments that manifest contradictions, "stressing their importance to the rhetorical force of narratives."[35] The double logic of these narratives of destiny is established by an implicit appeal to their destination, the audience that registers their force. Here we begin to move from double logic to the dialogical: a narrative can exert force only in the medium of an answering interest or desire; the irresolvable tensions in structuralist models impel us toward a transactional account.

That is the explicit aim pursued by Barbara Herrnstein Smith, who advances a more radical critique of the dualistic story–discourse model.[36]

---

[32] Jonathan Culler, "Story and Discourse in the Analysis of Narrative," in *The Pursuit of Signs* (Ithaca: Cornell University Press, 1981), p. 171.

[33] Culler, "Story and Discourse," pp. 175–76.

[34] "Force" appears eighteen times, an average of once per page, "forces" an additional eight times, "power" five, "powerful" three, and "impact" once.

[35] Culler, "Story and Discourse," pp. 175, 177, 178.

[36] Barbara Herrnstein Smith, "Narrative Versions, Narrative Theories," in *Critical Inquiry* 7 (1980): 213–36. Like Culler's essay, Smith's was originally presented at a major conference

Against the idea of a prediscursive structure or "basic story" that can be presented from different perspectives or transposed into different media, she sets an account of narrative transactions in which versions multiply dialogically. "For any particular narrative, there is no single *basically* basic story subsisting beneath it but, rather, an unlimited number of other narratives that can be *constructed in response* to it or *perceived as related* to it."[37] Some of these versions may be called "plot summaries," others "interpretations" or "variants," but the relations among them will be determined by the circumstances and purposes of those who produce and receive them, not by some general structural principle. Relativizing narrative in this way dismantles the hierarchy of story and discourse instead of momentarily inverting it and offers a more open sense of narrative as a social process. If structuralist models fail to grasp narrative form, we can now see more clearly, it is because they cannot contain this dialogical productivity.

Through critiques such as Culler's and Smith's, late-twentieth-century narrative theory seeks to correct the lapse of attention to force, but in a notably dispassionate way compared with the engagement of Lubbock and Barthes. Culler's sense of "force" is not very forceful, and Smith's version of "versions" lacks the sense of struggle, the dynamics of domination and resistance that we have already glimpsed in "The Turn of the Screw." Culler's deconstructive argument confirms Lubbock's sense of inevitable defeat in the effort to grasp form but with none of his fascination and frustration. Instead, he calmly concludes, "In the absence of the possibility of synthesis, one must be willing to shift from one perspective to the other, from story to discourse and back again."[38] Smith even seems to harbor the therapeutic aim of altogether curing critical fascination with the imaginary object of narrative. Since she defines narrative as basically *"someone telling*

---

on narrative, each held in the late 1970s. Along with other work like the previously mentioned books by Brooks and Chambers published a few years later (see n. 20), they signal the turn from structural to transactional models. For a recent attempt to supplement structural narratology with an account of narrative effects, see Michael Kearns, *Rhetorical Narratology* (Lincoln: University of Nebraska Press, 1999).

[37] Smith, "Narrative Versions," p. 221.

[38] Culler, "Story and Discourse," p. 187. This alternation can be taken not only as advice for narratologists but as the basic recipe for the narrative comedy of Shandyism, shifting attention erratically between the story and self-conscious discourse about the difficulties of telling it. The affinity accounts for Shklovsky's choice of Sterne to illustrate the theory of *sjužet* construction, as well as his notorious claim that *"Tristram Shandy* is the most typical novel in world literature." See Victor Shklovsky, "Sterne's *Tristram Shandy:* Stylistic Commentary," in *Russian Formalist Criticism,* trans. Lee T. Lemon and Marion J. Reis (Lincoln: University of Nebraska Press, 1965), pp. 25–57.

someone else that something happened . . . narrative discourse is, at one extreme, hardly distinguishable from description or simply assertion." The problem of narrative form can thus be solved by dissolving it into a general account of "the nature of verbal transactions and the dynamics of social behavior generally."[39] While such a comprehensive view may have its advantages, it requires us to abandon our sense of narrative as a distinctive and irreducible cultural practice. Here not just the phantasmal form of a book but the whole category of narrative threatens to slip from our grasp.

Questions of theoretical definition, whether we distinguish narrative or subsume it in a broader conception of social practices, may seem remote from our concern with Gothic reflections, but they are only a more abstract version of problems we have been engaged with from the beginning, problems of drawing boundaries. Lubbock's fascinating, impossible vision of form with its sharply defined outlines is one version, as are the linear structures that constrain the boundless galaxy of signifiers Barthes imagines. The enabling, problematic narratological distinction between story and discourse is, as we have just seen, yet another contested boundary. Even to consider Gothic as a genre or mode requires making demarcations that do not simply follow intrinsic features of the literary landscape: we construct a version through the examples we choose and the readings we give them. In all these cases, as in the fundamental one of considering narrative as a distinct object of study, we need both to draw and to cross boundaries, to impose and resist what Poe calls "the force of a frame."

Gothic fiction repeatedly involves us in such problems, as in the competing readings provoked by "The Turn of the Screw." Are the ghosts preternatural or natural, outside or inside the governess's mind? Do her efforts to set the boundaries between self and other (excluding the ghosts, claiming possession of Miles) make her a site for our identification, or fearfully other? And do our own efforts to relocate those boundaries (remarking her doubling with Quint and Miss Jessel) enable us to avoid her errors or do they implicate us in a similarly troubling use of force? In all these uncertainties, as in our struggles with many other Gothic disturbances, the lines we draw are also story lines, narrative versions among which we try to decide. Gothic fictions often dramatize narration, as in the opening social exchange of strange tales that frames "The Turn of the Screw" or the self-awareness of the governess's private written account, but they also make us aware of the roles we may play as readers, sharing in "a common thrill" or constructing alternative versions. Above all they make us aware of the role of force, of our own acting and being acted upon in all narra-

[39] Smith, "Narrative Versions," pp. 232, 236.

tive transactions, an often uneasy awareness that is their greatest contribution to the history of narrative reflection.

The issues and terms we have drawn from our readings of both "The Turn of the Screw" and narrative theory have introduced several of our main concerns in considering Gothic as a reflexive mode. Before pursuing them in a series of writers and texts, I want to give a fuller sense of the leading conceptions informing that approach and the interests organizing that series.

The crucial issue is how we conceive narrative reflection itself. As my earlier brief discussion of Shandyism indicates, we need to expand our conception of reflexivity to recognize Gothic versions. The familiar, narrower sense that focuses on the sort of explicit self-reference and metanarrative commentary typified in Tristram Shandy's self-conscious performances is bound up with the theoretical understanding of reflection developed in modern philosophy. The reflexive project inaugurated by Descartes and continued in various forms of idealism and phenomenology is an inward turn where thinking becomes its own object as the mind seeks a certain ground for all knowledge in knowledge of itself. In this sense of reflection, thought turns back on itself, "turning away from any straightforward consideration of objects and from the immediacy of such an experience toward a consideration of the very experience in which objects are given." Further, "with such a bending back upon the modalities of object perception, reflection shows itself to mean primarily self-reflection, self-relation, self-mirroring."[40] Though the most unsystematic of all "isms," Shandyism clearly engages with this restricted inward sense, and Tristram's *Life and Opinions* can and often have been read in the same way he reads Locke's *Essay Concerning Human Understanding*, as "a history . . . of what passes in a man's own mind."[41] But for all its investment in exploring inwardness and narrating subjectivity, *Tristram Shandy* is at least equally concerned with narrative intersubjectivity, as Tristram continually calls attention to his shifting relations with his audience. Whether confiding ("Shut the door" [I, 4, 8]) or confronting ("How could you, Madam, be so inattentive in reading the last chapter?" [I, 20, 56]), he repeatedly stresses the dependence of narra-

[40] Rodolphe Gasché, *The Tain of the Mirror: Derrida and the Philosophy of Reflection* (Cambridge: Harvard University Press, 1986), p. 13.

[41] Laurence Sterne, *The Life and Opinions of Tristram Shandy, Gentleman*, ed. James Aiken Work (New York: Odyssey Press, 1940), vol. II, chap. 2, p. 85. Subsequent references are to this edition by volume, chapter, and page numbers. For a reading that sets the novel in the tradition of philosophical reflection, see James E. Swearingen, *Reflexivity in Tristram Shandy: An Essay in Phenomenological Criticism* (New Haven: Yale University Press, 1977).

tive on a dialogical interaction in which the reader plays an active role. "Writing, when properly managed (as you may be sure I think mine is) is but a different name for conversation: As no one, who knows what he is about in good company, would venture to talk all;——so no author, who understands the just boundaries of decorum and good breeding, would presume to think all: The truest respect which you can pay to the reader's understanding, is to halve this matter amicably, and leave him something to imagine, in his turn, as well as yourself" (II, 11, 108–9).[42]

Nineteenth-century fiction offers numerous instances of such reflection, staging narrative as a social transaction in an age when the novel had become a central cultural institution. Whether in Thackeray's narrative stance as the puppet master of *Vanity Fair* or Trollope's as the reader's companion ("And now, if the reader will allow me to seize him affectionately by the arm, we will together take our last farewell of Barset and of the towers of Barchester"), in Dickens's narrator invoking "the custom on the stage, in all good murderous melodrama" to reflect on his own "sudden shiftings of the scene" or George Eliot's requiring the story to pause a little for an exposition on realism, Victorian novels carry on the dialogue of writer and reader.[43] In all these cases, to which we could add many more examples from these and other novelists, it is the figure of the "author" who self-consciously reflects and provokes the reader to reflect on the narrative transactions in which they are both engaged.

Gothic reflections seldom work this way. They arise more indirectly from figures engaged in narrative transactions like James's governess and the guests gathered around the fire in his opening frame, from metaphorically charged settings like Poe's enclosures, or from plots like those of "The Turn of the Screw" and numerous other Gothic fictions that solicit the reader's participation in constructing alternative versions. These differences may have hindered critical recognition of Gothic reflexivity, but as we shall see its effects have much in common with those of more overt and familiar kinds, including an awareness of the dialogical production of narrative that is heightened by the active inferences its indirection requires.

---

[42] Compare James on engaging the reader's imagination in "The Turn of the Screw." "Only make the reader's general vision of evil intense enough, I said to myself . . . and his own experience, his own imagination, his own sympathy (with the children) and horror (of their false friends) will supply him quite sufficiently with all the particulars." *Art of the Novel*, p. 176.
[43] Anthony Trollope, *The Last Chronicle of Barset* (Harmondsworth: Penguin, 1967), p. 861; Charles Dickens, *Oliver Twist* (Harmondsworth: Penguin, 1966), pp. 168–69. Eliot's well-known chapter 17 of *Adam Bede*, "In Which the Story Pauses a Little," opens with a device straight out of *Tristram Shandy*: "'This Rector of Broxton is little better than a pagan!' I hear one of my lady readers exclaim." George Eliot, *Adam Bede* (Harmondsworth: Penguin, 1980), p. 222.

This heightened awareness comes, however, with a characteristic tinge of anxiety. Like James's governess and her precursors, we cannot be certain how much of the reflexive implications we sense in Gothic arises from our own aroused imagination. Uncertainty about whether reflections are in the text or outside it is another instance of the problem of boundaries, of the effort to grasp something intrinsic, as well as of the power texts have to determine our response. My accounts of Gothic reflexivity typically take the form of statements about how a set of narratives work on us, but like all interpretations they ultimately aim to show how we can work with these narratives to realize neglected possibilities and so read them differently. Like all interpretations, their success will mainly depend on the persuasiveness of the individual readings I give, but there are also some general considerations that support a reflexive reading of nineteenth-century Gothic.

One is that many writers, such as Godwin, Shelley, Poe, and James, show in their essays, prefaces, and other nonfiction writing an awareness of issues of narrative form and force that is also reflected in their Gothic fiction. Shelley's 1831 preface to *Frankenstein* is a familiar example, in which she draws analogies between her "hideous progeny" and the creature produced by "the pale student of unhallowed arts."[44] Are these connections already at work in the original 1818 version, as many readers are now likely to feel, or only produced in retrospect? Becoming a reader of her novel, Shelley herself crosses and redraws the boundaries between inside and outside, before and after, just as we must. In the case of *Frankenstein,* whose story has been retold in so many versions (including some that preceded Shelley's 1831 preface), these questions are intensified, but like several other cases we will encounter it shows that the reflexive possibilities of Gothic were clearly available to nineteenth-century writers and readers.

Those possibilities arise from two closely linked aspects that were prominent from the beginnings of Gothic but took on special significance in the nineteenth century: its affective economy of disturbance and control and its representational preoccupation with isolated individuals and extreme experiences. Together they become the basis for self-conscious reflections on narrative force and dialogical transactions. In the alarms and struggles of characters, their efforts to make narrative sense of their disturbing experiences, to tell their stories or impose their versions, and in the reader's corresponding agitation, sympathy, or resistance, we can find reflections of fundamental cultural concerns. Beyond all the specific ways Gothic reflects

[44] Mary Wollstonecraft Shelley, *Frankenstein; or, The Modern Prometheus,* ed. James Rieger (Chicago: University of Chicago Press, 1982), pp. 228–29.

on narrative force, deeper than any ideological effects of subversion or containment, we can sense the fear that nothing but sheer power can decide between opposing narrative versions, that force alone determines meaning and value. This nightmare of a world where all transcendental support or guarantees of the intrinsic have disappeared may be the deepest terror of nineteenth-century Gothic, but it is also confronted by persistent reminders of dialogical possibilities that resist such reduction. Disclosing the necessarily social conditions of both narrative and the self, Gothic reflections likewise counter the introspective fascination of "self-reflection, self-relation, self-mirroring" and help us understand Gothic extremity in dialogue with the realist social representation to which it is usually opposed.

Although the following chapters are all concerned with narrative, they do not themselves follow a single, continuous story line. Instead, they reflect on Gothic and develop Gothic reflections on narrative under three related aspects, each in a set of three chapters and each with a distinct theoretical and historical perspective. Part 1, "The Force of a Frame," concentrates on the questions of reflexivity I have just sketched out. Rather than begin by tracing their emergence through earlier Gothic fiction, I start in the nineteenth century with Poe, one of the most openly self-conscious Gothic writers, whose theory and practice insistently dwell on issues of narrative power and control. Poe's theory of the tale as a unified, self-contained form sets it in opposition to the looseness of the novel and so poses in formal and rhetorical rather than representational terms tensions between Gothic and realism that he allows us to recognize within each mode. After this initial account, supported by a reading of "The Tell-Tale Heart," I turn back to earlier Gothic, using Poe to frame studies that stress its reflexivity from its inception with Walpole through its later-eighteenth-century development in Radcliffe and Lewis and the Romantic versions of Godwin, Maturin, and Hogg. The prominence of doubling in Romantic Gothic, seen as an instance of multiple versions, then provides a basis for returning to Poe and considering the different senses of reflection implicated in his use of doubles in "William Wilson" and "The Fall of the House of Usher."

These fictions probe narrative power by staging confrontations between extremes and norms, between isolated, often deviant subjectivities and collective beliefs and values. Part 2, "Monster Stories," pursues the problem of deviance in its most extreme, memorable nineteenth-century versions, *Frankenstein, Dr. Jekyll and Mr. Hyde,* and *Dracula.* Set beyond the boundaries of humanity, monsters are represented as absolutely singular, yet *Frankenstein*'s creature, Hyde, and Dracula are also intimately linked to others through the mirroring and antagonism of doubling. Their unstable tensions between exclusion and bonding invite us to read these texts for their politics of difference, which have brought them much recent attention. Less noted, however, is how in narrating the conflicts monsters provoke, each shows through its formal complexity the ways narrative itself serves as an arena of struggle and an instrument of power. From the nested triple narrative of *Frankenstein* to the shifting voices of *Dr. Jekyll and Mr. Hyde* to the assembly of a collective account in *Dracula,* we can trace a movement from Romantic to Victorian Gothic, from competing to complementary versions that again manifests the tension between disparate individual perspectives and the power of the group. Monstrosity also animates the reception of these texts, whose narrative force reaches beyond their formal boundaries into the multiple versions that sustain their extraordinary afterlives. As pervasive popular myths they have become story-monsters that have escaped the discursive control of their original forms, reaching destinations their authors could hardly have foreseen, and yet in reflecting on the uncontrollable forces of writing and reading each narrative also anticipates its strange destiny.

Part 3, "The Language of Destiny," turns directly to that notion, the retrospective logic Barthes attributes to all narrative by which outcomes and endings determine the meaning of what precedes them. Gothic fiction often intensifies this logic in plots and figures of fate, but here I pursue such narrative tropes beyond the boundaries of what are commonly considered Gothic fictions to show how Gothic infiltrates the more realistic social representation that predominates in mainstream Victorian fiction. Stories of characters pursued by an oppressive fate or drawn by an exceptional destiny are clearly driven by such teleological force, but the novels and tales in which these characters figure also often resist that force by offering alternative versions. The Gothic tale itself offered Victorian novelists an alternative form that could generate far-reaching narrative reflections, as we have already seen in "The Turn of the Screw," and each of the three chapters in this part draws on the dialogical relation of tale and novel. Dickens returns to the form of the Gothic tale throughout his career, especially in the confessional monologues of aberrant figures, and by incorporating Miss Wade's remarkable "History of a Self-Tormentor" in *Little Dorrit* he develops reflections on both the novel's vision of converging destinies and the recurring versions of fate that arise from his own haunting past. George Eliot's only Gothic tale, "The Lifted Veil," uses its protagonist's preternatural powers of "insight" and "foresight" to reflect on both narrative omniscience and the determinism of foregone conclusions, issues that return in the questions of "second-sight" and the force of destiny in *Daniel Deronda*. Several of James's ghostly tales develop similarly reflexive implications, but the one most concerned with destiny, "The Beast in the Jungle," also sheds a revealing light on *The Ambassadors,* a novel that seems far removed from the Gothic.

Here the effects of realism appear as alternative versions of characteristic Gothic conflicts and anxieties, and the opposition between the expansive social representation of the novel and the self-enclosure of the tale reappears as a tension within the novels themselves, whose large and diverse fictional worlds can also be seen as the projections of secret fears and desires. A brief conclusion drawing on Eliot's *Middlemarch* pursues the implications of such tensions for our understanding of realism, suggesting how the self-consciousness found in Gothic reflections on narrative force informs some of the greatest achievements of nineteenth-century fiction.

Part I

The Force of a Frame

1

Poe and the Tale

In 1839 the *Southern Literary Messenger* rejected Poe's "The Fall of the House of Usher." Its Gothic terror, he was told, was no longer in vogue. "I doubt very much whether tales of the wild, improbable and terrible class can ever be permanently popular in this country. Charles Dickens, it appears to me, has given the final death blow to writings of that description."[1] Over a century and a half later, when this and several other of Poe's tales of the terrible class appear to have achieved a popularity as permanent as Dickens's, such a judgment seems curious, but it can alert us to a struggle to win and hold readers that not only was played out in the production and reception of his tales but is also inscribed within them. Much of Poe's writing, including his criticism and poetry, his detective stories, burlesques, parodies, and hoaxes, pursues and reflects on this struggle for the control of reading, which reaches its greatest intensity and complexity in his tales of terror.

As a reviewer, Poe gave high praise to Dickens's early fiction, but he also used it to stage a formal conflict between the looseness of the serialized novel and the concentration of the tale.[2] Concerned, as always, with "unity of effect," he stresses the potential and demands of the "brief article" as

---

[1] Letter from J. E. Heath, quoted in Michael Allen, *Poe and the British Magazine Tradition* (New York: Oxford University Press, 1969), p. 139.

[2] Poe reviewed both *Sketches by Boz* and *Pickwick Papers* in 1836, *The Old Curiosity Shop* (together with *Master Humphrey's Clock*) and the early installments of *Barnaby Rudge* in 1841, and the completed *Barnaby Rudge* in 1842. All citations of these and Poe's other essays are from Edgar Allan Poe, *Essays and Reviews* (New York: Library of America, 1984). For a detailed survey, see Gerald C. Grubb, "The Personal and Literary Relationships of Dickens and Poe," *Nineteenth-Century Fiction* 5 (1950): 1–22, 101–20, 209–21.

opposed to the "common novel" (205) and celebrates the force of such unity when he finds it in the *Sketches* ("the *Pawnbroker's Shop* engages and enchains our attention" [206]). Similarly, in *Pickwick* he passes over the main narrative to demonstrate Dickens's "powers as a prose writer" by reprinting one of the interpolated tales, "A Madman's Manuscript" (207), while in reviewing *The Old Curiosity Shop* he points out inconsistencies the serial writer had no chance to remove, "one among a hundred instances of the disadvantage under which the periodical novelist labors" (213), and extricates from the awkward framework of *Master Humphrey's Clock* "the 'Confession Found in a Prison in the Time of Charles the Second' . . . a paper of remarkable power" (212). The tales Poe praises are like several of his own, brief first-person narratives of madness and crime that trace the growth of obsession, the destruction of innocent victims, and the exposure of guilt.[3] In acclaiming Dickens he turns him into his double, a writer whose power is more evident in the intensity of such self-enclosed forms than in the looser extended narratives that surround them.

This appropriative strategy of reading as identification is carried further in Poe's best-known discussion of Dickens, his two reviews of *Barnaby Rudge*. The first, written after only the first three installments had appeared, offers a detailed solution to the mystery of Haredale's murder, confidently claiming an understanding of the plot's logic that equals, or perhaps even surpasses, the author's: "This is clearly the design of Mr. Dickens—although he himself may not at present perceive it" (222–23). The second considers the completed novel and analyzes the mystery plot in terms of the distinction between what the Russian Formalists would call *fabula*, "the events . . . in the order of their occurrence" (232), and *sjužet*, the order of their presentation, showing how their disparity heightens and preserves the mystery until the dénouement. As Poe demonstrates, "*The intention once known*, the *traces* of the design can be found upon every page" (232). He calls attention to his earlier solution, which he claims was essentially correct though mistaken on some minor points, and goes on to argue that his version would have been better: "If we did not rightly prophesy,

---

[3] Beyond such general resemblances, there are some closer ones that might interest a reader who followed Poe's lead as an aggressive detector of supposed plagiarism, especially between the exposure scene in "Confession Found in a Prison" and those of "The Tell-Tale Heart" and "The Black Cat," both written in 1843. These and other parallels have been noted by Edith Smith Krappe, "A Possible Source for Poe's 'Tell-Tale Heart' and 'The Black Cat,'" *American Literature* 12 (1940): 84–88. Stephen Rachman claims that Poe's "The Man of the Crowd" plagiarizes *Sketches by Boz*. See "'Es lässt sich nicht schrieben': Plagiarism and 'The Man of the Crowd,'" in *The American Face of Edgar Allan Poe*, ed. Shawn Rosenheim and Stephen Rachman (Baltimore: Johns Hopkins University Press, 1995), pp. 49–87.

yet at least our prophecy *should have been* right" (235).[4] Poe recognizes that the mystery plot does not dominate the completed novel as he had anticipated, but for him this is only further evidence of the defects of serialization. "It is, perhaps, but one of a thousand instances of the disadvantages, both to the author and the public, of the present absurd fashion of periodical novel-writing, that our author had not sufficiently considered or determined upon *any* particular plot when he began the story now under review" (236). With a shrewd and detailed argument, he makes his case "that the soul of the plot, as originally conceived, was the murder of Haredale with the subsequent discovery of the murderer in Rudge—but that this idea was afterwards abandoned, or rather suffered to be merged in that of the Popish Riots" (238). Poe concludes that Dickens's gifts are better suited to "the most fluent and simple style of narration. In tales of ordinary sequence he may and will long reign triumphant. He has a *talent* for all things, but no positive *genius* . . . for that metaphysical art in which the souls of all *mysteries* lie" (244).

Here reading passes from doubling to dispossession, as Poe advertises his superiority in the "metaphysical art" of creating and solving mysteries. We should recall that at the time he was reviewing *Barnaby Rudge,* Poe was also inventing the detective story, writing "tales of ratiocination" that include extended reflections on detection as just such a strategy of identification.[5] In "The Murders in the Rue Morgue" the narrator illustrates "the higher powers of the reflective intellect" with the example of an endgame in draughts: "The analyst throws himself into the spirit of his opponent, identifies himself therewith, and not infrequently sees thus, at a glance, the sole methods . . . by which he may seduce into error or hurry into miscalculation" (398). The lesson is repeated in "The Purloined Letter" in terms of the guessing game of odd and even, where again success depends on "an identification of the reasoner's intellect with that of his opponent" (689). This process of rivalrous identification offers a model of writing as well as

---

[4] By Grubb's reckoning, Poe made five predictions, of which only one, the identity of the murderer, was correct. See "Personal and Literary Relationships," pp. 8–11.

[5] "The Murders in the Rue Morgue" was written in 1841, "The Mystery of Marie Rogêt" in 1842–43, and "The Purloined Letter" in 1844. All citations of these and Poe's other fiction are from Edgar Allan Poe, *Poetry and Tales* (New York: Library of America, 1984). The complex logic of identification is a leading concern in Jacques Lacan's "Seminar on 'The Purloined Letter,'" which has prompted several further investigations that are collected with it in *The Purloined Poe: Lacan, Derrida, and Psychoanalytic Reading,* ed. John P. Muller and William J. Richardson (Baltimore: Johns Hopkins University Press, 1988). For a more recent study of Poe's detective fiction, including its thematization of reading, see John T. Irwin, *The Mystery to a Solution: Poe, Borges, and the Analytic Detective Story* (Baltimore: Johns Hopkins University Press, 1994).

reading, a model that informs several of Poe's Gothic tales as well as his detective stories, but before turning to his fiction we need to return to his criticism in order to see more clearly how the model bears on writing, the competition for readers, and the rivalry between the novel and the tale.

In 1842, four months after he reviewed *Barnaby Rudge,* Poe wrote a review of Hawthorne's *Twice-Told Tales* that presents his most general account of narrative form. Beginning with his basic premise that "in almost all classes of composition, the unity of effect or impression is a point of the greatest importance," he maintains that "the short prose narrative, requiring from a half-hour to one or two hours in its perusal," is superior to "the ordinary novel," a form to which the objections should be obvious.

> As it cannot be read at one sitting, it deprives itself, of course, of the immense force derivable from *totality*. Worldly interests intervening during the pauses of perusal, modify, annul, or counteract, in a greater or less degree, the impressions of the book. But simple cessation in reading would, of itself, be sufficient to destroy the full unity. In the brief tale, however, the author is enabled to carry out the fulness of his intention, be it what it may. During the hour of perusal the soul of the reader is at the writer's control. (572)

It is the tale's potential for controlling reading that makes it superior. Recalling Poe's complaints about the "absurd fashion" of serialized publication, we can see how for him it exacerbates the inherent defects of the novel. Imposing numerous interruptions in which worldly interests intervene, it disrupts the writer's control of the reader just as it invites the inconsistencies produced by changing intentions. To make the most of the opportunities offered by the tale, however, to realize "the immense force derivable from totality," requires subordinating all narrative elements to the severe demands of unity.

> A skilful literary artist has constructed a tale. If wise, he has not fashioned his thoughts to accommodate his incidents; but having conceived, with deliberate care, a certain unique or single *effect* to be wrought out, he then invents such incidents—he then combines such events as may best aid him in establishing this preconceived effect. If his very initial sentence tend not to the outbringing of this effect, then he has failed in his first step. In the whole composition there should be no word written, of which the tendency, direct or indirect, is not to the one pre-established design. (572)

Poe's conception of the tale as offering "the fairest field for the exercise of the loftiest talent, which can be afforded by the wide domains of mere prose" (571) has often been taken as a theoretical manifesto for the modern short story, superior to the novel because closer to the intensity and purity of lyric poetry.[6] Readers today may still choose to reaffirm those values, but other positions are readily available. We could, for instance, invoke Bakhtin's arguments for the superiority of the novel, with its many voices, its "dialogized heteroglossia," to the monological lyric.[7] We could then go on to make unfavorable comparisons between the claustrophobic enclosure of Poe's tales and the openness of the Dickensian novel, perhaps finding it particularly telling that Poe resists the move in *Barnaby Rudge* from the private sphere of domestic crime and guilt to the public sphere of historical action. Such readings, however, are less interesting and productive than those that recognize that the formal and imaginative tensions expressed in the nineteenth-century opposition between the tale and the novel are actually internal to both.

If we were to consider Dickens in these terms, we could follow Poe's lead by focusing on the tales that inject isolated monologues into the broad, polyphonic compositions of his novels, not only such early examples as Poe singled out but also Miss Wade's remarkable "History of a Self-Tormentor" in *Little Dorrit,* tracing the ways these narratives both contribute to and challenge those that surround them; that will indeed be one of the lines of inquiry we will pursue later. In reading Poe's tales, the lead is less clear, but we have already touched on several indicators. The writer's dream of total mastery, subordinating representation and meaning to unity of effect, aims at reducing the otherness of the reader to a register of his power, so that "the soul of the reader is at the writer's control." Such a reader is passive, utterly possessed by the writer's potent spell—and incapable of the sort of active, critical reading Poe himself performs. This is the anonymous common reader, typifying the popular audience Poe wants to dominate, whose actual resistance is implied in his fantasy of total control. The reader who produces Poe's criticism, on the other hand, is the elite counterpart of the author, capable of contemplating his design "with a kindred art" (572). In the review of *Twice-Told Tales,* the social positioning of such reading becomes explicit as Poe comments on one of Hawthorne's tales.

[6] In the later nineteenth century Poe's doctrines were widely promulgated by Brander Matthews in "The Philosophy of the Short Story" (1884). A century later they are still presented as fundamental principles of the form in Valerie Shaw, *The Short Story: A Critical Introduction* (London: Longman, 1983). For an extended discussion of Poe in relation to modernist theories of the short story, see Douglas Tallack, *The Nineteenth-Century American Short Story: Language, Form and Ideology* (London: Routledge, 1993).

[7] For an instance of this polemical opposition, see M. M. Bakhtin, "Discourse in the Novel," in *The Dialogic Imagination,* trans. Caryl Emerson and Michael Holquist (Austin: University of Texas Press, 1981), especially pp. 275–300.

"The Minister's Black Veil" is a masterly composition of which the sole defect is that to the rabble its exquisite skill will be *caviare*. The *obvious* meaning of this article will be found to smother its insinuated one. The *moral* put into the mouth of the dying minister will be supposed to convey the *true* import of the narrative; and that a crime of dark dye, (having reference to the "young lady") has been committed, is a point which only minds congenial with that of the author will perceive. (574–75)

Again Poe takes control of reading by identifying himself with the author, opposing his privileged grasp of the hidden, insinuated mystery plot to the obvious but false didactic reading of the rabble, those common readers who fail to appreciate the exquisite skill of both Hawthorne and Poe. Both as a writer and as a reader of Dickens and Hawthorne, Poe is engaged in a characteristically premodernist cultural struggle, fascinated with the possibilities of a growing popular audience he longs to master while attempting to establish his own elite critical authority.[8]

To appreciate at least the singularity if not the exquisite skill of Poe's reading of Hawthorne, one must recall that "The Minister's Black Veil" is subtitled "A Parable," inviting the reader to expect or formulate some "moral." From the tale's opening scene, where Mr. Hooper first appears wearing the black veil, it is insistently presented as a problematic sign, a "symbol," "type," or "emblem" that provokes and resists the interpretations offered by several of the characters. It seems likely that the minister intends his sustained symbolic gesture as a representation of that pervasive "secret sin" that forms the theme of both his sermon and his last words: "I look around me, and lo! on every visage a Black Veil!"[9] The tale, however, also suggests a more particular and psychological account of Hooper's estrangement, in which this universal vision becomes a subjective projection

---

[8] Compare his stated intention in writing "The Raven" "of composing a poem that should suit at once the popular and the critical taste," and his elaborate account in "The Philosophy of Composition" of how "the work proceeded, step by step, to its completion with the precision and rigid consequence of a mathematical problem" (15). On Poe's tales as elite appropriations of the "popular irrationalism" of contemporary sensational literature, see David S. Reynolds, *Beneath the American Renaissance: The Subversive Imagination in the Age of Emerson and Melville* (New York: Knopf, 1988), pp. 225–48. See also Terence Whalen, *Poe and the Masses: The Political Economy of Literature in Antebellum America* (Princeton: Princeton University Press, 1999).

[9] Nathaniel Hawthorne, *Tales and Sketches* (New York: Library of America, 1982), p. 384. In his second essay on Hawthorne (1847) Poe voices his objections to "the strain of allegory which completely overwhelms the greater number of his subjects, and which in some measure interferes with the direct conduct of absolutely all" (582). It is again an issue of control: allegory is tolerable only "where the suggested meaning runs through the obvious one in a very profound undercurrent, so as never to interfere with the upper one without our own volition,"

and the moral only that viewing the world through a black veil will "give a darkened aspect to all living and inanimate things" (372). In further reducing this account to the detection of "a crime of dark dye," Poe assimilates Hawthorne's ambiguous metaparable of interpretation to the mode of his own current detective stories. As in "The Murders in the Rue Morgue" and "The Mystery of Marie Rogêt," he makes the narrative turn on the rational reconstruction of an eroticized act of violence against a female victim, but here the role of the detective is assigned only to the reader.[10]

This strategy, assuming control of a narrative by rejecting the obvious meaning in favor of some hidden true import and constructing an alternative version of the story, defines a reading position offered by most of Poe's Gothic tales, most obviously in the possibilities of irony that open up once we doubt the narrator's reliability.[11] But the control offered by such maneuvers may be deceptive. In his later Hawthorne essay, which restates his theory of the tale, Poe suggests how the sense of privileged understanding and affinity with the author may be deliberately produced in the reader. "They two, he fancies, have, alone of all men, thought thus. They two have together created this thing. Henceforward there is a bond of sympathy between them, a sympathy which irradiates every subsequent page of the book" (581). Here reading with a kindred art slides into the illusion of reading with a kindred heart; the bond of sympathy may be a subtler form of subjection. As in the identification and conflict between the detective Dupin and his rival the Minister D—— in "The Purloined Letter," the alternation of dominance here is potentially perpetual, the struggle for control irresolvable.

It is in the Gothic tales, however, that these issues receive their most complex development, where Poe's theories and interpretive ploys are not just

---

and even then "it must always interfere with that unity of effect which, to the artist, is worth all the allegory in the world" (582–83). Compare Poe's "Never Bet the Devil Your Head: A Tale with a Moral," which mocks the common critical demand for didactic meaning: "Every fiction should have a moral; and what is more to the purpose, the critics have discovered that every fiction has" (458).

[10] This is a possibility Poe had already anticipated in his first review of *Barnaby Rudge*. The protracted building of mystery and "intimation of horror," he predicts, must inevitably produce disappointment in the end—except in the case "where there is no dénouement whatever—where the reader's imagination is left to clear up the mystery for itself" (219). In "The Minister's Black Veil" there is only slight support for Poe's reading, though some characters speculate "that Mr. Hooper's conscience tortured him for some great crime, too horrible to be entirely concealed, or otherwise than so obscurely intimated" (Hawthorne, *Tales and Sketches*, p. 380). The "young lady" Poe casts as Hooper's victim is presumably the one at whose funeral he presides on the same day he assumes his veil.

[11] For a reading that systematically pursues those possibilities, see G. R. Thompson, *Poe's Fiction: Romantic Irony in the Gothic Tales* (Madison: University of Wisconsin Press, 1973).

expounded and applied but figuratively embodied and dramatically played out. There, the dynamics of identification work through numerous forms of doubling between their characters, while the dream of total authorial control is figured in their claustrophobically enclosed settings, as Poe clearly indicates in his comment on "locale" in "The Philosophy of Composition": "It has always appeared to me that a close *circumscription of space* is absolutely necessary to the effect of insulated incident:—it has the force of a frame to a picture. It has an indisputable moral power of keeping concentrated the attention" (21). Of course, as in "The Raven," the Gothic scene of concentrated attention also typically displays a protagonist losing his grip; the tale of terror is centrally concerned with both control and the loss of control, and it is through this fundamental generic preoccupation that Poe's tales probe the power relations of reading and writing narrative.

These propositions could be applied to many of Poe's tales, but for now it will be most useful to concentrate our attention on the one that most insistently and concisely raises the issue of tale telling. "The Tell-Tale Heart" is remarkable even among Poe's tales for both its formal and its spatial compression, completing its trajectory of obsession, murder, and exposure in only five pages and confining its action almost entirely to a single room. Concentrating attention through the circumscription of space and time is only part of the effort to control reading here. The struggle is also staged within the narrative frame as the tale's opening outburst foregrounds the positions of teller and listener, setting them immediately in dialogical confrontation and interpretive conflict. "True!—very, very, dreadfully nervous I had been and am; but why *will* you say that I am mad?" (555). The reader seems to have little choice of position here (how can we *not* say he's mad?) and so is drawn into taking up the narrator's challenge ("How, then, am I mad?") by questioning his account and constructing an alternative.

In urging his case, the narrator repeatedly insists on his control, both as narrator ("Hearken! and observe how healthily—how calmly I can tell you the whole story") and as protagonist: "Now this is the point. You fancy me mad. Madmen know nothing. But you should have seen *me*. You should have seen how wisely I proceeded—with what caution—with what foresight—with what dissimulation I went to work!" This correlation between the projects of action and narration continues as he recounts his most elaborate exercise of control, the grotesque deliberation of his repeated intrusions into his victim's room, slowly opening the door and advancing his head: "I moved it slowly—very, very slowly, so that I might not disturb the old man's sleep. It took me an hour to place my whole head within the opening so far that I could see him as he lay upon his bed. Ha!—would a madman have been so wise as this?" His exaggerated caution is not just the expression of anxiety but a means of savoring his mastery, as he makes clear in describing his "more than usually cautious" final approach: "Never before that night, had I *felt* the extent of my own powers—of my sagacity" (556). These powers are peculiarly those of a narrator: the control of pace and the capacity for privileged observation. Standing silent and invisible in the doorway, he claims the powers of narrative omniscience to report the feelings and thoughts of another: "I knew what the old man felt. . . . He had been saying to himself . . . but he had found all in vain" (556). In such ways the tale's story figures what its discourse enacts, the assertion of narrative control.

But the rhythm of gradual progression and the claim to extraordinary perception also lead to the narrator's loss of control. Twice his "sharpened senses" detect "a low, dull quick sound," which he identifies as "the beating of the old man's heart" (557) and whose intolerable crescendo drives him to the violent release first of murder and then of confession. His triumphant knowledge of another's thoughts gives way to the knowledge and "derision" he attributes to the police officers: "They heard!—they suspected!—they *knew*!" (559). Both the promised calm of his narration and his proclaimed control within the story are undone by the accelerating rhythm that leads to his final outburst, in whose violence they both end: "'Villains!' I shrieked, 'dissemble no more! I admit the deed!—tear up the planks!—here, here!—it is the beating of his hideous heart!'" (559).

Yet even this spectacular breakdown does not fundamentally disrupt the narrator's power to control our reading. As long as we accept the terms in which he frames his account we remain enclosed within his experience, subject to the terror both of his unmotivated violence and of the preternatural power that exposes it.[12] The validity of such a reading is undeniable, or in Poe's terms "obvious." Indeed, none of his tales better displays the concentrated force demanded by his theory, the unity of effect enabled by the reader's submission to the writer's control and reception of a narrative on its own terms. The enduring popularity of Poe's tales of terror demonstrates the continuing possibility of such reception. At the same time, none shows more clearly how such intense effects depend on the suppression of any context that could let us escape the tale's tight confinement. The characters of

---

[12] It may be worth noting that the traditional motif of the victim's body exposing its murderer, which Poe adapts in the accusatory beating of the dismembered old man's heart, might also be detected in "The Minister's Black Veil" if one were intent on reading it as he proposes. As the minister bends over the young lady's coffin, his veil hangs down "so that, if her eyelids had not been closed forever, the dead maiden might have seen his face. Could Mr. Hooper be fearful of her glance, that he so hastily caught back the black veil? A person, who watched the interview between the dead and the living, scrupled not to affirm, that, at the instant when the clergyman's features were disclosed, the corpse had slightly shuddered, rustling the shroud and muslin cap, though the countenance retained the composure of death" (375).

"The Tell-Tale Heart" are given no names, no prior histories; there is little to suggest the existence of any larger world beyond the single room in which the story takes place. Such drastic circumscription seems to confirm Auden's observation that Poe's concentration on intense "states of being" requires the exclusion of all "historical existence," or, we might add, of the densely populated social world of the Dickensian novel.[13] Enclosed within this absolutely private sphere, we are hardly entitled to appeal to the public norms that would allow us to call the narrator "mad."

But of course we do; we already have through the proxy of the fictional audience, and to maintain that view we must contest and eventually replace the narrator's version. An early opening for such reinterpretation appears when the narrator finds it hard to explain his motive. "Object there was none. Passion there was none. I loved the old man. He had never wronged me. He had never given me insult. For his gold I had no desire. I think it was his eye! yes, it was this!" (555). Recalled with difficulty, then eagerly embraced as a reason for murder, the "pale blue eye, with a film over it" indicates his own lack of insight into the forces that drive him. We, however, can see that he has dissociated the eye and invested it with an autonomous, threatening power ("it was not the old man who vexed me, but his Evil Eye" [556]), displacing a threat originating in his own unconscious conflicts. His delight in secret observation is the counterpart of his compulsion to destroy the gaze of the other that manifests an unacknowledged part of himself, a relation dramatized in a deadlocked specular confrontation when the single ray of his lantern falls "as if by instinct" directly on the old man's eye (557).[14] The privileged knowledge he claims is as much a projection as the lantern's beam: "He was sitting up in the bed, listening;—just as I have done, night after night. . . . I knew the sound [of the old man's 'groan of mortal terror'] well. Many a night, just at midnight,

---

[13] W. H. Auden, "Introduction to Edgar Allan Poe: Selected Prose and Poetry," in *The Recognition of Edgar Allan Poe,* ed. Eric W. Carlson (Ann Arbor: University of Michigan Press, 1966), p. 221. One could also note the way "The Minister's Black Veil" sets its protagonist's extreme and willful gesture in a social and historical context that motivates and sustains its preoccupation with emblems and secret sin, as well as the way its mobile point of view also represents the multiple perspectives of the community.

[14] A classical Freudian analysis would probably, and plausibly, attribute the narrator's paranoia to suppressed homoerotic impulses. I am less concerned with filling in Poe's blanks with specific psychological content than with outlining an interpretive strategy for resisting the narrator's account. In terms of such narrative transactions, paranoia appears as the negative image of dialogical engagement. See, however, Eve Kosofsky Sedgwick's reading of Gothic paranoia as "the psychosis that makes graphic the mechanisms of homophobia" in *Between Men: English Literature and Male Homosocial Desire* (New York: Columbia University Press, 1985), p. 91.

when all the world slept, it has welled up from my own bosom, deepening, with its dreadful echo, the terrors that distracted me" (556). Everything in the narrator's world appears to be a dreadful echo of his terror-ridden mind and body, and pursuing that insight allows us ultimately to reinterpret the uncanny tell-tale heartbeats as his own, an inciting and accusing inner agency that he again misrecognizes as outside himself.

Such a naturalistic reconstruction of the story enables us to take control and move outside the narrator's "mad" version by relocating the division between inside and outside. It replaces "obvious" with "insinuated" meaning in the way Poe proposes in his reading of "The Minister's Black Veil," by establishing what has "really" happened, and it likewise permits us to claim the privileged position of "minds congenial with that of the author" who grasp "the *true* import of the narrative." As we do, however, we replicate the narrator's self-aggrandizing strategy of identification even as we triumph over his delusion and confidently confirm his otherness. The public norms of rationality and the private aberrations of madness thus become mirroring rivals, locked in an endlessly renewable contest that can be decided only by superior force. This is the essence, the deepest terror of Gothic, as Poe so thoroughly understood, a vision of a world where truth and all other values have lost any transcendental support and seem no more than masks of power, whether embodied in an individual will or in the instruments of social control. Though figured in private nightmares, this vision implies as broad a cultural scene as any represented in the most multifarious nineteenth-century novels—and is at least as pertinent to our own time. In "The Tell-Tale Heart," where tale telling is inseparable from (self) betrayal, a reader who undertakes to retell the story runs the same risks of incrimination as the narrator, of falling into an equally fixed and dubious position already marked out in the figures of the text. The condemning audience, threatening eye, accusing heartbeat, and smiling police officers all offer images of the reader's opposition and eventual ascendance, so that even as we suppose we are assuming a position outside the narrator's account we find ourselves inscribed within it.

That, at least, is how a Gothic metareading might go, but we can also drop such rhetoric of confinement, with its endless ploys and ruses, to consider more directly how Poe's fictional practice reflects on his theory. Clearly, and most remarkably, when he dramatizes his authorial project of total control in his fiction he presents it as both crazy and impossible. The narrator of "The Tell-Tale Heart," with his false identifications, grandiose pretensions, and radical instability, figures Poe's aesthetic aims as a pathological derangement of the imaginary, even as the tale pursues those aims. Not only do the narrator's monological efforts to dominate the other fail in both story and discourse, but the success of any alternative account we may construct also remains doubtful, allowing us to recognize the necessarily open and dialogical nature of even the most insistently self-enclosed narrative or authoritative reading.[15] The dialogical nature of the narrator's discourse is, of course, marked from his first words and doubly marked in his last, addressed to both the police and his audience. Like both, we may try to arrest the narrator and his tale, enclosing him in the category of madness and substituting a sane version, but those moves involve us too in a process that can be arrested only by an arbitrary imposition of limits, by the force of a frame.

These struggles for control all turn on drawing and crossing boundaries, between inside and outside, self and other, private and public, madness and sanity, narrator and author, and even the tale and the novel. For all its circumscription of space, "The Tell-Tale Heart" dwells on the penetrable division between inside and outside, as the narrator lingers in both action and description over crossing the threshold of the old man's room, and it gets its power less from maintaining enclosure than from rupturing it in the narrator's intrusions, the intervention of the police, and most of all in the insistent beating of the tell-tale heart. Since for Poe the novel entails the intervening of worldly interests and the breaking of totality, these disruptions, like the reader's interpretive interventions, are how his tale figures and registers the tension between "novel" and "tale," which like all its other oppositions requires any reading both to draw and cross its boundaries, to acknowledge and resist its power. The controlling force of any interpretive frame is always divided and uncertain, like the location of a picture's frame, which is neither completely inside nor outside, neither part of the picture nor of its surroundings.[16] No text can fully anticipate its reception or determine how it will be read; no reading can ever be complete or final. This too is obvious, and must have been as much so to Poe as it is to us, which may account for his insinuated self-mockery.[17] For it is also part of the nature of Gothic to play with terror, though not to master it.

[15] Tensions between the identification involved in both writing and reading such monological tales of isolated, aberrant figures and the dialogical processes that constitute the norms by which they are evaluated arise repeatedly in the earlier nineteenth-century first-person Gothic narratives considered in the next chapter.

[16] Jacques Derrida develops this undecidability into a deconstructive critique of Kantian aesthetics in *The Truth in Painting*, trans. Geoff Bennington and Ian McLeod (Chicago: University of Chicago Press, 1987), pp. 37–82. See also his discussion of formal and generic boundaries (as well as a tale of madness) in "The Law of Genre," trans. Avital Ronell, *Critical Inquiry* 7 (1980): 55–81.

[17] Poe can also openly mock himself, representing his own practice in the mode of farcical caricature in "How to Write a Blackwood Article" and its companion piece, "A Predicament," where the tale of terror is exposed as a formularized commodity.

2

Gothic Reflexivity from Walpole to Hogg

There is more to the story of Poe's efforts both to probe and to exercise narrative power, and to follow it we will need to consider more of his fiction. But first I want to take up the larger question of Gothic reflexivity and its earlier history. To claim that Poe's idiosyncratic, insistently theorized and self-referential practice discloses the "essence" of Gothic amounts to proposing that we read the genre through the frame of his work, that we think of earlier Gothic fiction as if in Poe it reaches its destination. Such an obviously restrictive imposition signals the effort to control a diverse field of texts required by any reflection on a genre or tradition; we need to recognize the artifice of this framing device, but it seems peculiarly appropriate for considering Gothic reflexivity. One reason is the remarkable history of Poe's reception, particularly in France, that has made his work the site or pretext for so much strenuous theoretical reflection. The story of Baudelaire's profound identification with Poe and its impact on Mallarmé and Valéry is well known;[1] more relevant here are the themes elaborated in Lacan's "Seminar on 'The Purloined Letter,'" Derrida's critique of Lacan, and various commentaries they have attracted. When we find Poe's work reaching this destination, we also find intense concern with the question of destination itself. Lacan asserts that "a letter always arrives at its destination"; Derrida counters that it always might not, "and from the moment that this possibility belongs to its structure one can say that it never truly arrives"; Barbara Johnson argues that "the letter's destination is . . . *wherever it is read.*"[2] At stake here

---

[1] See Patrick Quinn, *The French Face of Edgar Poe* (Carbondale: Southern Illinois University Press, 1957).

[2] John P. Muller and William J. Richardson, eds., *The Purloined Poe: Lacan, Derrida,*

are general claims about truth and meaning, but we do not need to decide whether Lacan merits Derrida's charge of "phallogocentrism," or, as Johnson says, "whether Lacan and Derrida are really saying the same thing or only enacting their own differences from themselves" (250). We need only recognize how it has become part of Poe's destiny to be linked with these issues and, further, how they are posed in terms of what Derrida calls the "question of the frame" (181), which includes both Lacan's neglect of Poe's narrative frame and the general impossibility of any "totalization of the bordering" (209). As we will see, destiny, destination, and framing frequently figure in Gothic fiction, but in our readings they will also necessarily be inflected by the way Poe figures in these debates.

Another, simpler reason for reading Gothic through Poe is that he concentrates and highlights its reflexive potential. His self-consciousness can be understood in part as a reflection of his belated, provincial position, deliberately taking up the form of the Gothic tale, theorizing it through a Romantic aesthetic of intensity, and amplifying its self-referential dimension. We need not extend the series of appropriating identifications that his own criticism and fiction repeatedly make, but we can recognize that Poe's unstable compounding of terror and play, and the preoccupation with power and control that underlies both, resonate throughout the Gothic tradition. By linking those concerns with the formal and interpretive effects of framing, Poe shows very clearly how Gothic can reflect on fundamental features of narrative. The possibility of alternative perspectives on or versions of a story presupposes the problematic distinction between its events and their discursive presentation that recurs in all efforts to grasp narrative form. In the dialogic contestation between Poe's narrators and their audience, as in the multiplied narrators and textual frames of so many other Gothic fictions, this basic structural feature becomes a means of dramatizing the force of narrative as a social transaction, as an instrument of domination or resistance, an affirmation or questioning of shared beliefs. Through Poe, we can look back to the beginnings of Gothic and see how it offered new reflections on narrative.

The first "Gothic Story," Walpole's *Castle of Otranto*, is doubly framed by his two prefaces, which offer the reader multiple perspectives. The first, preceding the pseudonymous first edition, is supposedly written by William Marshall, who has found and translated the original Italian text of Onuphrio Muralto and who speculates about its origins and motivation.

---

and Psychoanalytic Reading (Baltimore: Johns Hopkins University Press, 1988), pp. 53, 201, 248.

Though its date is 1529, its "principal incidents are such as were believed in the darkest ages of christianity" much earlier. The purity of its language suggests that "the date of the composition was little antecedent to that of the impression. Letters were then in their most flourishing state in Italy, and contributed to dispel the empire of superstition, at that time so forcibly attacked by the reformers." To reconcile the story's content with its style, Marshall proposes that the author was "an artful priest" engaged in reactionary propaganda, working "to confirm the populace in their ancient errors and superstitions. If this was his view, he has certainly acted with signal address. Such a work as the following would enslave a hundred vulgar minds beyond half the books of controversy that have been written from the days of Luther to the present hour."[3]

Already, before the first Gothic story has even begun, we can recognize the fascination with narrative's imagined power to enslave that later animates Poe's writing, as well as the division of readers and writers into the vulgar and the enlightened or the passive and the artful—positions that are explicitly linked with the crisis of authority produced by secularizing modernity. We can also recognize, much more clearly than in Poe, how the question of narrative power is linked with the characteristic Enlightenment conception of ideology, of systems of belief as instruments of domination.[4] This politics of reading, however, is displaced into the past and onto an exotic setting. Walpole, as Marshall, can slyly praise himself, as Muralto, for his "address" in reanimating outmoded credulity, but addressing contemporary readers requires a different basis for appreciation. "Whatever his [the author's] views were, or whatever effects the execution of them might have, his work can only be laid before the public at present as a matter of entertainment." From this standpoint, "miracles, visions, necromancy, dreams, and other preternatural events" become the object of neither belief nor skepticism but an aesthetic judgment of propriety: "Belief in every kind of prodigy was so established in those dark ages, that an author would not be faithful to the *manners* of the times who should omit to mention them. He is not bound to believe them himself, but he must represent his actors as believing them" (4). When Walpole acknowledges his authorship

---

[3] Horace Walpole, *The Castle of Otranto: A Gothic Story* (New York: Oxford University Press, 1964), pp. 3–4.

[4] The first formulation of "ideology" as a positive science came a generation after *Otranto* in the work of Destutt de Tracy, who coined the term in 1796, and it was Condorcet who gave it the sense of mystifying political manipulation later developed by Marx and Engels. But the conception of traditional beliefs and superstitions as blocking progress and serving the interests of a ruling elite was clearly available to Walpole. See David Braybrooke's article "Ideology" in *The Encyclopedia of Philosophy* (New York: Macmillan, 1967), 4:124–27.

in his preface to the second edition, however, this historical alibi is replaced by the expressive project of unblocking "the great resources of fancy." Instead of just representing discredited superstitions, the narrative of preternatural events can assume new imaginative functions and metaphorical values; instead of signifying subjection it offers release from the restrictions of common life, "leaving the powers of fancy at liberty to expatiate through the boundless realms of invention" (7).[5]

The intersection of all these perspectives can be observed at a single point in the narrative when Manfred announces the villainous scheme by which he and Frederick will each marry the other's daughter. "As he spoke those words three drops of blood fell from the nose of Alfonso's statue. Manfred turned pale, and the princess sunk on her knees. Behold! said the friar: mark this miraculous indication that the blood of Alfonso will never mix with that of Manfred!" (93). This is the sort of thing that keeps happening to Manfred. From the beginning, when the gigantic helmet (a nightmarishly enlarged version of the one on Alfonso's statue) crushes his son Conrad, preternatural events continually thwart his attempts to secure his claim to Otranto. The bleeding image of the castle's last rightful owner readily joins this series and so seems to warrant Friar Jerome's interpretation. As one of those incidents calculated to strengthen the empire of superstition, this miraculous indication can be set within the ideological frame of "the darkest ages of christianity," which encloses the actors of the drama but not necessarily its implied author or audience. If we suppose the author to be Marshall's "artful priest," it can recall the many awe-inspiring prodigies like weeping images of the Virgin featured in both Catholic legends and Protestant denunciations of deception and idolatry, offering readers the opportunity to distinguish themselves from vulgar minds and enjoy the satisfactions of enlightened superiority, as well as partial identification with the power that enslaves the credulous.[6]

If we take this incident as a matter of entertainment, however, it can offer the aesthetic pleasure of make-believe, playing at and with the fear of the preternatural. The image of a statue with a nosebleed is ludicrous enough to distance most readers, but we can recognize in it an appeal more

---

[5] On Walpole's two prefaces in relation to contemporary expectations and the novel's reception, see E. J. Clery, *The Rise of Supernatural Fiction, 1762–1800* (Cambridge: Cambridge University Press, 1995), pp. 53–67.

[6] For examples of such seventeenth- and eighteenth-century religious polemics, see Anne McWhir, "The Gothic Transgression of Disbelief: Walpole, Radcliffe and Lewis," in *Gothic Fictions: Prohibition/Transgression*, ed. Kenneth W. Graham (New York: AMS, 1989), pp. 29–47. McWhir argues that Gothic produces an aesthetic suspension of disbelief that reconciles the claims of reason and imagination.

successfully realized in Poe's tell-tale heart, displacing a naturalistic framework and allowing us to share in the characters' loss of control. For Manfred, as for Poe's narrator and so many other Gothic protagonists, that loss is devastating, instilling terror and baffling desire; for Gothic readers, it can become an object of desire, a thrill, a touch of the sublime. The sublime has received considerable attention in recent years, in its eighteenth-century, Romantic, postmodern, and even its Gothic versions.[7] What matters most here is the way it designates a reading position from which the inability to grasp, the failure of an interpretive frame, assumes a high value, offering an experience of narrative force that allows the powers of fancy to expatiate through the boundless realms of invention. From this perspective, we no longer have a simple opposition between enslavement to superstition and emancipated rationality but a liberation that depends on imaginary regression to a supposedly superseded form of life.

Here we might note that inanimate objects that seem to be alive, like the bleeding statue, are the starting point for Freud's investigation of the uncanny, which he explains as the effect of just such a return. "An uncanny experience occurs either when repressed infantile complexes have been revived by some impression, or when the primitive beliefs we have surmounted seem once more to be confirmed."[8] Freud is referring not to the superstitions of the darkest ages of Christianity but to the animistic beliefs of "savages," yet his analogy of individual and collective progress, with its equation of infantile and primitive magical thinking, is not far removed from Walpole's compound frame. Both the psychoanalytic and the Gothic narratives tell of an uncertain or incomplete development threatened by the return of a repressed past. *The Castle of Otranto*'s plot is of course a version of this story. Manfred, whose family has held power for three generations, is pursued by the repeated mysterious interventions of the gigantic form of Alfonso ("an ancient prophecy . . . was said to have pronounced, *That the castle and lordship of Otranto should pass from the present family, whenever the real owner should be grown too large to inhabit it*" [15–16]), who appears at the end to declare Theodore the rightful heir and prompts Manfred's disclosure of his grandfather's crimes of murder and usurpation. The way to this revelation of family secrets is prominently marked by Manfred's semi-incestuous attempts to possess Isabella, leading

---

[7] See Vijay Mishra, *The Gothic Sublime* (Albany: SUNY Press, 1994), which surveys theories of the sublime from Burke and Kant to Baudrillard and Lyotard and reads the Gothic as "a genre of fissure and fracture, a kind of antilanguage, which heralds and foreshadows the postmodern" (54).

[8] Sigmund Freud, "The 'Uncanny,'" in *On Creativity and the Unconscious: Papers on the Psychology of Art, Literature, Love, Religion* (New York: Harper and Row, 1958), p. 157.

to his fatal stabbing of his daughter Matilda, which leads in turn to his final guilty surrender of Otranto.[9] Like Freud's doubly caused uncanny, this mélange of dark passions is not only motivated by Walpole's story of a returning repressed but licensed by the simulated archaism of his Gothic story, whose narrative force mobilizes the uncanny threat and allure of regression in both individual and social terms.

Walpole's plot contains these disturbances, but its rigid moral scheme is reframed in his first preface, where Marshall includes it among "my author's defects."

> I could wish that he had grounded his plan on a more useful moral than this; that *the sins of the fathers are visited on their children to the third and fourth generation.* I doubt whether in his time, any more than at present, ambition curbed its appetite of dominion from the dread of so remote a punishment. And yet this moral is weakened by that less direct insinuation, that even such anathema may be diverted by devotion to saint Nicholas. Here the interest of the monk plainly gets the better of the judgment of the author. (5)

From this perspective, transgression and retribution appear equally savage; the nemesis that punishes the protagonist's appetite of dominion stems from the same appetite in the "author."[10] The canny monk Muralto, like his surrogate Friar Jerome, may try to marshal uncanny effects to advance his interests, but Walpole and the reader who acquiesces in those effects are also implicated, impelled by their desire to produce and consume "a constant vicissitude of interesting passions" (4).[11] The most genuinely uncanny effect of *The Castle of Otranto* may be this collapsing of superstition and enlightenment into the common terms of narrative power.

The many descendants of Walpole's "new species of romance" (12) that proliferated in the 1790s and continued to thrive into the 1820s developed in several new directions, but they all return to the question posed in his

[9] Walpole's play *The Mysterious Mother,* whose material is closely akin to *The Castle of Otranto*'s, includes actual mother–son and potential father–daughter incest. See Mishra, *Gothic Sublime,* pp. 64–69.

[10] Manfred has a point, though he typically regards his children's deaths only as *his* afflictions, when he complains of being punished far more heavily than the original transgressor, Ricardo. "His crimes pursued him—yet he lost no Conrad, no Matilda! I pay the price of usurpation for all!" (109).

[11] The surrogate of the Gothic reader as consumer of emotions appears in Theodore, who after long grieving for Matilda finally marries Isabella, "persuaded he could know no happiness but in the society of one with whom he could forever indulge the melancholy that had taken possession of his soul" (110).

first preface, the status of the preternatural. Whether prodigies such as Walpole deployed are central or marginal, literal or figural, confirmed or ultimately reduced to naturalistic terms, their possibility is a crucial feature of early Gothic, the apparent origin of its tendency to multiply versions, which are in turn frequently the basis for narrative reflections. Commentators from the eighteenth century to the present assume the importance of this issue in continually reproducing the opposition between the explained and asserted supernatural, reaffirming its significance.[12] As we have already seen in our readings of Poe and Walpole, the opposition plays an important tactical role in the narrative transactions they propose. Such uncanny part-objects as the tell-tale heart and the bleeding statuary nose violate the boundary between life and death or animate and inanimate and incite readers to take positions in constructing naturalistic or preternaturalistic versions.[13] But we have also seen that resolving this tension may be less significant than what we learn in the process of struggling with it, so that any outcome will seem less than satisfactory.

The comparison of Radcliffe and Lewis, a familiar trope in Gothic criticism, offers a good test case. The two are usually contrasted: Radcliffe provides rational explanations for apparently preternatural events, while Lewis insists on the reality of the demonic, and this difference in their fictional worlds is often correlated with their very different artistic qualities, with (depending on which is favored) Radcliffe's conservative caution or artistic subtlety and Lewis's radical daring or crude sensationalism. Overlooked in such quite plausible contrasts is these authors' common use of deferred explanations, separated from the events they reinterpret not, as in Walpole's prophecy and its fulfillment, by the suspense of mystery plotting but by long intervals of neglect. Hundreds of pages intervene between Emily St. Aubert's mysterious experiences in the castle of Udolpho or Vin-

---

[12] One of the more interesting contemporary comments on this dichotomy, notable for its stress on effect rather than on ideological content, comes from the Marquis de Sade, who observed that in an age of "revolutionary shocks" novelists found it "necessary to call upon hell for aid in order to arouse interest. . . . But this way of writing presented so many inconveniences! The author of *The Monk* failed to avoid them no less than did Mrs. Radcliffe; either of these two alternatives was unavoidable; either to explain away all the magic elements, and from then on to be interesting no longer, or never raise the curtain, and there you are in the most horrible unreality." Quoted in Mario Praz, "Introductory Essay," in *Three Gothic Novels,* ed. Peter Faircloth (Harmondsworth: Penguin, 1978), p. 14. Compare Tzvetan Todorov's restatement of the opposition in *The Fantastic: A Structural Approach to a Literary Genre,* trans. Richard Howard (Ithaca: Cornell University Press, 1975), which locates "the fantastic" on the border between "the uncanny" (strange but natural) and "the marvelous."

[13] On Melanie Klein's theory of the part-object in relation to Gothic, see David Punter, "Narrative and Psychology in Gothic Fiction," in Graham, *Gothic Fictions,* pp. 2–27.

centi di Vivaldi's at the ruined fortress of Paluzzi and their eventual natural explanations, pages in which we hear nothing more of them. Had these scrupulous clarifications never arrived, they would scarcely have been missed. In *The Monk,* the final revelations are more spectacular and gratuitous. Lucifer himself appears and, having secured Ambrosio's soul, scornfully informs him that Matilda, his partner in perdition, was actually "a subordinate but crafty spirit" commissioned to corrupt him.[14] Since Ambrosio's fall has seemed to proceed throughout from his own pride, weakness, and violent passions, this last-minute recasting of his story in terms of demonic manipulation is at least as reductive as Radcliffe's naturalization and has as little power to control the significance of the whole narrative.[15]

In these belated and unsatisfactory explanations, we can observe a separation of alternative versions that attenuates Barthes's hermeneutic code, weakening its linear logic and opening spaces for the elaboration of subjectivity. Radcliffe's protagonists are endowed with sensibility and imagination that make them responsive to intimations of the preternatural and the appeal of sublimity. While she is careful to note the possible dangers of imagination, these qualities are linked with moral as well as aesthetic refinement and figure as sources of her heroines' growing strength. Delaying naturalistic deflation permits more expansive accounts of their inward dramas of alarm, doubt, and exaltation.[16] Lewis presents sensibility and imagination only as sources of vulnerability, as in the doomed Antonia's confiding response to Ambrosio or Don Raymond's subjection to the ghost of the Bleeding Nun,[17] and his hero's inward dramas are of violent com-

---

[14] Matthew G. Lewis, *The Monk* (New York: Grove Press, 1952), p. 418.

[15] This is not to deny that the earlier narrative allows rereading Matilda as a petty demon, just as it occasionally hints that Ambrosio's victims Elvira and Antonia are, as Lucifer also reveals, actually his mother and sister. The late introduction of this diabolus ex machina corresponds to the way Radcliffe's deferred explanations also involve belated appearances by significant characters, Du Pont in *Udolpho* and Nicola in *The Italian.* Austen recalls this practice at the end of *Northanger Abbey* when she marries off Eleanor Tilney to a previously unknown "man of fortune and consequence" and adds "(aware that the rules of composition forbid the introduction of a character not connected with my fable)" that he is the one whose washing bills Catherine discovered in the mysterious black cabinet.

[16] This expansiveness can be recognized more clearly by comparing cases where it collapses, as when Vivaldi encounters the mysterious monk in the dungeons of the Inquisition. "He almost fancied . . . that he beheld something not of this earth. . . . But he checked the imperfect thought, and, though his imagination inclined him to the marvellous, and to admit ideas which, filling and expanding all the faculties of the soul, produce feelings that partake of the sublime, he now resisted the propensity, and dismissed, as absurd, a supposition, which had begun to thrill his every nerve with horror." Ann Radcliffe, *The Italian* (New York: Oxford University Press, 1981), p. 347.

[17] On Lewis's "cynical" treatment of sensibility in contrast to Radcliffe's and its relation to

pulsion rather than a struggle toward autonomy, but they too gain fullness and intensity by being detached from his explanatory frame. For all their obvious differences, both novelists show how the preternatural, whether asserted or withdrawn, serves the characteristic Gothic interplay of disturbance and control.

Whether that interplay also yields reflexive implications is a different question. The preternatural always produces disturbance, not just in the characters or readers who thrill with terror but to the cultural norms of a world that has relegated belief in such prodigies to a surmounted past. Seeking to regain control, we may try to construct alternative accounts, like the naturalistic reading of the tell-tale heart, and if those do not seem to be available, we may consider the entire narrative as an alternative world whose self-enclosure marks off a private sphere of the imagination. Instead of expatiating through the boundless realms of invention, kings of infinite space, Gothic writers may then seem bound in Hamlet's nutshell with their own bad dreams, and we can read *The Castle of Otranto* or *The Monk,* for example, as projections of their authors' unresolved oedipal conflicts.[18] More generously, and productively, we can link those imagined worlds metaphorically with our own, as when we consider the dungeons, crypts, and secret passageways of Gothic settings as figures for the unconscious. These are familiar and useful strategies of reading, but we should recognize that all of them, including the honorific conflation with psychoanalysis, are means of mastering disturbance. Yet even though such processes are always in play, they are not always called to our attention. The Gothic novels and tales that develop the genre's reflexive potential are those that make us most aware of the frames we impose and the partiality of the versions we construct.

There are several ways of prompting such awareness, but they all involve questioning narrative authority by indicating multiple reading positions. "Whatever his views were," Walpole does this with his doubled prefaces, and some later Gothic fiction deploys comparable apparatuses, of which the most interesting is the "Editor's Narrative" that forms fully half of Hogg's *Private Memoirs and Confessions of a Justified Sinner.* More common are framing narratives such as Walton's in *Frankenstein* or Lockwood's in *Wuthering Heights,* devices that may be reduced to opening accounts of a discovered or transmitted text, as in "The Turn of the Screw,"

---

their different uses of the marvelous, see Jacqueline Howard, *Reading Gothic Fiction: A Bakhtinian Approach* (New York: Oxford University Press, 1994), pp. 205–9.
[18] As we shall see, the possibility of collapsing into private fantasy and encrypted autobiography repeatedly returns to haunt Gothic writing, including the Gothic elements in the more realistic social representation of novelists like Dickens, Eliot, and James.

or elaborated into dizzying feats of embedding tales within tales, as in *Melmoth the Wanderer.* Throughout the nineteenth century, Gothic fictions tend to display more complicated narrative schemes and so call more attention to form than their more realistic contemporaries, which is the most obvious way they produce reflections on narrative force. Unlike most of their eighteenth-century predecessors, however, nearly all of them embody the question of authority in the uncertain reliability of one or more first-person narrators, the problem that Poe reduced to its purest terms. To explore the implications of this strategy, we need to look next at the first Gothic novel that systematically exploited it.

"By the way, are you aware that Godwin wrote his 'Caleb Williams' backwards? He first involved his hero in a web of difficulties, forming the second volume, and then, for the first, cast about him for some mode of accounting for what had been done." Poe quotes this note from Dickens, "alluding to an examination I once made of the mechanism of 'Barnaby Rudge,'" as the opening move of "The Philosophy of Composition."[19] Poe's claims for the "mathematical" precision of the process of composing "The Raven" in this essay of 1846 closely follow the model of Godwin's 1832 preface to *Fleetwood,* published thirty-eight years after *Caleb Williams* appeared, in which he claims to have proceeded by the sort of retrograde logic Dickens describes. Beginning with "the conception of a series of adventures of flight and pursuit," working back to the discovery of "a secret murder" as the cause, and from there to the motivating qualities of both pursuer and victim, Godwin presents himself as the possessor of a powerful and certain method. "I felt that I had a great advantage in thus carrying back my invention from the ultimate conclusion to the first commencement of the train of adventures upon which I purposed to employ my pen. An entire unity of plot would be the infallible result; and the unity of spirit and interest in a tale truly considered, gives it a powerful hold on the reader, which can scarcely be generated with equal success in any other way."[20] Godwin prefigures nearly every feature of Poe's authorial self-image, with his rigorous methods, his stress on unity of both form and effect, and his desire for power over the reader. "I said to myself a thousand times, 'I will write a tale, that shall constitute an epoch in the mind of the reader, that no one, after he has read it, shall ever be exactly the same man that he was before'" (338).

Of course, the revolutionary mental epoch Godwin anticipated was, unlike the power Poe seeks, overtly political, exposing the injustice of "things

[19] Edgar Allan Poe, *Essays and Reviews* (New York: Library of America, 1984), p. 13.
[20] William Godwin, *Caleb Williams* (New York: Norton, 1977), p. 337.

as they are." His story of compulsion and persecution, offering "a general review of the modes of domestic and unrecorded despotism," is closely keyed to contemporary debates over the French Revolution, and even to specific episodes of radical agitation and official repression.[21] Telling the story of his story nearly forty years later, however, Godwin says nothing of this topical significance, dwelling instead on his artistic procedures, and while he includes many details in his "true history of the concoction and mode of writing of this mighty trifle," he also says nothing of his last-minute change of the "ultimate conclusion," which originally had Caleb failing in his public indictment of Falkland and ending in prison and madness. The political implications of this version ("Alas! alas! it too plainly appears in my history that persecution and tyranny can never die!" [332]) are far removed from those of the emotional reconciliation with which Godwin replaced it; the possibility of both endings unsettles the teleology of his narrative.

More unsettling to any straightforward reading is Godwin's change in narrative stance.

> I began my narrative, as is the more usual way, in the third person. But I speedily became dissatisfied. I then assumed the first person, making the hero of my tale his own historian. . . . It was infinitely the best adapted, at least, to my vein of delineation, where the thing in which my imagination revelled the most freely, was the analysis of the private and internal operations of the mind, employing my metaphysical dissecting knife in tracing and laying bare the involutions of motive, and recording the gradually accumulating impulses. (339)

As in his formalistic account of plot construction, Godwin's account of his choice of perspective omits any social or political context, but because any reader of Caleb's narrative must continually try to gauge its reliability, the representation of private and internal operations of the mind is repeatedly framed and reframed in public terms. Caleb's alternating moods of grandiosity and abjection, like his conflicting feelings of reverence and resentment toward Falkland, invite both participation and questioning at every point. Like the reversibility of the positions of persecutor and persecuted or righteousness and guilt between Caleb and Falkland, these shifting perspectives project alternating versions of the novel's adventures of flight and pur-

[21] See Pamela Clemit, *The Godwinian Novel: The Rational Fictions of Godwin, Brockden Brown, Mary Shelley* (Oxford: Oxford University Press, 1993), pp. 35–45. Godwin's description of his political aims appears in his preface to the first edition (1794), withdrawn out of fear of prosecution, pp. 2–3.

suit. Just as domesticating and naturalizing the Gothic drama of hidden crime, persecution, and struggle brings out its political implications, making Caleb his own historian dramatizes the act of narration itself and foregrounds its relation to power. Whatever his novel's impact on its first readers may have been, Godwin's shift of perspective constitutes an epoch in the development of Gothic reflexivity. More than any other, this move opens up nineteenth-century Gothic's characteristic reflections on narrative force.

Like his author, Caleb also experiences a change in his narrative perspective and aim in the course of composition. "I began these memoirs with the idea of vindicating my character. I have now no character that I wish to vindicate" (326). Having begun by addressing his story to "posterity" in hopes of receiving "a justice which my contemporaries refuse" (3), he ends in apostrophe and an effort to do justice to the dead Falkland: he will finish his memoirs "that thy story may be fully understood; and that, if those errors of thy life be known which thou so ardently desiredst to conceal, the world may at least not hear and repeat a half-told and mangled tale" (326). Framed between these moments, Caleb's tale repeatedly turns on telling stories, where seeking or doing justice, exerting or resisting power, defining the self and its relation to others, all work through the unreliable medium of narrative. His effort to vindicate his character is a counternarrative to widespread accounts of "the notorious housebreaker, Kit Williams" (235–36) and pamphlets telling "the most wonderful and surprising history, and miraculous adventures of Caleb Williams" (268–69), and it incorporates others' narratives such as Collins's account of Falkland's earlier history or Falkland's own confession, where "character" always appears as a narrative construct, always subject to being told otherwise.

Character as the private and internal operations of the mind is equally formed by narrative. Caleb traces "the whole train of my life" from his leading trait of curiosity, which "produced in me an invincible attachment to books of narrative and romance" (4; compare the "heroic poets of Italy" from whom Falkland "imbibed the love of chivalry and romance" [10]). Romance takes on a markedly Gothic flavor when Caleb retells Collins's story of Tyrell's response to Falkland's vivid prediction (the multiple embedding is quite appropriate) of social ostracism. "Mr. Tyrell, in spite of himself, was blasted with the compunctions of guilt. The picture Mr. Falkland had drawn was prophetic. It described what Mr. Tyrell chiefly feared. . . . It was responsive to the whispering of his own meditations; it simply gave body and voice to the spectre that haunted him, and to the terrors to which he was an hourly prey" (78).[22] Again, after Tyrell's barbarous

---

[22] Note how this highly mediated account of Tyrell's state of mind claims knowledge of an-

treatment has led to the death of Miss Melvile, "in the indignation of all around him he found a ghost that haunted him with every change of place and a remorse that stung his conscience and exterminated his peace" (92). When the preternatural enters the secularized world of *Caleb Williams*, it is as a figure for the social dependence of even this brute. Falkland, "the fool of fame" (135), sacrificing everything to preserve his reputation, and Caleb, "cut off from the whole human species" by Falkland's slanders, are further instances of the principle Caleb voices: "The pride of philosophy has taught us to treat man as an individual. He is no such thing. He holds, necessarily, indispensibly, to his species" (303).[23] This insistently social view of the self foregrounds the operations of narrative as a discursive transaction, showing how the tales we take in and tell, as well as the tales told about us, shape our lives.[24]

The stress on social interconnections also offers a fuller understanding of narrative unreliability. The standard account features only individuals, the questionable version of a first-person narrator measured against the values of the implied author,[25] but Godwin shows how such judgments mobilize a large array of collective norms, positions, and interests, and how questions of reliability can challenge the beliefs that inform both the social and the individual. To the youthful Caleb, "innocence and guilt [are] the things in the whole world the most opposite to each other" (160); Mr. Forester believes "that it is not in the power of ingenuity to subvert the distinctions of right and wrong" (172); and Laura Denison believes "the good man and the bad, are characters precisely opposite, not characters distin-

---

other's private and internal operations that is supposedly inaccessible to homodiegetic narrators like Caleb and Collins. The effect is to make the self continuous with publicly circulated discourses like the rhetoric of Gothic.

[23] Caleb elaborates this account with a remarkable figure of monstrosity: "He is like those twin-births, that have two heads indeed, and four hands; but, if you attempt to detach them from each other, they are inevitably subjected to miserable and lingering destruction" (303). Here the norm of social existence appears as monstrous deviation, an effect that will be extensively developed in the great nineteenth-century monster stories, beginning with that Godwinian progeny *Frankenstein*.

[24] There are several other episodes in which telling, hearing, and reinterpreting stories play a crucial role. Caleb begins his efforts to discover Falkland's secret when he becomes dissatisfied with the "obvious sense" of Collins's narrative: "In the original communication it appeared sufficiently distinct and satisfactory; but, as I brooded over it, it gradually became mysterious" (107). The growing tensions between Caleb and Falkland are illustrated by a scene in which they argue about the story of Alexander the Great, which becomes an allegory of Falkland's nobility and/or crime (110–13). It is hardly surprising, after so many struggles have been staged over controlling narrative power, when near the end Caleb speculates that "the contents of the fatal trunk from which all my misfortunes originated" were "a faithful narrative" of the murder, which his own account may replace (315–16).

[25] See Wayne C. Booth, *The Rhetoric of Fiction* (Chicago: University of Chicago Press, 1961).

guished from each other by imperceptible shades" (299). As not only Caleb's failures to vindicate himself but his own shifting perspective on his innocence and guilt makes us realize, all are mistaken, and their errors obviously implicate general beliefs in such absolute oppositions.

Less obvious, though, are the ways unreliability bears on plotting, which may be recognized by comparing the logics of narrative destination and destiny. An ideally reliable narrative would be a communication in which the message received is always the same as the one sent. In these terms, an unreliable narrator's message has not reached its destination. It has gone astray, and another has arrived in its place, like a Gothic double usurping its identity. A plot whose conclusion seems inevitable also pursues an undeviating course, which can take on the preternatural aura of Destiny, a prominent Gothic motif. Caleb repeatedly draws on this retrospective sense of fatality, as when he recounts the moment he became certain of Falkland's guilt. "'Mr. Falkland is the murderer! He is Guilty! I see it! I feel it! I am sure of it!' Thus was I hurried along by an uncontrollable destiny. The state of my passions in their progressive career, the inquisitiveness and impatience of my thoughts, appeared to make this determination unavoidable" (130). In the slight uncertainty of "appeared" the possibility of other courses, other outcomes may be intimated, but Caleb's narrative hindsight works rather to confirm the inevitability of what has happened.[26] Questions of moral freedom and psychological determination hover here, as well as the suspicion of bad faith that haunts invocations of destiny. In the revised ending, Caleb blames himself for his "dreadful mistake" of insisting on a public hearing of his accusation. "I am sure that, if I had opened my heart to Mr. Falkland, if I had told him privately the tale that I now have been telling, he could not have resisted my reasonable demand" (323). Even without the evidence of the original ending, we cannot be so sure. Whether it insists on his uncontrollable destiny or on his culpability, Caleb's narrative, like any other, cannot reliably control its destination.

We have encountered this point already at the end of our reading of "The Tell-Tale Heart": the version of indeterminacy, of uncontrollable force, that arises from the structural potential of narrative to generate multiple versions. Since neither a text's grasp on its readers nor a reader's grasp of a text can ever be assured or final, this point could be considered the destined conclusion of reflecting on any narrative transaction, but it returns each time with a difference. Here, through the analogy of destiny and destina-

[26] Caleb also confides that the consoling sense of inevitability is "one of the motives which induced me to the penning of this narrative. . . . I derive a melancholy pleasure from dwelling upon the circumstances which imperceptibly paved the way to my ruin" (123; cf. 303).

tion, which will itself return several times in the following chapters, we see more clearly how by foregrounding the process of framing, Gothic fiction can produce a heightened and conflicted sense of narrative linearity in the terror and consolation of an inevitable fate and of narrative communication in the urgency and fallibility of a narrator's efforts to control meaning. In comparing Caleb Williams with Poe's narrator, we also see how differently the failure of those efforts can signify. "The Tell-Tale Heart" presents narrative control as domination, a force that produces an equal and opposite reaction. A similar sense of narrative power appears in Caleb's struggle to establish his version, as when he imagines denouncing Falkland: "I will tell a tale—! The justice of the country shall hear me! The elements of nature in universal uproar shall not interrupt me! I will speak with a voice more fearful than thunder!" (314).[27] But this grandiosity is a sign of his desperation and, in either version of the conclusion, a prelude to disaster. Whether the "vehemence" of his denunciation leads to failure, imprisonment, and madness or his anguished self-accusation leads to Falkland's surrender ("Williams, said he, you have conquered! I see too late the greatness and elevation of your mind" [324]), the persistent aim of his narrative is not domination but understanding, the shared meaning that would end his isolation and that always eludes him.

With its explicit political concerns and its thematic insistence that "man . . . holds, necessarily, indispensibly, to his species," *Caleb Williams* can acknowledge much more directly than any of Poe's tales the necessarily dialogical nature of narrative, but it is typically Gothic in dwelling on the breakdown of dialogue and the fraying of social bonds, while the strongest bond it develops cannot be socially accommodated. The intense moment of mutual recognition in the revised conclusion when Falkland throws himself into Caleb's arms stands out as a wish fulfillment of homosocial longing that complements Caleb's equally intense experience of Falkland's persecution as "like what has been described of the eye of omniscience pursuing the guilty sinner" (305). Both reduce their relations to a concentrated private sphere whose fantasmatic self-enclosure approaches that of narrator and victim in "The Tell-Tale Heart." The link between Gothic motifs and the loss of social connections also appears at the end of the original conclusion, as Caleb descends toward the indifference of "being like a stone." "Well, it is all one at last—I believe there was nothing in life worth

---

[27] Caleb's fantasy of narrative power invites comparison with his author's ("I will write a tale, that shall constitute an epoch in the mind of the reader . . . "). In Godwin, as in Poe, there is a powerful tension between the compulsions that drive the characters and authorial claims to conscious calculation and control.

making such a bustle about—no, nor in SECRETS—nor in MURDERS neither, for the matter of that—when people are dead, you know, one cannot bring them to life again!—dead folks tell no tales—ghosts do not walk these days—I never saw Mr. Tyrell's—Only once!" (334). The ghost that had been a figure for Tyrell's fear of being shunned returns here to mark the extremity of Caleb's estrangement from both others and himself. As good as dead, he will tell no more tales. If ghosts no longer walk in his secularized world, if the eye of divine omniscience no longer supervises it, their images can still register the terror of being cut off from the whole human species, of discovering the self's utter dependence on its relation to others.

The most impressive Gothic fictions written in the period between *Caleb Williams* and Poe's tales continue to investigate narrative force through the effects of framing. Shelley's *Frankenstein,* with its multiplication of narrative voices and thematic stress on the demand for recognition, clearly belongs to this group, but because it also introduces the new problematic of monstrosity, I will defer discussing it to part 2. Here, before returning to Poe, I want only to glance at two more examples that confirm and extend my account of Gothic as a reflexive mode, Maturin's *Melmoth the Wanderer* (1820) and Hogg's *Confessions of a Justified Sinner* (1824). Poe scornfully commented on "the devil in 'Melmoth,' who plots and counterplots through three octavo volumes for the entrapment of one or two souls, while any common devil would have demolished one or two thousand."[28] It is easy to understand his impatience with the inefficient length of this formidable wandering narrative, but he might also have recognized how it produces moments that concentrate the sense of narrative compulsion and control. Its tales within tales can be disorienting, as we lose track of the relation of its nested narratives and become absorbed in the story, but they can also produce sharp reminders of our own position as readers.

This effect occurs several times in the segment of the "Tale of the Spaniard" that presents Alonzo Monçada's attempted escape from the monastery. As he recounts the terrors of being guided by the fearsome parricide monk through the labyrinthine underground vaults, Monçada also reminds us, through the surrogate audience of John Melmoth, that we have been here before in the novels of Walpole, Radcliffe, and Lewis. "Romances have made your country, Sir, familiar with tales of supernatural horrors. All these, painted by the most eloquent pen, must fall short of the breathless horror felt by a being engaged in an enterprise beyond his powers, experience, or calculation, driven to trust his life and liberation to hands that

---

[28] "Henry Cockton," in *Essays and Reviews*, p. 178. Poe repeats the joke almost verbatim in "Letter to B——," p. 7.

reeked with a father's blood."[29] At one crisis, when he is caught in a narrowing passage, another narrative precedent occurs to him.

> In situations of peril, the imagination is unhappily fertile, and I could not help recollecting and *applying* a story I had once read of some travellers who attempted to explore the vaults of the Egyptian pyramids. One of them, who was advancing, as I was, on his hands and knees, stuck in the passage, and whether from terror, or from the natural consequences of his situation, swelled so that it was impossible for him to retreat, advance, or allow a passage for his companions. The party were on their return, and finding their passage stopped by this irremovable obstruction, their lights trembling on the verge of extinction, and their guide terrified beyond the power of direction or advice, proposed, in the selfishness to which the feeling of vital danger reduces all, to cut off the limbs of the wretched being who obstructed their passage. He heard this proposal, and, contracting himself with agony at the sound, was reduced, by that strong muscular spasm, to his usual dimensions, dragged out, and afforded room for the party to advance. He was suffocated, however, in the effort, and left behind a corse. (149)

The recollection fuels Monçada's panic, but the sensational effect turns out to be helpful. "I tried to crawl backwards,—I succeeded. I believe the story I recollected had an effect on me, I felt a contraction of muscles corresponding to what I had read of. I felt myself almost liberated by the sensation, and the next moment I was actually so." The episode is not only a little gem of induced claustrophobia but a shrewd reflection on the interplay of disturbance and control, imaginative subjection and liberation in the reader.[30]

Maturin seems to be as alert as Poe to the correspondence between circumscription of space and the force of a narrative frame, as Monçada suffers from the terrors of both oppressive enclosure and his companion's tales.

---

[29] Charles Robert Maturin, *Melmoth the Wanderer* (Lincoln: University of Nebraska Press, 1961), p. 148. In his brief preface, Maturin defends himself against a friend's criticism of the "Spaniard's Tale" "as containing too much attempt at the revivification of the horrors of Radcliffe-Romance" (3). His friend might well have had in mind Ellena and Vivaldi's attempted escape from the abbey in *The Italian,* which Monçada's ordeal closely resembles, just as the later death of the parricide at the hands of a mob recalls the riot in *The Monk.*

[30] Compare Poe's "The Premature Burial," which also plays claustrophobic terror off against narrative self-consciousness, producing an unresolved oscillation between the farcical deflation of manipulative "bugaboo tales—*such as this*" and the reassertion that "the grim legion of sepulchural terrors cannot be regarded as altogether fanciful." Edgar Allan Poe, *Poetry and Tales* (New York: Library of America, 1984), p. 679.

Forced to remain in the vaults while the day passes, he is subjected to the sleeping monk's dream-monologue in which he compulsively relives his father's murder. "At these horrible expressions, repeated over and over, I called, I shrieked to my companion to awake. . . . 'I cannot sustain your horrible eloquence of sleep. . . . I am willing to famish with hunger, to shudder with cold, to couch on these hard stones, but I cannot bear your dreams'" (156). Monçada tries to regain control by insisting that they stay awake, but this only leads to his renewed subjection as the monk tells the story of how he helped to trap two lovers in the same vault, gloating as he describes their degradation and death. The sequence renders an image of narrative as itself the sort of demonic bargain that Melmoth keeps offering, an abject bond between a sadistic narrator ("He was now in his element. He was enabled to daunt a feeble mind by the narration of horrors, and to amaze an ignorant one with a display of crimes" [158]) and a repelled but fascinated audience drawn by "that curiosity that brings thousands to witness a tragedy, and makes the most delicate female feast on groans and agonies" (163).[31]

Of course, the point of Maturin's framing story, and the condition of his continuing narrative, is that no one, no matter how desperate, will accept Melmoth's bargain.[32] Monçada's own narrative, struggling to escape from enclosure in the frightening tale he tells himself or in another's nightmares, seeks sympathetic understanding of his ordeals rather than power over his listener, and in the wider context of the novel's recurring themes we can read the parricide's tale as one more instance of the refusal of sympathy and the perversion of religion into a system of cruelty and oppression. But the reassurance we may derive from this reframing does not neutralize the corrosive doubt such moments inspire. Unlike Melmoth's bargain, the narrative pact cannot be simply refused: whatever his motives, Monçada must reenact the narration of horrors, occupying the position of oppressor as well as victim, and this structure is replicated in any reading.[33] Its in-

---

[31] As Robert Kiely observes, Monçada's relationship with the monk is sexualized from their first encounter and presented as "a strange courtship and marriage." *The Romantic Novel in England* (Cambridge: Harvard University Press, 1972), p. 203.

[32] Maturin's preface traces the origin of his story from a passage in one of his own sermons: "At this moment is there one of us present, however we may have departed from the Lord, disobeyed his will, and disregarded his word—is there one of us who would, at this moment accept all that man could bestow, or earth afford, to resign the hope of his salvation!—No, there is not one—not such a fool on earth, were the enemy of mankind to traverse it with the offer!" (3).

[33] As an indication of this complicity, note how Monçada's parenthetical remark about "the selfishness to which the feeling of vital danger reduces all" in his tale of the pyramid is echoed both in outlook and imagery of bodily mutilation in the monk's cynical account of how the extremity of the lovers' torment destroys their love. "In the agonies of their famished sickness

evitability is the most telling consequence of the Gothic reduction of all relations to terms of power. Caleb Williams recoils "with unspeakable loathing of those errors, in consequence of which every man is fated to be more or less the tyrant or the slave" and resolves "to hold myself disengaged from this odious scene, and never fill the part either of the oppressor or the sufferer" (156), but he cannot avoid playing both parts. Maturin insistently shows us how this necessity governs our own part in the narrative contract.[34] We may not lose our hope of salvation, which would be to embrace the parricide's savage despair, but we do lose our innocence.

The Private Memoirs and Confessions of a Justified Sinner is also concerned with salvation and damnation, inflected through Scottish Calvinist doctrines of predestination that conceive our lives as stories whose endings are irrevocably determined in advance. That is only one of several ways Hogg's novel raises questions about narrative force; others are indicated in its subtitle: *Written by Himself: With a Detail of Curious Traditionary Facts, and Other Evidence by the Editor.* Hogg's name is absent from the original title page, though it appears, significantly, near the end of the novel. Instead there are the doubled authorial figures of the sinner and the editor, whose twin accounts expand and complicate the Gothic investigation of narrative reliability. Hogg's scheme recalls the antiquarian gambit with which Walpole inaugurated the Gothic novel, framing the simulation of a recovered text (the first edition even included a facsimile of the sinner's manuscript) between the "Editor's Narrative," which recounts a version of the story based on "traditionary facts," and a brief concluding account of the discovery of the sinner's preserved body and memoirs. But because the two narratives overlap so much yet offer sharply differing perspectives, the novel also anticipates later Victorian experiments such as the alternating authorial and personal narratives of Dickens's *Bleak House*, setting "the account as . . . publicly handed down to us" against the private version of "one who knew all the circumstances—was deeply interested in them, and whose relation is of higher value than any thing that can be retailed out of the stores of tradition and old registers."[35]

---

they loathed each other,—they could have cursed each other, if they had had breath to curse. It was on the fourth night that I heard the shriek of the wretched female,—her lover, in the agony of hunger, had fastened his teeth in her shoulder;—that bosom on which he had so often luxuriated, became a meal to him now" (164–65).

[34] Compare the later moment when Monçada describes in horrifying detail the parricide's death at the hands of an enraged mob, occupying the positions of both narrator in telling his tale and audience as he watches in helpless fascination and shrieks in concert with both the mob and its prey. "The drama of terror has the irresistible power of converting its audience into its victims" (197).

[35] James Hogg, *The Private Memoirs and Confessions of a Justified Sinner* (Harmondsworth:

What is this higher value? The editor's apparent strategy is to present the partial and inconclusive public version of the deadly fraternal rivalry between George Colwan and Robert Wringim before offering Robert's own fuller and more authentic private account, so that questions posed by the first will be answered by the second. The comments on the relation between the two appear at the point where the description of Robert's intensifying persecution of his brother has pushed the editor's narrative beyond naturalistic terms.

> A fiend of more malignant aspect was ever at his elbow, in the form of his brother. . . . George became utterly confounded; not only at the import of this persecution, but how in the world it came to pass that this unaccountable being knew all his motions, and every intention of his heart, as it were intuitively. (58)

> The attendance of that brother was now become like the attendance of a demon on some devoted being that has sold himself to destruction; his approaches as undiscerned, and his looks as fraught with hideous malignity. (60)

> He could not get quit of a conviction that he was haunted by some evil genius in the shape of his brother, as well as by that dark and mysterious wretch himself. (66)

Robert's narrative offers a possible solution to these enigmas in the figure of his mysterious companion Gil-Martin, who first appears, at the moment when Robert has just been assured that he is one of the justified, as his perfect likeness. Gil-Martin's preternatural powers of knowing others' thoughts and assuming others' forms could account for these uncanny effects, as well as for the duplicate of Drummond that Bell Calvert sees before George's murder, who strikes her as "some spirit, or demon, in his likeness" (90) and the duplicate of George that both she and Mrs. Logan see later, "walking arm in arm with his murderer" (99).

Reading the two narratives according to a hermeneutic code of enigma and solution engages us in the sort of detective work we have already traced in "The Tell-Tale Heart," replacing Robert's unreliable version with a more

---

Penguin, 1983), p. 68. Besides the formal features that link it to later experiments in multiple narration, Hogg's embedding of a recovered text from the previous century in a contemporary editorial commentary dramatizes the tensions between traditional religious belief and enlightened modernity in specifically Scottish terms. On the Scottish "association between the *national* and the *uncanny or supernatural*," see Ian Duncan, "Walter Scott, James Hogg and Scottish Gothic," in *A Companion to the Gothic*, ed. David Punter (Oxford: Blackwell, 2000), pp. 70–80.

coherent one. Here, however, the explanation reverses the usual naturalizing project of detection. There are several moments in Robert's confessions
that invite a psychological reading,[36] but several others prompt us to identify Gil-Martin as the devil ("'I have no parents save one, whom I do not
acknowledge,' said he proudly" [136–37]), and constructing a consistent
narrative requires us to consider him as an independent agent, not a projection of Robert's madness. As we saw in Radcliffe and Lewis, resolving
the tension between natural and preternatural explanation may matter less
than the struggle for narrative control it provokes. Robert, recounting his
increasingly terrifying experiences, despairs of making sense of them: "I
have now lost all hopes of ever discovering the true import of these events"
(128); and when he declares, "I seemed hardly to be an accountable creature," it bears as much on narrative intelligibility as on moral responsibility.

> I was a being incomprehensible to myself. Either I had a second self, who
> transacted business in my likeness, or else my body was at times possessed
> by a spirit over which it had no control, and of whose actions my own soul
> was wholly unconscious. This was an anomaly not to be accounted for by
> any philosophy of mine, and I was many times, in contemplating it, excited
> to terrors and mental torments hardly describable. To be in a state of con-
> sciousness and unconsciousness, at the same time, in the same body and
> same spirit, was impossible. (181)

We can try to account for these mysteries by crediting demonic doubling
or possession or by affirming the psychological coexistence of consciousness
and unconsciousness, but the whole novel also offers a warning and resistance against such attempts to grasp it securely. Robert's downfall begins
with a moment of narrative certainty, his assurance of salvation, while the
brief conclusion that follows his memoirs stresses the difficulty of deciding
what to make of them. "What can this work be? Sure, you will say, it must
be an allegory; or (as the writer calls it) a religious PARABLE, showing the
dreadful danger of self-righteousness? I cannot tell" (230). The editor, resuming here, pursues the questions of authenticity and origin, first by in-
serting part of an "authentic letter, published in *Blackwood's Magazine* for
August, 1823," and "signed JAMES HOGG" describing the discovery of the
sinner's remarkably well-preserved body. "It bears the stamp of authentic-

---

[36] See, for example, David Punter: "Hogg produces a detailed and terrifying account of schiz-
ophrenia, tracing it through its stages of development with considerable psychological skill."
The Literature of Terror: A History of Gothic Fictions from 1765 to the Present Day (London: Longman, 1980), p. 149.

ity in every line; yet, so often had I been hoaxed by the ingenious fancies displayed in that Magazine, that . . . I did not believe it" (234). The editor's investigation leads to a brief encounter with "Hogg," who is more interested in selling sheep than "ganging to houk up hunder-year-auld banes" (236), and then to exhuming the body and discovering the text of the memoirs. None of this, however, brings the editor any closer to comprehension. "With regard to the work itself, I dare not venture a judgment, for I do not understand it." Like Walpole's Marshall, he cannot entertain a literal preternatural reading: "It is certainly impossible that these scenes could ever have occurred, that he describes as having himself transacted. . . . In this day, and with the present generation, it will not go down, that a man should be daily tempted by the devil, in the semblance of a fellow-creature"; but neither can he discern a figurative meaning: "It was a bold theme for an allegory, and would have suited that age well had it been taken up by one fully qualified for the task, which this writer was not." The only explanation he can offer is the writer's aberration: "We must either conceive him not only the greatest fool, but the greatest wretch, on whom was ever stamped the form of humanity; or, that he was a religious maniac, who wrote and wrote about a deluded creature, till he arrived at that height of madness, that he believed himself the very object whom he had been all along describing" (241–42).

As the frame closes with this final reflection on the process of doubling itself, the positions of writer and reader shift, multiply, merge, and dissolve. The editor becomes another protagonist in his story of discovery and another unreliable narrator in his bafflement; Hogg at last appears as an author, but only, in his persona of canny Ettrick shepherd, of a letter tainted with the suspicion of literary hoax and wrong in most of its authenticating particulars ("hardly a bit o't correct," says the guide [236]). Like the uncertain location of his grave, the position of the writer of the memoirs becomes a difficult question; like his body, which "could not bear handling" and is "all shaken to pieces" (239), his narrative disintegrates as we try to grasp it. A supposed suicide, he becomes, in the editor's final speculation, a figure of authorial breakdown, not only losing control over his narrative's allegorical potential but losing himself to the point of self-destruction in the process of imaginative projection and identification that fictional creation requires. This version reflects a persistent anxiety in nineteenth-century Gothic, the threat of psychic collapse that haunts its representations of isolated subjectivity, in which the private becomes completely solipsistic. Glimpsed already in "The Tell-Tale Heart" and the original ending to *Caleb Williams,* this "height of madness" figures the fate that threatens both writing and reading, the anomie in which the "higher value" of the private and the collective norms of the public accounts are finally incommensurable.

Caleb Williams, Melmoth the Wanderer, and *Confessions of a Justified Sinner* all plumb the terror of persecution, of the self cut off from others. They are, as David Punter says, "nightmare books" that can also be considered "paranoiac texts, for it is very difficult to know where the reader is situated in an encounter with a story of persecution told by the persecuted."[37] Eve Sedgwick also groups these novels, together with *Frankenstein,* as classic instances of "paranoid Gothic," which she takes to be "about what we would today call 'homosexual panic.'"[38] Whether we focus on their themes of political or religious persecution or trace in their private dramas the effects of "homophobia as a tool of social control," we can recognize that these novels significantly extend the Gothic investigation of power and subjectivity, and recognize as well that they do this through the processes of identification and dissociation that generate character doubling. Doubling will be a prominent issue as we return to Poe in the next chapter, and we will also pursue it further in the discussion of monster stories in part 2; here I want to dwell for a moment on its relation to narrative versions.

The structural potential for telling a story otherwise is a primary resource for producing effects of subjectivity, since a first-person or internally focalized account offers a perspective to which there are always possible alternatives and so seems to be determined by a character's distinctive qualities and interests. When multiple perspectives are actually presented, they usually heighten this individualizing effect, creating a sense of independent consciousnesses that each view the world at a different angle. We commonly think of these fictive subjectivities as the source of narrative points of view, but it is also possible to consider them as results of transforming one version into another, a consequence of the reversible priority of story and discourse. *Confessions of a Justified Sinner* allows us to sense more acutely how different versions entail subject positions through the troubling relation between its doubled narratives. As they tell the "same" story twice, their perspectives seem to be at first complementary and eventually incommensurable, yet their distinctness is also compromised at moments such as those where the editor seems compelled to adopt preternatural terms or where Robert cannot account for the evidence of his double existence, as if a version of events that neither can accommodate is imposing itself and disrupting their self-possession. This blurring of boundaries corresponds to the subversion of identity by doubling, the splitting of a self or

[37] Punter, *Literature of Terror,* pp. 127–28.
[38] Eve Kosofsky Sedgwick, *Between Men: English Literature and Male Homosocial Desire* (New York: Columbia University Press, 1985), p. 116.

the encounter with another who is also oneself. Both narratives suffer from increasing confusion as they approach their conclusions, and in the final section the identities of Robert, Gil-Martin, the editor, the writer of the memoirs, and Hogg all threaten to collapse into "that height of madness," endemic identification.[39] As when Falkland becomes a persecuting figure in Caleb's imagination or Monçada becomes the parricide's narrative accomplice, these uncanny effects testify to the disturbing power of Gothic reflexivity, the doubling that constitutes narrative reflection itself.

This power manifests itself here as narrative dispossession, the counterpart and opposing force to the writer's attempt to control meaning and secure a narrative's grasp on its reader. Robert Wringham ends his memoirs with such an attempt: "I will now seal up my little book, and conceal it; and cursed be he who trieth to alter or amend!" (230), but his prohibition is necessarily futile. The editor says he first "altered the title to *A Self-justified Sinner,* but my booksellers did not approve of it; and there being a curse pronounced by the writer on him that should dare to alter or amend, I have let it stand as it is" (241). Yet of course he has also made the alteration, as has any reader who views Robert's justification ironically, opening it to revision by assigning it to the "self" and so producing an alternative version. The uncanny effects of doubling in *Confessions of a Justified Sinner* dramatize the inevitable dialogism of narrative. The divided self appears here not as the splitting of a primal unity but as an apprehension of the other that already inhabits us as a condition of our existence in a supplementary relation that is as much intersubjective and social as it is intrapsychic and private. The final framing moment, in which all the narrative figures can seem to merge into the self-enclosed mind of the author, like figments of a dream, is also the moment at which the narrative is finally given over to its readers for reframing.

---

[39] Compare the moment near the end of the editor's initial narrative where Mrs. Logan, Mrs. Calvert, and the landlady are seized by mimetic contagion in response to the reappearance of George Colwan after his murder. "Their looks encountered, and there was an unearthly amazement that gleamed from each, which, meeting together, caught real fire, and returned the flame to their heated imaginations, till the two associates became like two statues, with their hands spread, their eyes fixed, and their chops fallen down upon their bosoms. An old woman who kept the lodging house . . . caught the infection, and fell into the same rigid and statue-like appearance. . . . 'It *is* he!' cried Mrs Logan, hysterically. 'Yes, yes, it *is* he!' cried the landlady in unison" (98). For the biographical basis of Hogg's potential identification with his characters, see John Carey, "Introduction," *The Private Memoirs and Confessions of a Justified Sinner* (Oxford: Oxford University Press, 1981), pp. xi–xxiii.

3

Poe and His Doubles

In the intensified doubling that concludes *Confessions of a Justified Sinner* we have again encountered the struggle for narrative control we first found in Poe. If he has offered a perspective that helps us recognize the reflexive dimension in Gothic writers from Walpole to Hogg, they in turn can help us extend our reading of him. Framed by that series of texts, Poe's tales may seem all the more abstracted from "historical existence," turned in on themselves in their pursuit of formal control and unity of effect. We could recall, for instance, earlier Gothic stories of political and religious persecution and compare Poe's use of such motifs in "The Pit and the Pendulum," where that standard agency of terror, the Inquisition, is reduced to the sparest schematic notation and the narrator's prior history completely elided in order to isolate and amplify the account of his torment in an oppressive space that again figures the concentration of the tale. Poe, we might claim, is utterly indifferent to the political significance of persecution, which functions only as the occasion for an elaborate phenomenology of terror, equivalent to the contrived physical predicaments of such sensational *Blackwood's* tales as "The Man in the Bell," "The Iron Shroud," or "The Involuntary Experimentalist."[1] This would of course reproduce

---

[1] Compare the advice of Mr. Blackwood to the aspiring writer Psyche Zenobia: "And then there was '*The Man in the Bell*,' . . . the history of a young person who goes to sleep under the clapper of a church bell, and is awakened by its tolling for a funeral. The sound drives him mad, and accordingly, pulling out his tablets, he gives a record of his sensations. Sensations are the great thing after all. Should you ever be drowned or hung, be sure and make a note of your sensations—they will be worth to you ten guineas a sheet." Edgar Allan Poe, "How to Write a Blackwood Article," in *Poetry and Tales* (New York: Library of America, 1984), p. 281.

within the Gothic tradition the contrast of Poe and Dickens, or tale and novel, that we have already considered and complicated. But we have now seen much more fully how from its beginnings Gothic poses questions of power and authority not just through its representational content but through reflections on its enabling conditions that heighten our sense of narrative as a social drama. Poe's tales, precisely because they are so often driven by the dream and nightmare of self-enclosure, intensify that drama all the more.

"William Wilson" offers a good illustration that repeats several features we have just been considering in *Confessions of a Justified Sinner,* including a story of perdition, doubling, the uncertain position of the author, and a failed allegory. The tale is also close to "The Tell-Tale Heart" in ways that allow us to add to our earlier reading.[2] Most striking is the repeated scene of the protagonist's stealthy intrusion into the bedroom of his sleeping counterpart and the resulting specular confrontation. Wilson too is "resolved to make him feel the full extent of the malice with which I was imbued" (346), though his object is some practical joke rather than murder, but in his case the effect of contemplating his unconscious rival is devastating, "an objectless yet intolerable horror."

> Gasping for breath, I lowered the lamp in still nearer proximity to the face. Were these—*these* the lineaments of William Wilson? I saw, indeed, that they were his, but I shook as if with a fit of the ague in fancying they were not. What *was* there about them to confound me in this manner? I gazed;— while my brain reeled with a multitude of incoherent thoughts. Not thus he appeared—assuredly not *thus*—in the vivacity of his waking hours. The same name! the same contour of person! the same day of arrival at the academy! And then his dogged and meaningless imitation of my gait, my voice, my habits, and my manner! Was it, in truth, within the bounds of human possibility, that *what I now saw* was the result, merely, of the habitual practice of this sarcastic imitation? (347)

Overwhelmed by the sight, which he leaves undescribed, Wilson flees from not only the room but the school. His nemesis, face always obscured, pursues him and repeatedly thwarts Wilson's schemes until their final confrontation, which yields a parallel scene. Here Wilson first mistakes his mortally wounded antagonist for his own mirrored image, then at last recognizes that there is "not a line in all the marked and singular lineaments

---

[2] Poe reprinted the two tales in successive weeks in the *Broadway Journal,* "The Tell-Tale Heart" on August 23, 1845, and "William Wilson" on August 30, 1845. In their original appearances, "William Wilson" (1839) preceded "The Tell-Tale Heart" (1843).

of his face which was not, even in the most absolute identity, *mine own!*"
(356).

If the earlier scene had not already prompted us to infer this duplication,
so uncanny that Wilson cannot acknowledge it, the second makes it explicit. But the tale has been inciting us from the beginning to produce an
alternative to Wilson's version, not only more explicit but providing a better explanation for what remains to him "the horror and the mystery of the
wildest of all sublunary visions" (338). He appeals to his readers to make
sense of his experience as an inevitable destiny: "I would wish them to seek
out for me, in the details I am about to give, some little oasis of *fatality*
amid a wilderness of error" (337); but we are more likely to concentrate
on explaining his crucial error, which takes the same form of misrecognition we found in "The Tell-Tale Heart." Before Wilson's narrative has even
begun, we have received a strong nudge in this direction from the epigraph:
"What say of it? what say CONSCIENCE grim, / That spectre in my path?"[3]
This makes the solution to the mystery obvious—perhaps, as Poe's Dupin
might say, a little too obvious.[4] Once again, we can reconstruct the story
by redrawing boundaries and locating Wilson's persecuting double within
himself. Certainly, there are several details in his account that encourage us
to interpret the double as the embodiment of Wilson's conscience, such as
his always speaking in "*a very low whisper*" (343), but there are others that
resist an allegorical reading.

What, for instance, should we make of the scene at Oxford where Wilson's cheating at cards is exposed by his double? Are we to suppose that,
suddenly overcome with shame, he confesses his transgression? In this
episode, unlike the preceding intervention where he is recalled from a fit of
"soulless dissipation" at Eton (348), Wilson is not the only one to perceive
the double here, since after hearing him reveal, "in a low, distinct, and
never-to-be-forgotten *whisper,*" Wilson's "true character," the other play-
ers seize him and find his prepared packs of cards (352). No one else, how-

---

[3] The lines are attributed to "*Chamberlain's* Pharronida," but an editorial note informs us
that "The correct spellings are *Pharonnida* and *Chamberlayne;* the lines quoted are not in the
work cited" (1392). To whom should we assign the lines (and the errors)? If we say "Wilson,"
we would locate him both inside and outside his mystified account, both knowing and not
knowing the identity of his double; if we say "Poe," we would have to reckon with the biographical details he shares with Wilson, such as his birthday, that make him another double,
inside as well as outside the tale. The upper border of "William Wilson" is blurred, like, as
we shall see, the lower. Compare Derrida on the uncertain borders of Blanchot's "The Madness of the Day," in "The Law of Genre," trans. Avital Ronell, *Critical Inquiry* 7 (1980): 55–
81.
[4] "'Perhaps the mystery is a little *too* plain,' said Dupin. . . . 'A little *too* self-evident.'" "The
Purloined Letter," p. 681.

ever, notices that the fur cloak his host scornfully hands him is the "exact counterpart in every, in even the minutest possible particular" of the one already on his arm, whose unique design Wilson has stressed at length (353). We may not be filled, like Wilson, with "an astonishment nearly bordering upon terror," but neither can we easily fit these details into a psychological allegory.[5]

Allegory, we might recall, is acceptable for Poe only "where the suggested meaning runs through the obvious one in a *very* profound undercurrent, so as never to interfere with the upper one without our own volition,"[6] but here it is the figurative sense that is obvious, the literal that interferes, and our volition in controlling meaning that is balked, like Wilson's as he rages over his "natural rights of self-agency so pertinaciously, so insultingly denied" (354). As in Poe's stricture, the traditional scheme for managing such difficulties is the spatial metaphor of levels, keeping literal and figurative senses separate and parallel, another source of confusion for Wilson in his early school experience of the disorienting effect of the labyrinthine house, with "its incomprehensible subdivisions. It was difficult, at any given time, to say with certainty upon which of its two stories one happened to be" (340). Stories, levels: these familiar ways of grasping narrative form and meaning falter here, and we may begin to suspect that our comprehension is not so clearly superior to Wilson's. "Have I not indeed been living in a dream?" he asks; we may not be entirely outside it either, since we cannot completely reconstruct his story.

The main obstacle to that reconstruction, however, is not in the textural details but in the large-scale structure of Wilson's narrative. The point of his tale, he announces at the beginning, is not just to recount his early experience or, certainly, to "embody a record of my later years of unspeakable misery and unpardonable crime," but to explain the transformation that joins them, the "sudden elevation in turpitude, whose origin alone it is my present purpose to assign. Men usually grow base by degrees. From me, in an instant, all virtue dropped bodily as a mantle. From comparatively trivial wickedness I passed, with the stride of a giant, into more than the enormities of an Elah-Gabalus. What chance—what one event brought this evil thing to pass, bear with me while I relate" (337). The final moment of the tale apparently presents this momentous event, his destruction of his

---

[5] We might consider these resistant elements as evidence of the tension between "novel" and "tale," produced here by a novelistic technique of verisimilitude, specifying details of costume; compare the "white kerseymere morning frock, cut in the novel fashion of the one I myself wore at the moment," in which the double appears in the Eton episode (348).

[6] Edgar Allan Poe, "Nathaniel Hawthorne," in *Essays and Reviews* (New York: Library of America, 1984), p. 582.

double, whose dying words pronounce his fate. "*You have conquered, and I yield. Yet, henceforward art thou also dead—dead to the World, to Heaven, and to Hope! In me didst thou exist—and in my death, see by this image, which is thine own, how utterly thou hast murdered thyself*" (357). If Wilson has indeed destroyed his conscience, that would explain a sudden leap into unchecked evil, but it makes an inexplicable mystery of his continual self-reproaches as he tells his story.[7] There seems to be no way to reconcile the narrative frame with the guilt-ridden narrator who presents what indeed seems comparatively trivial wickedness as if it were already unpardonable crime: beginning and end, story and discourse, literal and figurative fail to mesh.

It is possible to salvage from these discrepancies the outlines of a coherent psychological portrait, if not a consistent story. We could begin with Wilson's rhetorical accusation of himself as another: "Oh, outcast of all outcasts most abandoned!" (337), where "abandoned" can carry the sense not only of depravity but of desertion, and we could recall his brief account of his parents' failure to control his "ungovernable passions. . . . Some feeble and ill-directed efforts resulted in complete failure on their part, and, of course, in total triumph on mine. Thenceforward my voice was a household law; and at an age when few children have abandoned their leading strings, I was left to the guidance of my own will, and became, in all but name, the master of my own actions" (338). Such a triumph might well feel like abandonment and leave a legacy of rage and guilt. To develop these suggestions would be a way of granting Wilson's wish that we seek out some little oasis of fatality amid the wilderness of his errors, and perhaps also of granting "the sympathy—I had nearly said the pity" that he longs for (337). Instead of a narrative transformation from being master of his own actions to being subjected to his double's "mysterious domination" (353), or from trivial wickedness to enormity, we might construct a version of a Wilson who continually, blindly reenacts the fury and despair, the bravado and self-contempt of an abandoned child.[8] In producing this version, we would be entering a dialogue that both contests and cooperates with Wilson's narrative, a relation that might avoid his stark, typically Gothic alternatives of mastery and subjection.

[7] A more consequential narrative logic might have produced such a blithely amoral narrator as we find in Mark Twain's comic version of conscience-killing, "The Facts Concerning the Recent Carnival of Crime in Connecticut."

[8] If we were to link such a reading to biographical interpretation, this would be the point to recall Poe's experience of abandonment, first in his father's desertion and his mother's early death and then in John Allan's withdrawal of support. It might then be easier to explain why Wilson's experiences at Dr. Bransby's school and Oxford parallel Poe's at Stoke Newington and the University of Virginia.

We might also expand this dialogue to include the epigraph and actually take up its questions instead of simply taking it as the obvious solution to Wilson's mystery. What to say of conscience, what does it say, and where does this haunting specter come from? The traditional allegory of a psychomachia, a split and battle within the self, will not easily contain Wilson's experience of attraction and rivalry, persecution and struggle. These recognizable features of the paranoid Gothic mode require a sense of the double as separate and other, not just a component of an enclosed psychic system: the specter in Wilson's path is both a fantasmatic version of himself and the intrusion or reminder of something that is not himself. We might then say of conscience that it is the spectral emanation of others who inhabit the self, that what it says always echoes their voices, and that its persistence shows how the self exists only in and as a dialogical relation. When Wilson addresses himself as an outcast ("to the earth art thou not forever dead? . . . and a cloud, dense, dismal, and limitless, does it not hang eternally between thy hopes and heaven?"), he echoes the last words of the double. Here end and beginning mesh tightly, but not to consolidate either Wilson's or his tale's self-enclosure. His thwarted will, his baffled account, and the reader's comparable frustrations all register the dependence of both the self and narrative on what escapes their control.

The repeatedly renewed and repeatedly frustrated bid for mastery in both his characters and his narrative dynamics, the recurring tension between his efforts to wield "the immense force derivable from *totality*" and the uncontainable force of dialogism, has been the main theme of our reading of Poe and his relation to Gothic reflexivity. To conclude that reading, I want to strengthen our sense of how Gothic reflects on narrative force by comparing it to the more narrowly philosophical sense of reflection, in terms of both the general process of doubling and the tale that pushes it to the furthest extreme, "The Fall of the House of Usher." As we saw in the introductory comparison of Gothic and Shandean reflexivity, philosophical reflection proposes an inward movement in which thought turns back on itself in a spiral of "self-reflection, self-relation, self-mirroring."[9] John Irwin has recently shown how much of Poe's work can be understood in terms of this pursuit of absolute self-knowledge, in which the many variations of doubling between his characters figure the inner division and duplication of self-consciousness. Irwin discusses "William Wilson" and "The Fall of the House of Usher" as "crucial steps in the development of the analytic detective story," which he considers the culmination of Poe's self-

[9] Rodolphe Gasché, *The Tain of the Mirror: Derrida and the Philosophy of Reflection* (Cambridge: Harvard University Press, 1986), p. 13.

reflexive project, interpreting their themes of doubling and incest as representations of the dangers of narcissistic self-absorption that threaten that inward quest.[10] This reading illuminates and connects many elements in Poe's thought, but in privileging the introspective work of ratiocination it leaves out his intense concern with narrative as a struggle for control. Framed by the Gothic tradition, his detective stories appear as only one version of that struggle, where the process of analysis or rational reconstruction is foregrounded and terror recedes. In Gothic fiction from Walpole onward, the effort to master terror never ceases because it never fully succeeds, and because it engages not only the characters but their authors and readers as well in a drama that has no set or final resolution.

The analytic process of self-reflexivity is likewise interminable, its solutions always yielding deeper mysteries: once the mind becomes both subject and object it can never completely coincide with itself. The sort of narrative reflection we have traced through Gothic, however, is less profound and inward, less concerned with what Poe, putting Dickens in his place, calls "that metaphysical art in which the souls of all *mysteries* lie." Because it stresses the construction of competing versions, its moments of self-reference and probing into its own conditions of possibility lead toward a heightened awareness of narrative as a social transaction, of both narrative and the self as ongoing dialogues that cannot be grasped as completed wholes. To pursue such reflections is not simply to shift our attention from metaphysical or psychological inwardness to social or political outwardness but, as we have seen in our readings of both Poe and his predecessors, continually to cross and redraw the boundaries between them. Gothic doubling typically enacts this transformation of shifting perspectives, turning inside out and outside in. The uncanny duplication that initially represents a division within the self turns out to disclose its inextricable involvement with others; the varied figures of a story turn into dreamlike projections of the protagonist or author. Doubling carries the drama of multiple versions from the level of narrative discourse into the heart of the story itself.

---

[10] John T. Irwin, *The Mystery to a Solution: Poe, Borges, and the Analytic Detective Story* (Baltimore: Johns Hopkins University Press, 1994), pp. 213–15. Reading Poe's tales as esoteric allegories of the mind is a well-established critical tradition, beginning with Richard Wilbur's "The House of Poe" (1959), which argues that "the scenes and representations of Poe's tales are always concrete representations of states of mind," so that, for example, "circumscription, in Poe's tales, means the exclusion from consciousness of the so-called real world, the world of time and reason and physical fact; it means the isolation of the poetic soul in visionary reverie or trance." See *The Recognition of Edgar Allan Poe*, ed. Eric W. Carlson (Ann Arbor: University of Michigan Press, 1966), pp. 260–61. For an account of Poe's allegories in relation to Romantic symbolism, see Leon Chai, *The Romantic Foundations of the American Renaissance* (Ithaca: Cornell University Press, 1987), pp. 17–38.

Of all Poe's tales, "The Fall of the House of Usher" carries this splitting and merging furthest. From its opening moments, when the narrator's "sense of insufferable gloom" at his first glimpse of the house is amplified by "a shudder even more thrilling" as he gazes at its reflection in the tarn, and when "the consciousness of the rapid increase of [his] superstition . . . served mainly to accelerate the increase itself" (317–19), multiplying and intensifying reflections proliferate both outward and inward. Once we enter this labyrinth of mirrors, it becomes difficult to distinguish reflection and origin or cause and effect, which in turn makes it difficult to reconstruct the story. What happens—from the narrator's arrival through Usher's progressive deterioration, Madeline's premature burial and violent return, and the final collapse of the house—seems clear, but not how to account for it. The decaying house, to which Usher attributes "sentience," may as he believes be the cause of his own decay, the "silent, yet importunate and terrible influence which for centuries had moulded the destinies of the family, and which had made *him* . . . what he was" (328). But the narrator also suggests that Usher may be the source rather than the result of the house's oppressive atmosphere, "a mind from which darkness, as if an inherent positive quality, poured forth upon all objects of the moral and physical universe, in one unceasing radiation of gloom" (324). Similarly, the "sympathies of a scarcely intelligible nature" between Roderick and Madeline (329) seem to invite the sort of interpretive move we have traced in "The Tell-Tale Heart" and "William Wilson," relocating boundaries to make her a part of himself whose attempted repression and inexorable return destroys him. But the same move can be made with Usher, who has been construed as the narrator's "inner and spiritual self,"[11] while the narrator feels himself becoming assimilated to Usher: "It was no wonder that his condition terrified—that it infected me. I felt creeping upon me, by slow yet certain degrees, the wild influence of his own fantastic yet impressive superstitions" (330).

Influences, sympathies, and correspondences propagate in all directions here, and while we may try to contain them in an allegorical framework we should also consider how the tale stages and restages the tactics of allegorical reading. The first version is of course the presentation of Usher's poem "The Haunted Palace," in which conventional correspondences of house and head (windows and eyes, door and mouth, interior and mind) are used to represent the passage from sanity to madness. The narrator glosses the text in advance when he reads it as Usher's self-reflection: "In the under or mystic current of its meaning, I fancied that I perceived . . . a full con-

---

[11] Wilbur, "House of Poe," p. 265.

sciousness on the part of Usher, of the tottering of his lofty reason upon her throne" (325). When we recall how Usher's house also has been given such emblematic features ("vacant, eye-like windows" [317]) and how he himself resembles it (his "hair of a more than web-like softness and tenuity" [321] matching the "fine tangled web-work" of the "minute fungi" hanging from the eaves [319]), and when we note how Usher's poem leads to his exposition on the house's baleful sentience, we find ourselves tracing well-marked correspondences between levels of meaning, outer and inner, physical and mental, whose coherence and significance seem obvious.

The second version, however, does not yield its meaning so readily. As the tale builds toward its climax we again encounter a recited text, the "Mad Trist," which gives rise to a series of correspondences that are as singular as those of "The Haunted Palace" are conventional. The precise coordination of the sounds the narrator hears with the descriptions he reads is powerfully uncanny and remains so even after Usher's explanation: "the breaking of the hermit's door, and the death-cry of the dragon, and the clangor of the shield!—say, rather, the rending of her coffin, and the grating of the iron hinges of her prison, and her struggles within the coppered archway of the vault!" (335). Madeline's return from the tomb appears to confirm his account but still leaves us with no explanation for this bizarre series of coincidences. As in allegory, we encounter a doubling of levels, both textual and architectural, in the mirrored stories of breaking in and breaking out, but their correlation seems completely arbitrary and does not produce a conventional hierarchy of meanings. Madeline's return is not the under or mystic current of the "Mad Trist" (the breaking of the hermit's door, for instance, does not *represent* the rending of her coffin), nor do these doublings express a self-reflexive consciousness.[12] Instead, the emphatic formal pattern of the parallel series pushes the process of doubling itself toward abstraction.

Abstraction, of course, is the leading trait of Usher's art, carried furthest in "the pure abstractions which the hypochondriac contrived to throw upon his canvass" (324). The narrator's account of these expressions of Usher's "excited and highly distempered ideality" stresses how they both turn away from the external world and dominate their viewer: "By the utter simplicity, by the nakedness of his designs, he arrested and overawed attention. If ever mortal painted an idea, that mortal was Roderick Usher."

---

[12] The closest narratological equivalent to these uncanny effects is the transgressive figure Gérard Genette calls metalepsis, the intrusion of one narrative level into another that occurs when, for instance, an extradiegetic narrator appears within the narrated world or characters in a fiction interact with their author. See *Narrative Discourse: An Essay on Method,* trans. Jane E. Lewin (Ithaca: Cornell University Press, 1980), pp. 234–37.

It is clearly possible to take Usher as Poe's double and his art as an idealized version of Poe's own aspirations, and in that perspective to see the tale's thrust toward abstraction as an approach to their visionary fulfillment.[13] It is equally possible, however, to read "The Fall of the House of Usher" as a cautionary tale, like Tennyson's "The Palace of Art," in which withdrawal into a private imaginative realm leads to madness and ultimate destruction. Embracing either of these opposed didactic versions, or striking an ambivalent compromise between them, would be a way of trying to control the tale's meaning and escape its oppressive enclosure, but it is more instructive to dwell a little longer on the difficulties of its design.

The abstractness of the doubling in the climactic scene, where we can become both disturbed and fascinated by insistent but baffling correspondences, is an effect that has been building throughout the tale. The multiplication of doubles, with its tendency to reverse and suspend causality or reference, leads to an extraordinary moment in which form predominates over any available content and the relation of inside and outside reaches a crisis. What makes the corresponding sounds uncanny is the violation of a boundary: events within a fictional narrative suddenly seem to be happening outside it. Is this a case of breaking out or breaking in? Does it enact the intrusion of an external reality into the artificial refuge of fiction or the final surrender to delusion? For a moment, the mirroring of the two sequences makes it impossible to orient ourselves, and we hesitate, like Madeline, "trembling and tottering to and fro upon the threshold" (335). Then directions quickly, violently diverge: Madeline falls "heavily inward," the twins merge and die, and the narrator flees as the house collapses into the mirroring tarn.

The possibility, even the necessity of this collapse and escape are bound up with the position of the narrator as both participant observer and teller of the tale. Unlike "The Tell-Tale Heart" and "William Wilson," "The Fall of the House of Usher" sets its narrative perspective at an oblique angle to its fictional world. Instead of framing his account as a dialogical confrontation or appeal, and instead of positioning himself as protagonist, the narrator appears as a witness to the final days of the house of Usher and as the reader's proxy in registering its disturbing effects. The story of his experience traces an apparent movement from outside to inside, which we can quickly review. He comes, at Usher's "importunate" request, to minister to

---

[13] Wilbur shows the curious consequences of pursuing this line: "*The Fall of the House of Usher,* then, is not really a horror story; it is a triumphant report by the narrator that it *is* possible for the poetic soul to shake off this temporal, rational, physical world and escape, if only for a moment, to a realm of unfettered vision." "House of Poe," p. 267.

his friend's self-declared "mental disorder . . . with a view of attempting, by the cheerfulness of my society, some alleviation of his malady" (318). Becoming immediately subject to the house's "insufferable gloom," he increasingly yields to the influence of Usher's "fantastic, yet impressive superstitions," and we may suspect that the allegory of "The Haunted Palace" also describes the tottering of the narrator's reason as he is drawn into Usher's world. Yet such suspicions do not empower the reader to regain control by constructing an alternative version like those we are offered in the other two tales, and attempts to grasp the true import of the narrative by symbolic interpretation still leave us enclosed in that world. Realizing the power of the tale requires our sharing something of the narrator's experience, especially his "wild amazement" at the unaccountable series of coincidences that bring it to its climax, and we may even feel ourselves touched by the stunning transference of Usher's epithet: *"Madman! I tell you that she now stands without the door!"* (335).

The development of the entire narrative, working toward Madeline's reappearance and the fall of the house, seems designed to enclose us in its solipsistic madness, yet the same devices that produce that enclosure also imply our location outside it. That doubled position is indicated throughout by the narrator's mediating role, inviting involvement while acknowledging the distance it seeks to bridge, and in turning our attention toward this aspect we are turning away from esoteric readings and their claim to a privileged grasp of hidden meanings, recalling the obvious effects on which the tale's continuing popularity has depended. But we can also find this divided location insinuated in the subtle details that frame and prepare for the house's fall. The long opening description of the house and its surroundings leads to the narrator's puzzled consideration of the "wild inconsistency between its still perfect adaptation of parts and the crumbling condition of the individual stones," reminding him of "the specious totality of old wood work" (319–20). Then he adds, "Perhaps the eye of a scrutinizing observer might have discovered a barely perceptible fissure, which extending from the roof of the building in front, made its way down the wall in a zigzag direction, till it became lost in the sullen waters of the tarn" (320). Did he himself make this discovery at the time? If so ("Noticing these things, I rode over a short causeway to the house"), why does he introduce the hypothetical "scrutinizing observer," who appears only in this sentence and only "might have discovered" this sign of incipient disintegration? When this prefiguration is fulfilled at the end of the tale, it is "that once barely-discernable fissure, *of which I have before spoken* as extending from the roof of the building, in a zigzag direction, to the base" that widens to precipitate the final collapse (335; emphasis added). For the story to work, the fissure must be located within its fictional world, but the text insistently displaces it into the discourse of narration. Indeed, the "fissure" *is* narration, barely perceptible but decisively rupturing the specious totality of the tale. The hypothetical observer figures the position of the narrator as teller rather than participant, in which prefiguration derives from retrospective knowledge rather than uncanny correspondences, and it also figures the reader, whose location outside and afterward, like the narrator's last-minute escape, is necessary for the tale to exist. Just as the inward fall of the house of Usher both completes and destroys its hermetic self-enclosure, the narrator's last moments trace a double movement, reaching the extreme point of involvement and achieving a saving distance. His flight serves not only his self-preservation but the preservation of the narrative, meeting a minimal requirement for plausibility and so acknowledging the rational norms that so much of the tale denies.[14] In fulfilling this clause of the standard narrative contract, the tale also acknowledges its dependence on its readers and the limits of its control.

We began considering Poe with the initial rejection of "The Fall of the House of Usher" and the question of whether such tales of terror could achieve permanent popularity. We can now see how much was at stake in that question, both for Poe and for the Gothic mode. This is the tale in which Poe takes to the limit his dream of wielding the immense force derivable from totality, of creating a circumscribed space in which the soul of the reader is at the writer's control, and it is thus all the more telling that it ends up disclosing, like so many previous Gothic reflections, the dialogical basis of narrative. In the following three chapters, we will see how these reflections on narrative as both the achievement and the loss of control are extended in some of the most remarkably popular Gothic fictions of the nineteenth century, where the threat and attraction of aberrant subjectivities are intensified in the problematic of monstrosity.

---

[14] Other of Poe's tales also engage with the problem of accounting for the existence of a first-person narrative that traces a movement beyond the point of no return. "MS. Found in a Bottle," whose narrator is carried "onwards to some exciting knowledge—some never-to-be-imparted secret, whose attainment is destruction" (198), includes its escape clause in its title. In *The Narrative of Arthur Gordon Pym,* the protagonist has somehow survived a similar voyage to the brink of a chasm at the South Pole but has died before completing his narrative and so explaining his escape. Compare "A Predicament," the bungled application of the precepts of "How to Write a Blackwood Article," whose narrator recounts her experience of being decapitated.

Part II

Monster Stories

4

Frankenstein

Early in the second volume of *Frankenstein* there is a charged moment that condenses much of the fascination that monsters and their stories hold for reflections on narrative. Across the great glacier of the Mer de Glace, Victor Frankenstein sees "the figure of a man . . . advancing towards me with superhuman speed," which he soon recognizes as "the wretch whom I had created."[1] Believing his creature responsible for the deaths of both his younger brother William and the falsely condemned Justine Moritz, Frankenstein furiously denounces him.

> "Devil!" I exclaimed, "do you dare approach me? and do not you fear the fierce vengeance of my arm wreaked on your miserable head? Begone, vile insect! or rather stay, that I may trample you to dust! and, oh, that I could with the extinction of your miserable existence, restore those victims whom you have so diabolically murdered!"
>
> "I expected this reception," said the dæmon. "All men hate the wretched; how then must I be hated, who am miserable beyond all living things!" (94)

These are the first words we hear from the creature, and they come as a surprise. In his previous approach, on that "dreary night of November" when his creator has brought him to life and then fled in "horror and disgust," he appears by Frankenstein's bedside. "He held up the curtain of the bed; and his eyes, if eyes they may be called, were fixed on me. His jaws opened,

[1] Mary Wollstonecraft Shelley, *Frankenstein; or, The Modern Prometheus,* ed. James Rieger (Chicago: University of Chicago Press, 1982), p. 94. All parenthetical references are to this edition, which reprints the 1818 text, along with Shelley's 1831 revisions.

and he muttered some inarticulate sounds, while a grin wrinkled his cheeks. He might have spoken, but I did not hear; one hand was stretched out, seemingly to detain me, but I escaped, and rushed down the stairs" (53). His only other appearance before their encounter in the Alps comes when Frankenstein sees him at night near the scene of William's murder. Here there is no question of communication; the creature figures only as a momentary apparition whose physical monstrosity declares his moral deformity. "Nothing in human shape could have destroyed that fair child. *He* was the murderer!" (71).

We could thus hardly have expected the creature's articulate reception of Frankenstein. His mere ability to speak is startling, but from his first words he displays an eloquence that surpasses his creator's.[2] After seizing the moral high ground by turning Frankenstein's attack into evidence of his own victimization, he quickly presses his rhetorical advantage. "Yet you, my creator, detest and spurn me, thy creature, to whom thou art bound by ties only dissoluble by the annihilation of one of us. You purpose to kill me. How dare you sport thus with life? Do your duty towards me, and I will do mine towards you and the rest of mankind. If you will comply with my conditions, I will leave you and them at peace; but if you refuse, I will glut the maw of death, until it be satiated with the blood of your remaining friends" (94). Clearly, the creature is capable of producing his own version of the situation; soon he will be telling his story so persuasively that Frankenstein does indeed comply with his conditions for a time. As we have seen, presenting or projecting multiple versions is the main way Gothic fiction reflects on narrative; here, by endowing the creature with speech, *Frankenstein* reflexively heightens its formal drama, lodging at the center of the novel an account whose perspective forcefully contests the authority of the one that frames it. The most remarkable feature of Mary Shelley's monster story, and what most distinguishes it from its nineteenth-century successors, is that it includes the monster's own story.

But for modern readers, whose reception of *Frankenstein* is inevitably mediated through the many popular versions of its story, the surprise of this moment is much greater. We come to the novel with the sense of knowing it before we even begin to read, and especially with the indelible image of Boris Karloff as the monster: slow, subhuman, and above all speechless.[3] Not only

---

[2] Frankenstein, however, seems to imagine his creature capable of speech from the beginning, believing "he might have spoken" by the bedside (53). And the next day, when Clerval asks the reason for his hysterical behavior, "'Do not ask me,' cried I, putting my hands before my eyes, for I thought I saw the dreaded spectre glide into the room; '*he* can tell'" (56).

[3] The power of that image reaches far beyond those who have actually seen James Whale's 1931 film or its successors. My (then) eleven-year-old stepdaughter, seeing my copy of Rieger's

do we not expect such eloquence, but its rhetorical formality may seem comically inappropriate even as it makes strange what we thought so familiar. Yet a crucial part of the strangeness of *Frankenstein* itself is its extraordinary destiny as a modern myth, the countless repetitions, transformations, appropriations, and allusions that have marked its cultural reception throughout the nineteenth and twentieth centuries, so that any reading now must at least implicitly struggle with the problem of multiple versions that reach far beyond the borders of the original text. What do we imagine Mary Shelley would say if she could view Karloff's performance: "I expected this reception"? What about *Abbott and Costello Meet Frankenstein,* or Mel Brooks's *Young Frankenstein?* What about Franken Berry cereal?[4]

Before we decide that such more or less remote and vulgar descendants have little bearing on the novel itself, or that its author could hardly have anticipated them, we should recall that they began to appear quite soon after its initial publication in 1818. Richard Brinsley Peake's melodrama *Presumption; or, The Fate of Frankenstein,* which started the tradition of a speechless monster, was a great success on the London stage in 1823, when Shelley herself saw it performed.[5] Within the next three years, at least fourteen other stage versions were produced, including several burlesques like Peake's own *Another Piece of Presumption,* featuring the Promethean tailor Frankinstitch, and while there is no mention of cereals, the French version, *Le monstre et le magicien,* apparently inspired "pamphlets, ribands, and sweetmeats . . . called by its name."[6] Every type of adaptation and

---

edition, with its cover illustration by Stephen Brayfield, declared, "That's not Frankenstein!" I then showed her a picture of Karloff as the monster. "*That's* Frankenstein," she said.

[4] For a comprehensive survey of versions and derivatives, see Donald F. Glut, *The Frankenstein Legend: A Tribute to Mary Shelley and Boris Karloff* (Metuchen, N.J.: Scarecrow Press, 1973).

[5] "The story is not well managed," she wrote to Leigh Hunt, "but Cooke played ———'s part extremely well. . . . I was much amused, & it appeared to excite a breathless eagerness in the audience." Betty T. Bennett and Charles E. Robinson, eds., *The Mary Shelley Reader* (New York: Oxford University Press, 1990), p. 404.

[6] This is the testimony of the *New Monthly Magazine and Literary Journal* (November 1, 1826), as quoted in Steven Earl Forry, *Hideous Progenies: Dramatizations of Frankenstein from Mary Shelley to the Present* (Philadelphia: University of Pennsylvania Press, 1990), p. 35. It is not clear by which name these products were called, though Forry assumes it was Frankenstein's. It seems to have taken a few more years for the creator's name to be transferred to his creature: Forry's earliest example is from 1832. How to name this character is a persistent problem: the novel designates him not only as "monster" but as "fiend," "dæmon," "creature," "wretch," and "devil." Recent usage seems to favor "creature" as least pejorative, and I follow this practice except where "monster," with all its complex connotations, seems more appropriate. The dramatis personae for Peake's *Presumption* listed him only as "———," which Shelley found extremely amusing: "This nameless mode of naming the unnamable is rather good." Bennett and Robinson, *Mary Shelley Reader,* p. 404.

commodification of *Frankenstein* with which we are now so familiar seems to have been at work throughout its reception.

Thus when Shelley concluded her introduction to the revised 1831 edition with "now, once again, I bid my hideous progeny go forth and prosper" (229), she could well have expected that in prospering it might wander far from her parental control. At the same time, her act of identifying herself there with "the pale student of unhallowed arts" and her book with his "hideous phantasm" is also a bid to renew and increase that control. The first edition had appeared anonymously and was attributed by some, notably Scott in his *Blackwood's* review, to Percy Shelley. Now, writing after his death, Mary credits him only with urging her to expand her original idea: "I certainly did not owe the suggestion of one incident, nor scarcely of one train of feeling, to my husband" (229). James Rieger calls this claim "the worst distortion in the 1831 Introduction" and after briefly reviewing the evidence for Percy's contributions concludes that "his assistance at every point in the book's manufacture was so extensive that one hardly knows whether to regard him as editor or minor collaborator" (xvii–xviii).[7] Mary's account of the book's genesis is devoted only to explaining "how I, then a young girl, came to think of, and to dilate upon, so very hideous an idea" (222), and like her protagonist, she appears as the sole progenitor.

This is only one of the ways Shelley attempts to regain control over her creation. Partly because of its association with Percy, who wrote the original preface, and its dedication to Godwin, the first edition was accused of subversive intent by some reviewers, who complained that "it inculcates no lesson of conduct, manners, or morality" and that it expressed views "bordering too closely on impiety."[8] Her 1831 introduction rebuts these accu-

---

[7] In his "Note on the Text" Rieger becomes less uncertain: "We know he was more than an editor" (xliv). On the basis of her survey of manuscripts, journals, and letters, Marie-Hélène Huet argues that "with the exception of the 1831 Preface and the changes made by Mary Shelley for the third edition, it is impossible to assign with absolute certainty either to Percy or to Mary Shelley *complete* creative responsibility for any part of the novel." *Monstrous Imagination* (Cambridge: Harvard University Press, 1993), p. 155. As we shall see, taking or assigning responsibility becomes a prominent and troubling issue in the novel itself. For a fuller discussion of critical debates about the extent and effect of Percy's revisions, see Zachary Leader, *Revision and Romantic Authorship* (Oxford: Oxford University Press, 1996), pp. 167–205.

[8] The *Quarterly Review* and the *Edinburgh Magazine*, as quoted in Chris Baldick, *In Frankenstein's Shadow: Myth, Monstrosity, and Nineteenth-Century Writing* (Oxford: Oxford University Press, 1987), p. 57. Baldick shows how "the myth of Frankenstein registers the anxieties of the period inaugurated in the twin social and industrial revolutions in France and Britain" (5) and how it became a vehicle for subsequent political anxieties such as those prompted by the 1832 Reform Bill or Irish nationalism.

sations by importing a pious moral into its account of the story's visionary inspiration. "Frightful it must be; for supremely frightful would be the effect of any human endeavour to mock the stupendous mechanism of the Creator of the world" (228). The same effect is produced by several of Shelley's revisions, such as the passages she added to the opening interviews between Walton and Frankenstein. As Walton confides his high ambitions and willingness to sacrifice everything to fulfill them ("One man's life or death were but a small price to pay for the acquirement of the knowledge which I sought"), Frankenstein is appalled. "Unhappy man! Do you share my madness? Have you drank also of the intoxicating draught? Hear me,—let me reveal my tale, and you will dash the cup from your lips" (231–32). Later, as he is about to begin his narrative, he again stresses its motivation: "When I reflect that you are pursuing the same course, exposing yourself to the same dangers, which have rendered me what I am, I imagine that you may deduce an apt moral from my tale" (232–33). If Peake's melodrama subsumed the novel under a moralizing rubric, Shelley too now frames Frankenstein's story as a cautionary tale of presumption. She both sends her hideous progeny forth and tries to rein it in, like the child in Freud's *Beyond the Pleasure Principle* playing the game of *fort/da,* struggling to control what cannot be mastered.[9]

That struggle clearly takes place in the interval between the 1818 and 1831 editions, including the reissue of 1823, which first named Mary Shelley as the author, and it continues in every reading that, like this one, considers the relation between *Frankenstein* and its many descendants. But the interplay of losing and reclaiming control happens not only after the novel is published; we can see it at work from the beginning. Shelley's story of her story's conception dramatizes the process: the ghost story contest, her repeated, futile attempts "to think of a story," and then at last the moment when deliberate effort yields to a power she does not control. "My imagination, unbidden, possessed and guided me, gifting the successive images that arose in my mind with a vividness far beyond the usual bounds of reverie. I saw—with shut eyes, but acute mental vision,—I saw the pale student of unhallowed arts kneeling beside the thing he had put together. I saw the hideous phantasm of a man stretched out, and then, on the working of some powerful engine, show signs of life, and stir with an uneasy, half vital motion" (227–28).[10] This is a more dramatic version of the moment of

---

[9] As Baldick observes, Shelley's revisions also have Victor describing the monster as "the living monument of presumption and rash ignorance which I had let loose upon the world" (245) and referring to his "unhallowed arts" (247). See *In Frankenstein's Shadow,* p. 61.

[10] Rieger cites evidence showing "it is unlikely that it took Mary Shelley all this time 'to think

animation than the novel itself offers; "the working of some powerful engine," absent from Frankenstein's account, anticipates the spectacular electrical apparatus of Whale's film and seems reflexively to figure the force of imagination that projects it.[11] Both possessing and possessed by imagination, guided by the unbidden and bidding her creature go forth, Shelley enacts her own drama of divided desire.

Each of the novel's three narrators also presents a story of origins, in which the formation of deliberate purpose alternates with a sense of blind compulsion. Walton can partly account for his dream of polar discoveries, but he adds (and Shelley added in revision), "There is something at work in my soul, which I do not understand" (231). Frankenstein could say the same as his long-meditated project comes to dominate him: "I could not tear my thoughts from my employment, loathsome in itself, but which had taken an irresistible hold of my imagination" (50). The creature offers the fullest and most intelligible account of developing motive ("I shall relate events that impressed me with feelings which, from what I was, have made me what I am" [111]), but he is also driven by the most extreme and conflicting passions. In murdering Clerval and Elizabeth, he tells Walton, "I was the slave, not the master of an impulse, which I detested, yet could not disobey" (218). Much more needs to be said about these stories and their motives, but already we can recognize in the features they share with Shelley's introduction a common concern with the sources of art and action, with the force of outward influences and inner impulses, with the limits of narrative understanding and the struggle for control. Working in both aesthetic and ethical registers, claiming and disowning both authorship and responsibility, these stories may seem at odds with the processes of cultural transmission and transformation we have considered in the reception of *Frankenstein:* on the one hand the motives and powers of individuals; on the other the social reworking of form and meaning. But we can also regard them all as versions of the *fort/da* in which both writers and readers are engaged, continually seeking and surrendering mastery.

This is the narratological fascination of the great nineteenth-century monster stories: they become story-monsters that escape their creators' dis-

---

of a story'" (226, n. 10), but of course it makes a better story for her to suffer repeated failures ("*Have you thought of a story?* I was asked each morning, and each morning I was forced to reply with a mortifying negative" [226]) before inspiration strikes.

[11] William Nestrick suggests one reason why the moment of animation should become so important in film versions: "In *Frankenstein* the filmmaker finds a story that offers a narrative analogy to film itself." "Coming to Life: *Frankenstein* and the Nature of Film Narrative," in *The Endurance of Frankenstein: Essays on Mary Shelley's Novel,* ed. George Levine and U. C. Knoepflmacher (Berkeley: University of California Press, 1979), p. 294.

cursive control, acquiring narrative force that breaks the grasp of their original form. Such is the destiny not only of *Frankenstein* but of *Dr. Jekyll and Mr. Hyde* and *Dracula,* whose stories all exert persistent cultural power.[12] As we shall see, they also all stage reflections on narrative that, as much as their themes and effects of terror, link them to the Gothic tradition, and as in the Gothic fictions we have already considered, these reflections turn on the problematic opposition of story and discourse. The monstrous proliferation of versions these texts have spawned draws on the fundamental possibility for any narrative to be told otherwise, to differ from itself, in a movement that joins inward origin and subsequent destination. Both the self-difference of something other at work in the soul and the difference of the endlessly retold story manifest the dialogical relations that animate both the self and the social. Monstrosity as an uncontrollable force, as a heterogeneous mixture, both excessive and deficient, and as a threatening otherness that can never be completely excluded figures in the narrative reflections of all these texts. We need to consider its larger implications before returning to *Frankenstein.*

Monstrosity has a long history; in fact, quite appropriately, it has more than one, as we can see in two recent accounts that intersect in their readings of *Frankenstein* yet appear to have remarkably little else in common. Chris Baldick traces the politics of monstrosity from its traditional features of physical and moral deformity through its frequent Renaissance figurations of ingratitude and rebellion, like Goneril's "monster ingratitude" toward Lear, to its prominence in polemics over the French Revolution, whether in Burke's denunciation of its unnatural "monster of a constitution" or Paine's insistence on the need "to exterminate the monster Aristocracy."[13] Here monstrosity is a discourse, a figural complex embodied in Frankenstein's creature, who can demonstrate either the uncontrollable destructiveness of revolution or the inevitable consequences of injustice.[14] For

[12] A striking example of this power may be found in both media representations and policy debates concerning genetic manipulation and embryo research. Robert Edwards, the test-tube baby pioneer, complains that "whatever today's embryologists may do, Frankenstein or Faust or Jekyll will have foreshadowed, looming over every biological debate." *Life before Birth: Reflections on the Embryo Debate* (London: Hutchinson, 1989), p. 70. For a study of how such stories figure in struggles over the control of biological research, see Michael Mulkay, "Frankenstein and the Debate over Embryo Research," *Science, Technology, and Human Values* 21 (1996): 157–76.

[13] Baldick, *In Frankenstein's Shadow,* pp. 10–29.

[14] "Read from the Burkean position, as it usually is, the novel seems to warn against the recklessness of the radical *philosophe* who tries to construct a new body politic. But read from the position of Paine, Wollstonecraft, or Godwin, it seems to suggest that the violence of the oppressed springs from their frustration with the neglect and injustice of their social 'parent.'"

Marie-Hélène Huet, however, monsters are real, and their politics are sexual. Her monster story is much longer and more diverse, reaching from Aristotle's *On the Generation of Animals* to *Invasion of the Body Snatchers,* but it continually focuses on the problem of accounting for monstrous progeny. She shows how from classical antiquity through the Enlightenment, responsibility for these failures of the child to resemble its father was persistently assigned to the mother's disordered imagination, and how this subversive power was transvalued and reclaimed as a Romantic metaphor for masculine artistic creativity. In this account *Frankenstein* plays a pivotal role, drawing on the long tradition linking monstrosity with maternal aberration but also, at least in Shelley's 1831 introduction, offering a "manifesto" for "the Romantic interpretation of Monstrosity as Art."[15]

These two versions are enough to show that monstrosity has no single, consistent meaning, but it always embodies disturbing difference, violating what is taken to be the natural order and often inwardly heterogeneous, whether in classical monsters and prodigies composed of incongruous animal and human parts or in Frankenstein's creature, constructed with diverse materials drawn from the grave, the dissecting room, and the slaughterhouse. Monsters threaten our categories with a crisis of unlikeness, matching none or mixing several, and so they have to be set apart or cast out.[16] In both its revolutionary and its reactionary articulations, the politics of monstrosity is one of exclusion, consolidating individual or collective identity by purging what is other.[17] In all the nineteenth-century monster stories, Judith Halberstam claims, the same forces of embodied horror are at work: "the monster . . . condenses various racial and sexual threats to nation, capitalism, and the bourgeoisie in one body."[18] This sort

---

Baldick, *In Frankenstein's Shadow,* pp. 54–55. Both warning and demonstration are implied in the derivation of "monster" from *monere,* to warn, and *monstrare,* to show.

[15] Huet, *Monstrous Imagination,* p. 162.

[16] The taxonomic incongruity of monsters can in some cases be more productive than threatening. See, for example, Michel Foucault on their role in eighteenth-century natural history, where "the monster provides an account, as though in caricature, of the genesis of differences." *The Order of Things: An Archeology of the Human Sciences* (New York: Vintage, 1973), p. 157. For a range of historical and theoretical views, see Jeffrey Jerome Cohen, ed., *Monster Theory: Reading Culture* (Minneapolis: University of Minnesota Press, 1996).

[17] In psychoanalytic terms this involves the process Julia Kristeva calls "abjection." See *Powers of Horror: An Essay on Abjection,* trans. Leon S. Roudiez (New York: Columbia University Press, 1982). The concept has frequently been applied to Gothic fiction, especially monster stories. See, for example, Jerrold E. Hogle, "The Gothic Ghost of the Counterfeit and the Progress of Abjection," in *A Companion to the Gothic,* ed. David Punter (Oxford: Blackwell, 2000), pp. 293–304.

[18] Judith Halberstam, *Skin Shows: Gothic Horror and the Technology of Monsters* (Durham: Duke University Press, 1995), p. 3.

of reading, which has now become commonplace, treats the monster as a symptom of cultural anxieties we no longer share, allowing us the opportunity for both detached diagnosis and self-congratulation, as in Halberstam's claims for recent horror films, in which "we no longer attempt to identify the monster and fix the terms of his/her deformity, rather postmodern Gothic warns us to be suspicious of monster hunters, monster makers, and above all, discourses invested in purity and innocence."[19] Such suspicions, however, are not just recent. They inform all the great monster stories, which with characteristically Gothic self-consciousness do not simply implement but reflect critically on the operations of narrative power. From the multiple epithets heaped on Frankenstein's nameless creature through the repeated efforts to fix the terms of Mr. Hyde's deformity to the narrative collaboration that identifies Dracula and plays a crucial role in his defeat, these novels continually show us how the struggle for purification can itself become monstrous, how the narratives that delineate monstrosity cannot remain innocent.

The reversal of perspective Halberstam describes is also not a recent development, though it has become much more common as a narrative strategy. Postmodern monster stories as various as John Gardner's *Grendel,* Jean Rhys's *Wide Sargasso Sea,* and Anne Rice's *Interview with the Vampire* all depend on the device Shelley introduced of letting the monster speak and so become less monstrous. What most often differentiates postmodern versions in both fiction and interpretive readings is a slackening of tension, a penchant for uncritical identification with the excluded other. The twentieth century's monstrous history of violence in the name of racial and other kinds of purification understandably motivates this resistance, which also finds theoretical expression in the production of terms that, like monsters, figure a heterogeneity that resists purifying reduction. Notions like hybridity in postcolonial studies or queerness in theories of sexuality clearly work this way, blurring binary oppositions and advancing the recognition that homogeneous identities are themselves chimerical, but these enlightened views again deprive the monstrous of its menace. The closest recent analogue to earlier monsters is the figure of the cyborg, a hybrid of organism and machine that has migrated from science and science fiction to feminist cultural studies. Regarded with an ambivalence comparable to that produced by its nineteenth-century predecessors, this fusion of nature and culture holds some of their power to inspire both the terror of dehumanization and the fascination of alternative forms of life.[20]

---

[19] Halberstam, *Skin Shows,* p. 27.
[20] "From one perspective, a cyborg world is about the final imposition of a grid of control

"Many see Mary Shelley's monster, Frankenstein's creature, as the first cyborg."[21] In this doubled designation we recognize the parallels between the student of unhallowed arts and his author, between their hideous progenies, monster and story, and thus can also recognize the differences as well as the similarities between *Frankenstein* and the later stories of dangerous technology for which it has become a precedent. The creature is an artifact of the laboratory, but as with the results of Dr. Jekyll's later experiments in "transcendental medicine," there is more concern with moral agency and responsibility than with the technology of monster making, which amounts to little more than naturalized magic.[22] It is in *Dracula,* whose monster is a preternatural creature of ancient folk beliefs, that modern technology becomes most prominent, but it figures there mainly in devices used by his adversaries. Photography, stenography, the telegraph, phonograph, and typewriter are all technologies of writing or reproduction, and all are used in the struggle against Dracula, whose greatest threat, Dr. Van Helsing explains, "is not mere life or death. It is that we become as him."[23] In Dracula's ability to turn his victims into vampires like himself we can see an alternate mode of reproduction that recalls monster making in *Frankenstein* and *Dr. Jekyll and Mr. Hyde,* deviant modes of engendering that all reflect on the production of the narratives that recount them.

Deviation, a turning aside from nature or change of direction, drives all the monster stories, indeed makes them both monstrous and stories. Monsters never match their makers' expectations, whether Frankenstein's dream of "a new species [that] would bless me as its creator and source" (49), Jekyll's anticipation of enjoying "the strange immunities of my position" by using Hyde to pursue his "undignified" pleasures (86), or even Dracula's boast that Mina is now "flesh of my flesh; blood of my blood; kin of my kin

---

on the planet, about the final abstraction embodied in a Star Wars apocalypse waged in the name of defense, about the final appropriation of women's bodies in a masculinist orgy of war. From another perspective, a cyborg world might be about lived social and bodily realities in which people are not afraid of their joint kinship with animals and machines, not afraid of permanently partial identities and contradictory standpoints." Donna Haraway, "A Manifesto for Cyborgs," in *Simians, Cyborgs, and Women* (New York: Routledge, 1989), p. 154.

21 Chris Hables Gray, ed., *The Cyborg Handbook* (New York: Routledge, 1995), p. 5. Chris Baldick rejects the description of the creature as "half human, half machine," which "may bear some relation to the post-Karloff myth, but is quite inapplicable to Mary Shelley's creature, who is not in the least mechanical; the most disturbing thing about him, indeed, is that he has fully human feelings." *In Frankenstein's Shadow,* pp. 7–8.

22 Robert Louis Stevenson, *The Strange Case of Dr. Jekyll and Mr. Hyde and Other Stories* [1886] (Harmondsworth: Penguin, 1979), p. 80.

23 Bram Stoker, *Dracula* (New York: Bantam, 1981), pp. 250–51. The question of whether, in their concerted opposition, Dracula's opponents are already becoming "as him" is, as we shall see, a crucial issue.

... and shall later on be my companion and my helper" (304). No sooner has Frankenstein succeeded in bringing his creature to life than "the beauty of the dream vanished, and breathless horror and disgust filled my heart" (53); the pleasures Jekyll seeks through Hyde "soon began to turn toward the monstrous"; and instead of becoming Dracula's companion and helper, Mina uses the bond he has formed with her to help bring about his destruction. Both the turns away from nature that engender monsters and the turns of events in which their makers lose control are closely related to the sort of turns we call narrative versions. This series may seem to move from the aberrant to the commonplace, but in each case deviation is measured against an imagined norm, origin, or outcome. The sense that a narrative discourse tropes some underlying story can never be grounded by producing the story in its original pure form: all we have are versions. This common condition of narrative also holds for stories about departures from nature, falls, or perversions, which must always construct their pure starting points retroactively from the mixed state whose heterogeneity is thereby figured as monstrous.

Deviation from an expected outcome, like the ways monsters turn on their makers, is also common in most narratives that hope to keep our interest, but such plot turns become particularly interesting when they figure the loss of control that turns monster stories into story-monsters. Only rarely and unpredictably do literary narratives become transformed into popular myths like *Frankenstein, Dr. Jekyll and Mr. Hyde,* and *Dracula,* but the dramatic escape of these stories from the grasp of their initial discursive forms is just a heightened version of what can happen with any narrative. In a vitalistic figure that monster stories elaborate, we often say the story takes on a life of its own. While it captures the uncanny sense of the story's independence from its creator's will, this narrative obscures as much as it illuminates by drawing a sharp boundary between before and after: first the story is wholly owned by its author, then somehow gains autonomy. But our stories, like all our utterances, are never wholly our own; they can exist only in and through their dialogical relations with their surroundings, with the discourses that precede, follow, and penetrate them. *Frankenstein* partially figures this interdependence in the assembly of the creature from fragments of other bodies, like the novel's assembly from the myth of Prometheus, *Paradise Lost,* and the many other predecessors it cites as well as in its formal construction as a dialogue of competing voices and versions, beginning the open series of reconstructions that continues in subsequent retellings.[24]

---

[24] The analogy between corporal and textual assembly in *Frankenstein* has often been noted, for example in Michael Holquist, *Dialogism: Bakhtin and His World* (London: Routledge, 1990), pp. 90–106.

In all these cases, all these occasions for narrative reflection, we find ourselves drawn along a line of thought that links the disturbing difference of monstrosity with the ordinary, endless play of differences that constitutes the self and its relations to others. Monster stories intensify the problematic of deviant subjectivity that we have already explored in Gothic fiction from Walpole to Poe, extending its reflections on narrative as a psychosocial transaction. Monsters not only generate and resemble narrative versions, they *are* versions, doubles of their makers, other characters, and ourselves. Our alertness to monstrosity's politics of exclusion makes it easier for us to recognize monsters as abjected versions of ourselves, scapegoats for those aspects we find threatening, but they are also always vehicles for desire, emancipated aspects of ourselves whose perceived monstrosity usually protects us from recognition. Jekyll offers an exceptional glimpse of this liberating possibility when he first regards Hyde in the mirror with "a leap of welcome. This too was myself. It seemed natural and human" (84), though his pleased acknowledgment soon yields to the more common horrified disavowals. Here, as in *Frankenstein,* doubling between the monster and its maker manifests divisions within the self, but the fearful versions these figures offer also reflect the communal life from which they emerge. This probing of the collective imagination goes furthest in *Dracula,* whose monster seems most alien and remote from those who oppose him, where we shall find the most extensive reflections on both the collaborative production of narrative and the social power of fantasy. It may well be because these monsters embody what we desire as well as fear that we continually retell their stories, deploying technologies of narrative reproduction whose deviant effects we can never completely control.

Attempts to exercise narrative control preoccupy all three monster stories, and our main concern in each will be how it engages in this struggle. In *Frankenstein* it emerges most clearly at the moment where we began, when the creature takes over the narrative. The shape of his story and its rhetorical aim are concisely stated in advance: "I was benevolent and good; misery made me a fiend. Make me happy, and I shall again be virtuous" (95). Offering a readily graspable form, his narrative traces the trajectory of a fall from natural innocence into murderous rage, revenge, and despair, from being a victim to victimizing others. Its coherence and cogency may well lead us to accept his account, but we should recall that, as in other stories of monstrous deviation, its initial state of purity is the product of a postlapsarian discourse and depends on his acquisition of the "godlike science" of language (107) as well as the cultural repertoire of narratives that enables him to tell his story by analogy to Adam's and Satan's. And if it tells the story of becoming monstrous, the creature's narrative also tells of discovering a monstrousness that already exists, as when comparing "the per- fect forms of my cottagers" and his own reflected image convinces him "that I was in reality the monster that I am" (109), or when learning how wealth and kinship confer status leads him to sense his exclusion from all social categories: "Was I then a monster, a blot upon the earth?" (116). The shifting senses of monstrosity—physical deformity, misfitting, and malig- nity—combine in an unstable compound that powerfully renders the crea- ture's pathos as well as his menace, so that we are urged to respond as Frankenstein does: "I compassionated him, and sometimes felt a wish to console him" (143). More than his rhetorical power, more than his claims as a victim of injustice, it is just this mixture that brings him closer to us and makes it possible to feel with him, to recognize ourselves in his mon- strousness.

As a story of how one becomes a monster, the creature's narrative invites comparison with Frankenstein's account of monster making. What con- vinces the creature of his monstrosity, drives him to violence, and leads him to demand a companion is his singularity, his painful lack of connection with others, while Frankenstein, who begins in a close domestic circle such as the creature yearns for and can never enjoy, leaves it for voluntary iso- lation to pursue his obsession. Yet when we consider their purposes in telling their stories, it is the creature who pursues a fixed aim, persuading Frankenstein to create a companion for him, while the motives offered for his creator's account shift and sometimes contradict one another. His aim of warning Walton by his example is, as we have seen, stressed mainly in Shelley's 1831 revisions; his account in the 1818 edition is prefaced only by the expectation that it "will afford a view of nature, which may enlarge your faculties and understanding" (24). But a cautionary purpose also ap- pears later in the original version: "Learn from me, if not by my precepts, at least by my example, how dangerous is the acquirement of knowledge, and how much happier that man is who believes his native town to be the world, than he who aspires to become greater than his nature will allow" (48). Frankenstein's didacticism becomes heaviest (enough to require an apology: "But I forget that I am moralizing in the most interesting part of my tale . . .") when he tells of how his obsession led him to "procrastinate all that related to my feelings of affection," a sure sign of danger: "If the study to which you apply yourself has a tendency to weaken your affec- tions . . . then that study is certainly unlawful" (50–51).

Frankenstein, however, is as much concerned with justifying as with blaming himself. Telling his story becomes a means of reviewing and re- composing his actions, and by the end he has constructed a version whose outlines support his claims as much as his creature's narrative supports his.

During these last days I have been occupied in examining my past conduct; nor do I find it blameable. In a fit of enthusiastic madness I created a rational creature, and was bound towards him, to assure, as far as was in my power, his happiness and well-being. This was my duty; but there was another still paramount to that. My duties towards my fellow creatures had greater claims to my attention, because they included a greater proportion of happiness or misery. Urged by this view, I refused, and did right in refusing, to create a companion for the first creature. He showed unparalleled malignity and selfishness, in evil; he destroyed my friends; he devoted to destruction beings who possessed exquisite sensations, happiness and wisdom; nor do I know where this thirst for vengeance may end. Miserable himself, that he may render no other wretched, he ought to die. (214–15)

This is a thoroughly rationalized version, smoothly eliding the turbulent interval between the moment of creation and the recognition of his duty, as well as the reversal between his promise to create a companion and his destruction of the half-finished female in a violent spasm ("trembling with passion, [I] tore to pieces the thing on which I was engaged" [164]) that he now replaces with a utilitarian calculation of the greatest good. Frankenstein urges his conclusion on Walton as a moral necessity, delivered from a position beyond all distorting passions. "Think not, Walton, that in the last moments of my existence I feel that burning hatred, and ardent desire of revenge, I once expressed, but I feel myself justified in desiring the death of my adversary" (214). Yet in his last days we recognize the same fanatical determination that at his first appearance led him to board Walton's ship only when assured it was bound northward, and he is roused to a final flight of passionate eloquence in his speech to the sailors urging them not to turn back. Instead of warning here against overreaching ambition, he makes it the demand of honor: "Oh! be men, or be more than men. . . . Do not return to your families with the stigma of disgrace marked on your brows" (212). The conflict continues in his last words. "Farewell Walton! Seek happiness in tranquility, and avoid ambition, even if it be only the apparently innocent one of distinguishing yourself in science and discoveries. Yet why do I say this? I myself have been blasted in these hopes, yet another may succeed" (215). As with his creature, it is not the coherence of his account so much as the troubled mixture of its motives that claims our compassion, and that marks their close kinship.

Frankenstein, however, appeals several times to one form of narrative coherence, the fixed pattern of destiny. When Walton announces that he is returning to England, Frankenstein replies, "Do so, if you will; but I will not.

You may give up your purpose; but mine is assigned me by heaven, and I dare not" (214). In place of the tangle of impulses that drives both creator and creature and binds them together, he substitutes a sacred destiny that requires him to continue his pursuit. Earlier, he invokes a darker determinism in retracing the steps that led to his momentous discovery. In the heavily revised ending to chapter 1, he tells of how for a time he turned from the study of alchemy to mathematics, which seems in retrospect to have been "the suggestion of the guardian angel of my life. . . . It was a strong effort of the spirit of good; but it was ineffectual. Destiny was too potent, and her immutable laws had decreed my utter and terrible destruction" (239). Similar reflections follow his account of his arrival at Ingolstadt and the interviews with Krempe and Waldman that set him on his course of study. In the 1818 version, Frankenstein concludes, "Thus ended a memorable day for me; it decided my future destiny" (43), sounding a note that the 1831 revisions amplify. They preface the first interview with "Chance—or rather the evil influence, the Angel of Destruction, which asserted omnipotent sway over me from the moment I turned my reluctant steps from my father's door—led me first to Mr. Krempe" (240), and after Waldman's panegyric on modern chemistry they insert two paragraphs recounting its profound effect: "Such were the professor's words—rather let me say the words of fate, enounced to destroy me" (214). In this doom-laden retrospect, disaster is not the consequence of his own errors; such wandering is not really possible because destiny allows no deviation from the course leading to its terrible predetermined conclusion.[25]

We have encountered such assertions of inevitability before in *Caleb Williams,* one of several features the two novels share.[26] Predestined destruction is a frequent version of narrative force in Gothic, darkening the atmosphere and lending a sense of tragic grandeur to the action by making it seem the work of baleful preternatural powers. When this rhetoric is deployed by an unreliable narrator, however, and in resolutely naturalistic fictions like Godwin's and Shelley's, it prompts suspicion and alternative versions. One alternative, stressed like the rhetoric of destiny in Shelley's

[25] Even the hint of error in the reference to his leaving home is withdrawn in "reluctant steps," as if he were being impelled by a force that overrules his will, which is quite inconsistent with his account of his mood on leaving, where initial trepidation soon yields to eagerness: "I ardently desired the acquisition of knowledge. I had often, when at home, thought it hard to remain during my youth cooped up in one place, and I had longed to enter the world, and take my station among other human beings. Now my desires were being complied with, and it would, indeed, have been folly to repent" (40).

[26] For a reading of *Frankenstein* as a Godwinian novel, and as a critique of revolutionary optimism, see Pamela Clemit, *The Godwinian Novel: The Rational Fictions of Godwin, Brockden Brown, Mary Shelley* (Oxford: Oxford University Press, 1993), pp. 138–74.

revisions, is the moral fable of presumption and its terrible punishment, whether it reintroduces religious terms ("supremely frightful would be the effect of any human endeavour to mock the stupendous mechanism of the Creator of the world") or transposes them into a psychological register where unconscious compulsions replace the "Angel of Destruction." Another version, more congenial to modern readers and capable of accommodating more of the text, holds that Frankenstein's "worst sin is not the creation of the Monster but his refusal to take responsibility for it."[27] Invoking destiny as he tells his story is one way of refusing responsibility, but in the story he tells the refusal begins the moment he perceives his creature as monstrous, which already entails the denial of relation. When the creature appears by his bed with "one hand . . . stretched out, seemingly to detain me" (53), we can read this gesture as an appeal rather than a threat, and Frankenstein's "escape" as a flight from responsibility, from the ethical demand to respond to another. From this point on, the creature alternately appeals and threatens, while Frankenstein alternates between acknowledgment and repudiation.

We might try to construct another moral fable in which Frankenstein's refusal of responsibility causes the destruction he attributes to destiny, but the novel's investigation of responsibility and responsiveness goes beyond simple questions of blame and includes our own responses through its staging of narrative reception. Each of the novel's narrators is also the receiver of a narrative he in turn reports, Walton of Frankenstein's, Frankenstein of the creature's, and the creature of the De Laceys', and in each case their responses mark possibilities for the reader. George Levine observes, "It is not clear that any of the three learn from the stories they hear," a fair assessment if by learning we mean extracting an effective lesson.[28] The creature, in his early innocence, comes closest to this way of grasping a story. Having gathered "the history of my beloved cottagers," he certainly thinks he has learned something: "I learned, from the views of social life which it developed, to admire their virtues, and to deprecate the vices of mankind" (122–23). In the narrative of his own bitter experience, however, this simple opposition breaks down as the whole sentimental account of the De Laceys' domestic and civic virtues becomes a preparation for the disaster of his appeal, in which their admirable qualities—Felix's courage and res-

[27] George Levine, "The Ambiguous Heritage of *Frankenstein*," in Levine and Knoepflmacher, *Endurance of Frankenstein*, p. 10. Levine's comprehensive outline of interpretive themes ("Birth and Creation," "The Overreacher," "Rebellion and Moral Isolation," "The Unjust Society," "The Defects of Domesticity," "The Double," and "Technology, Entropy, and the Monstrous") remains a useful guide to possible readings.

[28] Levine, "Ambiguous Heritage of *Frankenstein*," p. 18.

olution, Agatha's sensibility—contribute to its failure. Yet his experience as hidden observer and secret sharer of their lives also gives him what Frankenstein initially offers Walton and his own story offers Frankenstein, the enlarged faculties and understanding produced by learning of possibilities they could not have otherwise imagined.

Openly soliciting imaginative and ethical responsiveness distinguishes *Frankenstein* from other Gothic presentations of narrative as a struggle for control, but that struggle still figures centrally in Frankenstein's reception of the creature's story, which forms the pivot for the events that follow. "Hear my tale," the creature appeals, "it is long and strange" (96), and having heard it, Frankenstein finds that "his words had a strange effect on me" (143), disclosing unexpected possibilities. "His tale . . . proved him to be a creature of fine sensations; and did I not, as his maker, owe him all the portion of happiness that it was in my power to bestow?" (142). His own sensibility allows him to accept the chance narrative offers to put oneself in the place of the other and recognize his claims not just as a matter of principle but through fellow feeling, yet it also produces an involuntary repulsion with which his awakened sense of duty must struggle. "I compassionated him, and sometimes felt a wish to console him; but when I looked upon him, when I saw the filthy mass that moved and talked, my heart sickened, and my feelings were altered to those of horror and hatred. I tried to stifle these sensations; I thought, that as I could not sympathize with him, I had no right to withhold from him the small portion of happiness which was yet in my power to bestow" (143).[29] The hope that their relation could be based on mutual acknowledgment proves impossible to sustain, and we can see that it was compromised from the start. The creature's appeal is always backed by his threat of further destruction, and his moving story is also a skillful·act of manipulation. Near the end, when he is urging Walton to "satisfy my vengeance in his death," Frankenstein warns of the creature's rhetorical power. "He is eloquent and persuasive; and once his words had even power over my heart: but trust him not" (206). The sense that to tell a story eloquently is to exercise a power never securely distinct from violence, that persuasion is just a disguised form of domination, contaminates Frankenstein's response and troubles our own.

[29] On the opposition of sight and speech here between "the hideous body and the persuasive tongue," see Peter Brooks, "What Is a Monster? (According to *Frankenstein*)," in *Body Work: Objects of Desire in Modern Narrative* (Cambridge: Harvard University Press, 1993), pp. 198–220. Brooks reads the opposition in terms of Lacanian psychoanalysis, but one could also consider it as a reflection on the power of literary narration, where language predominates, as opposed to stage and film versions that stress the hideousness of a speechless creature.

The sense of subjection after having given his promise robs Frankenstein of autonomy and purpose: "Through the whole period during which I was the slave of my creature, I allowed myself to be governed by the impulses of the moment" (131). Recovering control requires revising the story of their encounter to stress the aspects of manipulation and intimidation: "I had before been moved by the sophisms of the being I had created; I had been struck senseless by his fiendish threats: but now, for the first time the wickedness of my promise burst upon me" (163). He tells himself hypothetical horror stories about the possible consequences of creating a female companion: "She might become ten thousand times more malignant than her mate . . . might refuse to comply with a compact made before her creation . . . might turn with disgust from him . . . might quit him, and he be again alone, exasperated," etc. Worst of all, "one of the first results of those sympathies for which the dæmon thirsted would be children, and a race of devils would be propagated upon the earth, who might make the very existence of the species of man a condition precarious and full of terror." This apocalyptic scenario (with its hint of sexual revulsion) provides the frame for the sudden reappearance of the creature, who comes "to mark my progress, and claim the fulfillment of my promise" and whose "countenance expressed the utmost extent of malice and treachery" (164). Constructing this demonic version works Frankenstein up to the necessary pitch of desperation in which, "with a sensation like madness," he can destroy the female "thing" that has come to represent his loss of control, displaying his own capacity for malice and treachery.

Reducing all relations to terms of power develops according to a demonic, self-confirming logic: Frankenstein's reassertion of his independence through such a reduction prompts the creature to respond in kind. "Slave, I before reasoned with you, but you have proved yourself unworthy of my condescension. Remember that I have power. . . . You are my creator, but I am your master;—obey!" (165). The same logic holds for our own response: if we question and try to replace the demonic version of the creature that Frankenstein constructs, we inevitably enter into a comparable struggle for control. There seems to be no escape from this double bind; the sense of narrative as an appeal for understanding remains monstrously mingled with that of narrative as an instrument of power. But *Frankenstein* continues to affirm the more hopeful sense even as it pursues its story of failure and destruction. Walton's letters to his sister, which form the outer frame, are inspired by his need for connection with the domestic life he has left behind, and his reception of Frankenstein's narrative is informed by his desire for a sympathetic friend. In Frankenstein he finds "a man who, before his spirit had been broken by misery, I should have been happy to have possessed as the brother of my heart. . . . He excites at once my admiration and pity to an astonishing degree" (22).[30] Of course, like his decision at the end to turn back rather than lead his sailors into danger against their will, these motives clearly serve to motivate and preserve his transmission of Frankenstein's narrative, but they also represent a sense of narrative that is not completely reducible to power relations.

Frankenstein too shows a concern for the preservation and transmission of his story, in which a sense of responsibility and the desire for control seem inseparable. "Frankenstein discovered that I made notes concerning his history: he asked to see them, and then himself corrected and augmented them in many places; but principally in giving the life and spirit to the conversations he held with his enemy. 'Since you have preserved my narration,' said he, 'I would not that a mutilated one should go down to posterity'" (207).[31] Since it is entirely through those conversations that we have gained any sense of the creature's own life and spirit up to this point, we owe our recognition of his claims to his creator's efforts to do justice to his enemy's version.

The creature also wants Walton to get the story right. In his last appearance his version is for once not mediated through his creator's or aimed at persuasion, and his "exclamations of grief and horror" (216) are at first addressed only to the dead Frankenstein, until Walton's reproaches move him to describe the "agony and remorse," "impotent envy and bitter indignation," and "excess of . . . despair" that led to the murders of Clerval and Elizabeth (217–18). He no longer appeals for compassion: "I seek not a fellow-feeling in my misery. No sympathy may I ever find" (218), yet he still wants to establish the perspective that only he can give.

> You, who call Frankenstein your friend, seem to have a knowledge of my crimes and his misfortunes. But, in the detail which he gave you of them, he could not sum up the hours and months of misery, which I endured, wasting in impotent passions. For whilst I destroyed his hopes, I did not satisfy my own desires. They were ever ardent and craving; still I desired love and fellowship, and still I was spurned. Was there no injustice in this? Am I to be thought the only criminal, when all human kind sinned against me? (219)

[30] In the revised version, Frankenstein agrees with Walton on the need for friendship: "We are unfashioned creatures, but half made up, if one wiser, better, dearer than ourselves—such a friend ought to be—do not lend his aid to perfectionate our weak and faulty natures" (232). He is presumably thinking of his relation with Clerval, but his terms also evoke his failed relationship with his own imperfectly fashioned creature and point toward a more general sense of how the self is fashioned through relations with others.
[31] Compare Caleb Williams's motive for completing his memoirs, his wish that Falkland's "story may be fully understood; and that . . . the world may at least not hear and repeat a half-told and mangled tale."

These moments of protest punctuate his repeated self-condemnations, intensifying the conflicts that marked his earlier narrative. Now, however, he has nothing to hope for but annihilation, the theme of his last, prospective narrative. "I shall die, and what I now feel be no longer felt. . . . My spirit will sleep in peace; or if it thinks, it will not surely think thus" (221).

Here, as throughout his story, the creature presents himself as utterly alone, yet the very act of his narration qualifies that account. Not only does his pursuit of recognition and revenge bind him to his creator, but every version he offers of himself—to De Lacey, Frankenstein, and finally Walton—confirms his dialogical relation to others. When he urges Frankenstein to create a female, he anticipates the beneficial effects of her companionship. "I shall feel the affections of a sensitive being, and become linked with the chain of existence and events, from which I am now excluded" (143). A "chain of existence and events" could serve as a general structural description of a story; he seems to think of entering into the relations with others he desires as becoming part of a narrative sequence, just as at the end he announces that his solitary death will "consummate the series of my being" (220). But whether solitary or social, the life represented in a narrative is already linked with others through the transaction of telling it, and while monsters may always be excluded, monster stories include them in a series that has no final consummation.

This open series reaches far beyond the communicative structure of narration, in ways that *Frankenstein* makes particularly clear. The creature anticipates the peace of final dissolution, but we know that he will be brought back to life and sent forth again and again in new versions of his story. In Shelley's 1831 introduction, and in many later commentaries, the animation of the creature becomes a powerful figure for the creative imagination or writing; it is equally a figure for reception, the bringing to life that happens in every reading or rewriting, the reception that a narrative expects but cannot determine. Frankenstein's act of creation, like Shelley's and our own, imposes the obligation to take responsibility for and toward what escapes control.

5

Dr. Jekyll and Mr. Hyde

Questions of responsibility and control return even more urgently in the later nineteenth-century monster story that owes so much to *Frankenstein,* Stevenson's *Dr. Jekyll and Mr. Hyde* (1886).[1] Again, a scientist produces and loses control over a creature who is both his double and his antagonist; again, they are caught in shifting relations of dissociation and conjuncture, the denial and reassertion of a bond that tightens into mutual destruction, and again, the questions of responsibility and control implicate the author and reader as well. "Is 'Dr. Jekyll and Mr. Hyde' a work of high philosophic intention, or simply the most ingenious and irresponsible of fictions?"[2] James's question draws its terms from the complaints of "many readers" who, dissatisfied with Stevenson's facility and charm, "manifest an impatience for some glimpse of his moral message" (292). *Dr. Jekyll and Mr. Hyde,* James declares, "has the stamp of a really imaginative production, that we may take it in different ways, but I suppose it would be called the most serious of the author's tales," and as such fulfills that authorial responsibility. "There is a genuine feeling for the perpetual moral question," but for James its main interest lies elsewhere: "It is, how-

---

[1] On the many features the stories share, see Gordon Hirsch, "*Frankenstein,* Detective Fiction, and *Jekyll and Hyde*," in *Dr. Jekyll and Mr. Hyde after One Hundred Years,* ed. William Veeder and Gordon Hirsch (Chicago: University of Chicago Press, 1987), pp. 223–28.

[2] Henry James, "Robert Louis Stevenson" (1888), in *Robert Louis Stevenson: The Critical Heritage,* ed. Paul Maixner (London: Routledge and Kegan Paul, 1981), p. 308. Compare James's description of "The Turn of the Screw" as "this perfectly independent and irresponsible little fiction," in *The Art of the Novel: Critical Prefaces,* ed. R. P. Blackmur (New York: Scribner's, 1934), p. 139. James seems to associate "irresponsibility" in both these fin de siècle Gothic tales with aesthetic autonomy.

ever, here, not the profundity of the idea which strikes me so much as the art of the presentation—the extremely successful form" (308). Genuine feeling and irresponsibility, the philosophic and the fictive, idea and form: such are the oppositions from which James's cautious appreciation is constructed, locating the tale in a cultural grid of moral and aesthetic values that repeats and amplifies its doubled protagonist's conflict between obligation and pleasure.[3]

Readers concerned with finding the tale's moral message or determining its philosophic intention are likely to focus on the general pronouncements in "Henry Jekyll's Full Statement of the Case" that also deal with oppositions. "With every day, and from both sides of my intelligence, the moral and the intellectual, I thus drew steadily nearer to that truth, by whose partial discovery I have been doomed to such a dreadful shipwreck: that man is not truly one but truly two."[4] Like his psychological investigations, Jekyll's scientific experiments in "transcendental medicine" are also based on duality. "I not only recognized my natural body for the mere aura and effulgence of certain of the powers that made up my spirit, but managed to compound a drug by which these powers should be dethroned from their supremacy, and a second form and countenance substituted, none the less natural to me because they were the expression, and bore the stamp of lower elements in my soul" (83). Good and evil, higher and lower, spirit and matter, soul and body: such are the oppositions from which Jekyll's philosophic discourse is constructed, and which for many readers have determined the meaning of the whole tale.

They are also the concern of another book, of indisputably high philosophic intention, also published in 1886, Nietzsche's *Beyond Good and Evil,* which begins by exposing and questioning precisely such assumptions. "The fundamental faith of the philosophers is *the faith in opposite values.*"[5] Nietzsche's polemical "Prelude to a Philosophy of the Future" strives

---

[3] We might add to these the opposition between high and popular culture, since the tale's success as a "shilling shocker," based on both its sensational appeal and its moral message, seems to lie behind James's reservations. Its elegantly condensed form, however, signals its claims to the status of high literary art. On Stevenson's own ambivalence toward the literary marketplace, stemming from "the fundamental contradiction between the sense of literature as a high calling and the desire for popular fame and fortune," see Patrick Brantlinger and Richard Boyle, "The Education of Edward Hyde: Stevenson's 'Gothic Gnome' and the Mass Readership of Late-Victorian England," in Veeder and Hirsch, *Dr. Jekyll and Mr. Hyde after One Hundred Years,* pp. 265–82.

[4] Robert Louis Stevenson, *The Strange Case of Dr. Jekyll and Mr. Hyde and Other Stories* (Harmondsworth: Penguin, 1979), p. 82. All parenthetical references are to this edition.

[5] Friedrich Nietzsche, *Beyond Good and Evil,* trans. Walter Kaufmann (New York: Vintage, 1966), p. 10.

to discredit this faith, as well as "the soul superstition which, in the form of the subject and ego superstition, has not even yet ceased to do mischief" (2), and "the worst, most durable and dangerous of all errors . . . Plato's invention of the pure spirit and the good as such" (3). To confront Jekyll's voice with Nietzsche's helps to bring out the strong conservative strain in his "Statement," his efforts to make sense of his terrible experience in conventional moral terms and as the reenactment of a traditional story. "Strange as my circumstances were, the terms of this debate are as old and commonplace as man . . . and it fell out with me, as it falls with so vast a majority of my fellows, that I chose the better part and was found wanting in the strength to keep to it" (89). Reading *Dr. Jekyll and Mr. Hyde* as a monster story requires us to heed both these voices, to consider whether its oppositions explain or produce the monstrous.

Jekyll's voice is of course only one among the many that compose the tale, but none of the others challenges his conservatism or opens up conflicting perspectives. For the reader who comes to the tale from *Frankenstein,* what is most striking about them is rather the ways they are all shaped to fit together like the pieces of a puzzle or mechanism. Thus the first narrative segment, Enfield's "Story of the Door," meshes with Utterson's knowledge of both Jekyll's house and will to trigger his "Search for Mr. Hyde." Coincidences help assemble information efficiently: the murder of Carew is quickly assimilated because the maid who witnesses it can identify Hyde and because the victim was carrying a letter addressed to Utterson, who, having already encountered Hyde, can provide *his* address. Just as these contrivances work to make connections, others work to avoid redundancy. Lanyon's narrative reveals the identity of Jekyll and Hyde, leaving to Jekyll's the task of explanation. (It is also necessary for Jekyll to know of Lanyon's letter, so he can instruct Utterson to read that account before his own.) Such devices not only serve to accelerate the narrative and make it the "masterpiece of concision" that James admired, they also implement a drive toward an all-inclusive coherence.

The form of that coherence, the mystery plot so tightly strung between the initial enigma of the relation between Jekyll and Hyde and its final solution, works by foregrounding the sequential narrative structure of question and delayed answer that Barthes calls the hermeneutic code.[6] In his conception of the five codes as interwoven textual voices, the hermeneutic is the "Voice of Truth," a purely formal truth of coherence produced by de-

---

[6] The prominence of the hermeneutic code in *Dr. Jekyll and Mr. Hyde* is evidenced by Kaja Silverman's use of the tale to illustrate each of the code's "morphemes." See *The Subject of Semiotics* (New York: Oxford University Press, 1983), pp. 257–62.

ferral, by prolonged expectation, and established by ultimate disclosure. "Truth is what completes, what closes."[7] For Barthes this closure is the mainstay of the classic, "readerly" text, in whose "circle of solidarities . . . 'everything holds together'" (156). Together with the proairetic code of actions, the linear, irreversible hermeneutic code works to constrain possibilities of reading, and "*it is precisely this constraint which reduces the plural of the classic text*" (30).

As in its thematic oppositions, so again in the narrative form of *Dr. Jekyll and Mr. Hyde* we encounter a strong conservative strain, a force that marshals the voices of the tale so that "everything holds together." This impulse toward integration is not just a peculiarity of Stevenson's tale but a general tendency of Victorian Gothic. In comparison with Romantic texts like *Frankenstein* or Hogg's *Confessions of a Justified Sinner*, with which *Dr. Jekyll and Mr. Hyde* also has much in common, later nineteenth-century fiction that draws most directly on Gothic conventions is less inclined to stress the tensions between narrative voices and versions than to present them as complementary parts of a larger whole. Mystery plotting is a powerful strategy for integrating multiple narratives, as Collins skillfully demonstrated in *The Woman in White* and *The Moonstone*, developing the model of gathered testimony that, as we shall see, also organizes *Dracula*. But along with their pursuit of a narrative coherence that contains and constrains plurality, these texts carry on the characteristic Gothic reflection on narrative that questions and unsettles their readerly solidarities. Instead of directly opposing alternative versions, they insinuate them by leading us to mistrust the authority of their narrative voices, the completeness of their supposedly full statements. We have brought out the conservative strain in *Dr. Jekyll and Mr. Hyde* by introducing the more skeptical or subversive perspectives of Nietzsche and Barthes, but Stevenson's tale itself offers possibilities of reading that point beyond good and evil and toward a less constrained plurality.

We can begin to locate those possibilities interwoven with the voice that tells the truth of plot and theme in Jekyll's "Full Statement." Even as he announces his rediscovery of "the thorough and primitive duality of man," confirming the traditional notion that "man is . . . truly two," Jekyll also offers his own speculative philosophy of the future. "I say two, because the state of my knowledge does not pass beyond that point. Others will follow, others will outstrip me on the same lines; and I hazard the guess that man will ultimately be known for a mere polity of multifarious, incongruous and independent denizens" (82). Such a radically disunified model of the self

[7] Roland Barthes, *S/Z*, trans. Richard Miller (New York: Hill and Wang, 1974), p. 76.

displaces traditional dualities and seems to anticipate postmodern decon-
structions of the unitary subject—although the idea was already well established in the nineteenth century.[8] The point here, however, is not the
progressive potential of conceiving the self as a polity but the tension within
Jekyll's account. As the ostensible guide to the philosophic intention of the
tale, he himself becomes multifarious, and his dualism begins to look like
a defense.

The supposed fullness of Jekyll's "Statement" lies in the way it provides
solutions to the tale's mysteries. It gathers up the threads of the preceding
episodes—the encounter with Enfield, the murder of Carew, the appeal to
Lanyon—and joins them in a continuous, intelligible series. As the end of
a hermeneutic sequence, its disclosures offer "a final nomination, the discovery and uttering of the irreversible word"[9] whose finality governs not
only events but the self. "Because the hermeneutic code moves toward disclosure, it . . . projects a stable subject about whom things can ultimately
be discovered although the process may be painstaking and full of delays—
a subject, in short, who can be defined and known."[10] It is such conclusive
knowledge that allows Chesterton, for example, to assert that "the real stab
of the story is not in the discovery that one man is two men; but in the discovery that the two men are one man."[11] Yet at the same time that the
"Statement" discloses and defines its divided subject, it also reopens the
questions it claims to answer. It begins a new narrative in the manner of a
conventional novelistic opening: "I was born in the year 18———" (81), presenting the relation of Jekyll and Hyde not as an established fact but as a
developing story. This sequence opens in a mood of unqualified identification as Jekyll observes his new form: "I was conscious of no repugnance,
rather of a leap of welcome. This too was myself. It seemed natural and human" (84), and it moves toward equally unqualified denial and dissociation. "He, I say—I cannot say I. That child of Hell had nothing human;
nothing lived in him but fear and hatred" (94).

These instances show how the drama of shifting relations between Jekyll
and Hyde is played out in terms of grammatical and narrative positions,
the permutations of "I," "he," and "it." As narrator and author of his
"Statement," Jekyll is "I," but as protagonist or object of his narrative he
is sometimes "I," sometimes "he" or "Jekyll," while "Hyde" is sometimes

---

[8] See Henri Ellenberger on the century-long debate among theorists of Mesmerism between
adherents of "dipsychism" and "polypsychism," in *The Discovery of the Unconscious* (New
York: Basic Books, 1970), pp. 145–46.

[9] Barthes, *S/Z*, p. 210.

[10] Silverman, *Subject of Semiotics*, p. 262.

[11] G. K. Chesterton, *Robert Louis Stevenson* (New York: Dodd, Mead, 1928), p. 50.

replaced by "I." See how quickly these positions shift in this summary of the early stages of divided existence.

> The pleasures which I made haste to seek in my disguise were, as I have said, undignified; I would scarce use a harsher term. But in the hands of Edward Hyde, they soon began to turn toward the monstrous. When I would come back from these excursions, I was often plunged into a kind of wonder at my vicarious depravity. This familiar that I called out of my own soul, and sent forth alone to do his good pleasure, was a being inherently malign and villainous; his every act and thought centered on self; drinking pleasure with bestial avidity from any degree of torture to another; relentless like a man of stone. Henry Jekyll stood at times aghast before the acts of Edward Hyde; but the situation was apart from ordinary laws, and insidiously relaxed the grasp of conscience. It was Hyde, after all, and Hyde alone, that was guilty. Jekyll was no worse; he woke again to his good qualities seemingly unimpaired; he would even make haste, where it was possible, to undo the evil done by Hyde. And thus his conscience slumbered. (86–87)

Tension between the splitting and joining of persons is both represented in the narrative and enacted in the narration of this passage. The "I" who seeks pleasures and wonders at his vicarious depravity is replaced by the formally distanced "Henry Jekyll"; the "I" who judiciously describes Jekyll's pleasures modulates into an unmarked "omniscient" voice that judicially condemns Hyde's and, like a typical Victorian authorial narrator, both ironically represents Jekyll's rationalizations and irresponsibility in indirect discourse and adds a summary moral comment.

Like Jekyll in his role as protagonist, the narrative voice of his "Statement" often refuses identification with Hyde, as in skirting "the details of the infamy at which I thus connived (for even now I can scarcely grant that I committed it)" (87). But this voice can also merge completely with Hyde, even in the account of his most extreme action, the assault on Carew. "With a transport of glee, I mauled the unresisting body, tasting delight from every blow" (90). The unnamed narrator who can speak for either Jekyll or Hyde is matched within the story by an indeterminate figure who is neither. "Between these two I now felt I had to choose" (89). Who is this anonymous agent? Who writes "Henry Jekyll's Statement"? The more we ponder its disclosures, the more mysterious and unstable it becomes.

We might say, like Jekyll, that strange as the circumstances are, the source of these uncertainties is as old and commonplace as narrative, the doubling of the subject that is always produced by telling one's story. That is already saying a great deal, since it indicates how Stevenson's tale estranges the commonplace by heightening tensions between story and discourse. The difficulties of representing the shifting relation of Jekyll and Hyde expose both narrative intelligibility and the equally commonplace notion of human duality as forms of control that here fail to secure their grasp. What eludes them is perhaps best suggested in Jekyll's horror as Hyde's power grows at his expense. "He thought of Hyde, for all his energy of life, as of something not only hellish but inorganic. This was the shocking thing; that the slime of the pit seemed to utter cries and voices; that the amorphous dust gesticulated and sinned; that what was dead, and had no shape, should usurp the offices of life" (95). The most extreme representation of Hyde's otherness also registers a force that collapses oppositions more fundamental than good and evil. Breaching the barrier between life and death, it suggests Freud's death drive, carrying Jekyll beyond the pleasure principle in a downward spiral of sadistic violence. We recognize in such boundary violations the mark of monstrosity, and this moment will become all the more significant as we go on to observe how not only Jekyll but others struggle to distance themselves from Hyde. Here, despite his inorganic remoteness, he is also an intimate part of Jekyll's organism. "And this again, that that insurgent horror was knit to him closer than a wife, closer than an eye; lay caged in his flesh, where he heard it mutter and felt it struggle to be born" (95).

As his "Statement" nears its end, Jekyll reasserts his separation from Hyde by identifying himself with his narrative, its last words with his death. "Will Hyde die upon the scaffold? or will he find the courage to release himself at the last moment? God knows; I am careless; this is my true hour of death, and what is to follow concerns another than myself. Here, as I lay down the pen and proceed to seal up my confession, I bring the life of that unhappy Henry Jekyll to an end" (97). As the last words of *Dr. Jekyll and Mr. Hyde*, these produce a poignant effect of narrative reflexivity, in which Jekyll's life is doubled and replaced by "the life of . . . Henry Jekyll," the written account. At the end, we might say, he reclaims through the form of his narrative the authenticity of his own death. But we can also reconstruct a different story, with rather different last words, from the narrative that precedes Jekyll's "Statement" and presents the events that follow its writing, a story that reaches its climax as Utterson stands before the door of Jekyll's cabinet and insists on being admitted.

"Jekyll," cried Utterson, with a loud voice, "I demand to see you." He paused a moment, but there came no reply. "I give you fair warning, our suspicions are aroused, and I must and shall see you," he resumed; "if not by fair means, then by foul—if not of your consent, then by brute force!"

"Utterson," said the voice, "for God's sake have mercy!"
"Ah, that's not Jekyll's voice—it's Hyde's!" cried Utterson. "Down with the door, Poole!" (69)

The desperate plea for mercy could well be taken for Jekyll's last words, addressed to his old friend, the man who has replaced Hyde as his heir. But Utterson believes he can identify the true source of these words, and this confident certainty authorizes the violence of foul means and brute force. In place of verbal dialogue, the crash of the axe against the door is answered by "a dismal screech, as of mere animal terror" (69). The "real stab of the story" may be not the discovery that one is two or that two are one (which commits suicide, Jekyll or Hyde?) but the discovery of the violence entailed in assigning any univocal meaning to these cries and voices.

Here we begin to move from the instabilities of Jekyll's "Full Statement" to those of its fuller narrative context and from the formal aspects of voice and person to the representation of character and action. The tension between splitting and joining reappears here as the basis of Jekyll's scientific project, his sense of the continual struggle between his "two natures" as a curse, which leads to his dream of "the separation of these elements" as in a process of chemical purification (82). He claims to have succeeded: Hyde's singular purity is shown by the invariable response he provokes in others. "I have observed that when I wore the semblance of Edward Hyde, none could come near me at first without a visible misgiving of the flesh. This, as I take it, was because all human beings, as we meet them, are commingled out of good and evil; and Edward Hyde, alone in the ranks of mankind, was pure evil" (85). The accounts of Enfield's, Utterson's, and Lanyon's responses to Hyde seem to anticipate this explanation, but there the stress is on the mysterious and disturbing quality of his effect on them, and as that effect is repeated and elaborated a different perspective emerges, in which we can see their unsuccessful efforts to describe, name, and analyze as failed rites of purification. Though Enfield declares he "can see him at this moment," he cannot describe him. "There is something wrong with his appearance; something displeasing, something down-right detestable. I never saw a man I so disliked, and yet I scarce know why. He must be deformed somewhere; he gives a strong feeling of deformity, although I couldn't specify the point. He's an extraordinary looking man, and yet I really can name nothing out of the way" (34). Utterson goes home to dream repeatedly of Hyde, but "the figure had no face, or one that baffled him and melted before his eyes; and thus it was that there sprang up and grew apace in the lawyer's mind a singularly strong, almost an inordinate curiosity to behold the features of the real Mr. Hyde" (37–38).

Yet when Utterson at last sees Hyde face to face, the effect of indescrib-
ability is not removed but intensified. "Mr. Hyde was pale and dwarfish;
he gave an impression of deformity without any nameable malformation,
he had a displeasing smile, he had borne himself to the lawyer with a sort
of murderous mixture of timidity and boldness, and he spoke with a husky,
whispering and somewhat broken voice,—all these were points against
him; but not all these together could explain the hitherto unknown disgust,
loathing and fear with which Mr. Utterson regarded him" (40). The effort
to resolve this enigma here becomes precisely what Barthes describes as the
goal of the hermeneutic code, an attempt at "a final nomination." "'There
must be something else,' said the perplexed gentleman. 'There *is* something
more, if I could find a name for it.'" He tries a series of descriptions: "hardly
human . . . troglodytic . . . the mere radiance of a foul soul," and ends not
by describing Hyde's appearance but by reading it as a sign, "Satan's signature upon a face" (40).

With Dr. Lanyon, we get not the lawyer's attempt at accurate testimony
but a more clinical account that dwells on Hyde's effect, "the odd, subjective disturbance caused by his neighbourhood. This bore some resemblance
to incipient rigour, and was accompanied by a marked sinking of the pulse.
At the time, I set it down to some idiosyncratic, personal distaste, and
merely wondered at the acuteness of the symptoms; but I have since had
reason to believe the cause to lie much deeper in the nature of man, and to
turn on some nobler hinge than the principle of hatred" (77). All of these
passages can be read as components of a hermeneutic sequence that concludes with Jekyll's "discovery and uttering of the irreversible word," the
explanation that Hyde is "pure evil." But we can also observe the repeated
struggle to master subjective disturbance through the power of naming, and
we may question how successfully it is resolved. Hyde remains as faceless
for us as he is in Utterson's nightmares, a blank to be filled in by each in-
terpreter who encounters him. His significance depends less on some pure
essence within him than on the purifying effect of considering him wholly
other, the flattering effect of considering hatred for him a confirmation of
"nobler" human instincts.

Believing he has succeeded in separating and projecting his evil nature,
Jekyll describes an asymmetrical relation between his "two characters . . .
one was wholly evil and the other was still the old Henry Jekyll, that incongruous compound" (85). His later account of their attitudes toward
each other elaborates this pattern.

My two natures had memory in common, but all other faculties were most
unequally shared between them. Jekyll (who was composite) now with the

most sensitive apprehensions, now with a greedy gusto, projected and shared in the pleasures and adventures of Hyde; but Hyde was indifferent to Jekyll, or but remembered him as the mountain bandit remembers the cavern in which he conceals himself from pursuit. Jekyll had more than a father's interest; Hyde had more than a son's indifference. (89)

Here there is no overt attempt at dissociation, but the claim of separation is clear: little of Jekyll but a vague memory remains in Hyde. The action of the story, however, displays a much more complicated relation and a stronger mix of memories, as in the episode of Jekyll's appeal to Lanyon, of which each gives a partial account. Here the two narrative versions, while presenting complementary parts of the action, also offer conflicting perspectives.

Jekyll's account in his "Statement" explains how the spontaneous transformation that produces this crisis arises from the slackening of his penitence and "fall" into the indulgences of "an ordinary secret sinner" (92). It is not deeds but impure thoughts, "the animal within me licking the chops of memory," that trigger the change into his more bestial form: "The hand that lay on my knee was corded and hairy." (One may recall Victorian cautionary tales about the consequences of sexual impurity.) Escape from the plight of being Hyde, "the common quarry of mankind, hunted, houseless, a known murderer, thrall to the gallows," also depends on memory. "I remembered that of my original character, one part remained to me: I could write my own hand" (93). Who owns the "hand" is a recurrent question that links the themes of identity and writing, from the check Hyde signs as Jekyll to the signature Jekyll creates for Hyde by "sloping my own hand backward" (87) to the "startling blasphemies" written in Jekyll's pious books "in his own hand" (71; cf. 96).[12] Here the letter to Lanyon is written by Hyde, but its voice, as we can observe from its transcription in Lanyon's narrative (74–75), seems entirely and convincingly Jekyll's. Whether we consider Hyde capable of extraordinary ventriloquism or rather suppose that much of Jekyll subsists within him, their relation here hardly matches Jekyll's description. It is precisely while telling of Hyde's journey to Lanyon's house that Jekyll's "Statement" pauses to insist on their radical sep-

---

[12] Other instances include Jekyll's "holograph" will and the letter from Hyde that Utterson suspects Jekyll of forging. The tale's elaborate thematization of writing as identity has attracted the attention of several recent commentators, such as Ronald Thomas, who considers how its version of "the death or disappearance of the author" anticipates such effects in modern writers like Beckett. See "The Strange Voices in the Strange Case: Dr. Jekyll, Mr. Hyde, and the Voices of Modern Fiction," in Veeder and Hirsch, *Dr. Jekyll and Mr. Hyde after One Hundred Years*, pp. 73–93.

aration—"He, I say—I cannot say I. That child of Hell had nothing human; nothing lived in him but fear and hatred" (94)—precisely at the point where we are best able to sense how much more lives in him.

Lanyon's account of their interview strengthens this sense. Once Hyde's desperation subsides and the potion is ready, he speaks in tones we do not hear elsewhere in the tale, offering a fateful choice between ignorance and "a new province of knowledge and new avenues to fame and power," and then, binding Lanyon by the "vows . . . of our profession," triumphantly displaying that power. "And now, you who have so long been bound to the most narrow and material views, you who have denied the virtue of transcendental medicine, you who have derided your superiors—behold!" (80). Not only are these words spoken as if by Jekyll but their melodramatic intensity offers a glimpse of the pride and ambition, as well as the desire for irresponsible pleasure, that went into the making of Edward Hyde, and that live on in him as well as fear and hatred.[13] Wherever we attempt to determine the relation of Jekyll and Hyde, we find neither unity nor purified duality but a mobile interweaving of traits and voices that resists any such stabilizing simplification.

A reading that dwells on these tensions and discrepancies should not aim at simply replacing a classic readerly coherence in which everything holds together with a writerly plurality in which nothing does. Such a symmetrical reversal, still governed by a faith in opposites, would do little to account for the power of *Dr. Jekyll and Mr. Hyde,* which depends to a large extent on holding together what both characters and readers try to separate. Like *Frankenstein,* Stevenson's tale has been retold countless times and its story reduced to an archetypal formula. The most consistent feature of all these versions is the reproduction and simplification of the dualism that the tale itself does so much to complicate and subvert. If one sense of *Dr. Jekyll and Mr. Hyde* as a monster story points toward the proliferation of subsequent versions, another confronts them with the monstrous heterogeneity their opposed values cannot accommodate. Jekyll realizes at the end that his supposed success in separating the elements so painfully mixed within him and in projecting a purified essence of evil depended on a crucial "unknown impurity" in one of the ingredients of the potion (96). This ironic discovery

---

[13] F. W. H. Myers, eager to see Stevenson perfect his near-masterpiece, offered a number of suggested revisions aimed at greater verisimilitude, of which the most important concerns this passage. "Style too elevated for Hyde," he observes. "These are not remarks that fit the husky broken voice of Hyde—they are Jekyllian." Maixner, *Critical Heritage,* p. 216. In his reply, Stevenson attributes this incongruity to the speed of composition: "Nothing but this white-hot haste would explain the gross error of Hyde's speech at Lanyon's" (219). Yet despite Myers's repeated urgings, Stevenson never corrected this "gross error."

applies to the tale as well, which achieves its most impressive and unsettling effects by compounding an impure, murderous mixture of motives.

Like Jekyll, several of the other characters try to dissociate themselves
from Hyde, but the "instinctive" repulsion they feel toward him also binds
them to him, as Lanyon is held by "a disgustful curiosity" (77). This fascination is presented most fully in Utterson's response to Enfield's story.

> Hitherto it had touched him on the intellectual side alone, but now his imag-
> ination was also engaged, or rather enslaved; and as he lay and tossed in
> the gross darkness of the night and the curtained room, Mr. Enfield's tale
> went before his mind in a scroll of lighted pictures. He would be aware of
> the great field of lamps of a nocturnal city; then of the figure of a man walk-
> ing swiftly; then of a child running from the doctor's; and then these met
> and that human Juggernaut trod the child down and passed on regardless
> of her screams. Or else he would see a room in a rich house, where his friend
> lay asleep, dreaming and smiling at his dreams; and then the door of the
> room would be opened, the curtains of the bed plucked apart, the sleeper
> recalled, and lo! there would stand by his side a figure to whom power was
> given, and even at that dead hour, he must rise and do its bidding. (37)

The two scenic images of the faceless Hyde are repeated and multiplied obsessively in Utterson's troubled dreams. Enfield has said of the scene he wit-
nessed, "It sounds like nothing to hear, but it was hellish to see" (31); here
the vision is recreated by Utterson's enslaved imagination and comple-
mented by another, recalling the specular bedroom confrontations of Poe's
"The Tell-Tale Heart" and "William Wilson" or the creature's awakening
of Frankenstein, which we will eventually realize to be literally impossible
but an accurate prefiguration of Hyde's ascendance. The images both represent and exercise power, figured in an interplay of accelerating movement
and compulsive repetition, as Utterson sees "the figure . . . move the more
swiftly, and still the more swiftly, even to dizziness, through wider laby-
rinths of lamp-lighted city, and at every street corner crush a child and leave
her screaming" (37). Utterson's efforts to break the spell that has enslaved
his imagination lead him to replace these repeated images with his own pur-
poseful movement, the search for Hyde, but that project also binds them
together in complementary roles: "If he be Mr. Hyde . . . I shall be Mr.
Seek" (38). It leads not just to their encounter by the outer door where the
tale began but to their final dialogue through the door of Jekyll's cabinet,
where it will be Utterson who presses on, "regardless of [the other's]
screams." Narrative movement yields in turn to an uncanny repetition of
violence and domination as these two exchange places.

The opposition between Hyde and others repeatedly begins to blur as soon as it is posited. In the account of his trampling the child, as in the later account of his attack on Carew, his evil is presented as uniquely gratuitous, violent aggression, which Jekyll amplifies by describing the monstrous turn of Hyde's depravity as "drinking pleasure with bestial avidity from any degree of torture to another" (86). But from the beginning there is a sense of him not just as an isolated embodiment of rage and cruelty but also as the occasion of them in others. Enfield tells how, after he has captured Hyde, he, the child's family, and even the unemotional doctor become possessed "with desire to kill him. . . . I never saw a circle of such hateful faces" (32). Those who confront and oppose Hyde seem to turn into his doubles.[14]

This effect of contamination takes a more complex course with Utterson, who at the outset displays a milder form of Jekyll's vicarious depravity, denying himself pleasures while maintaining "an approved tolerance for others; sometimes wondering, almost with envy, at the high pressure of spirits involved in their misdeeds; and in any extremity inclined to help rather than to reprove" (29). His investigations turn this tendency into a source of guilt, which arises first through identification with Jekyll: supposing Hyde to be connected with "the ghost of some old sin," he uneasily broods on his own "fairly blameless" past and "the many ill things he had done" (42). After the murder of Carew, his anxieties implicate him more with Hyde. Driving with the officer seeking Hyde through fog-darkened Soho, "like a district of some city in a nightmare," he is "conscious of some touch of that terror of the law and the law's officers, which may at times assail the most honest" (40). At the end, however, Utterson betrays no sign of any such disturbing identifications, and it is he, rather than the more single-minded and self-righteous Enfield or Lanyon, who at last discharges the violence that has gathered around Hyde throughout the tale. Breaking down the door is justified by considering Hyde as completely other, deserving no mercy, but this outburst of brute force actually removes the separation between them.

As the character through whom most of the earlier narrative is focused and the receiver of Lanyon's and Jekyll's accounts, Utterson is the reader's main representative, and his compulsive investigation, his moments of identification and dissociation, figure our own possible relations to the unfolding story, registering its force. In the delayed shock delivered by rereading the door-breaking scene after finishing Jekyll's "Statement" we can sense our implication in Utterson's violent final nomination: "That's not Jekyll's

---

[14] Once more, Nietzsche's voice offers an apt warning: "Whoever fights monsters should see to it that in the process he does not become a monster." *Beyond Good and Evil*, p. 89.

voice—it's Hyde's!" For these effects of contamination are not confined to the characters; they can be traced in the motives of the tale itself and all the ways it involves the reader as the taint of sadistic aggression spreads from Hyde to opposed figures and at last to the whole narrative. Wherever we try to locate the real stab of the story, we should recognize that it really means to stab. It may arouse guilty identification like Utterson's, the sense of a corresponding doubleness ("You are certainly wrong about Hyde being overdrawn," Gerard Manley Hopkins wrote to Robert Bridges: "my Hyde is worse"),[15] but even without or apart from such recognition, there is a covert cruel streak in the narrative that also seeks to implicate us. It appears most clearly in the presentation of the maid who views the encounter between Hyde and Carew, "brilliantly lit by the full moon. It seems she was romantically given; for she sat down upon her box, which stood immediately under the window, and fell into a dream of musing. Never (she used to say, with streaming tears, when she narrated that experience), never had she felt more at peace with all men or thought more kindly of the world." As Carew approaches he becomes the focus of this romantic reverie, "an aged and beautiful gentleman with white hair. . . . The moon shone on his face as he spoke, and the girl was pleased to watch it, it seemed to breathe such an innocent and old-world kindness of disposition" (46). Hyde's ferocious attack on Carew also violates the maid's moony dreams with an insistent demonstration of human evil. She too is a victim: "At the horror of these sights and sounds, the maid fainted" (47), but we are induced not to sympathize but to participate in her victimization. By focusing the account through her and alluding to her subsequent tearful narration, the passage makes her a kind of unreliable narrator from whose naive innocence the superior, knowing tone of the enclosing narrative ("It seems she was romantically given") invites us to separate ourselves. We are offered instead the vicarious depravity of a philosophical rape.[16]

The impulse to violate and destroy innocence or optimistic contentment finds other victims, and in each case the reader is nudged into alignment with that impulse. After his first encounter with Hyde, Utterson feels "a

---

[15] Maixner, *Critical Heritage*, p. 229.

[16] Compare the earlier female victim, the girl Hyde tramples. That scene may also be read as an equivalent for sexual assault, which seems to be the way Hopkins read it: "The trampling scene is perhaps a convention: he was thinking of something unsuitable for fiction" (Maixner, *Critical Heritage*, p. 229). The maid's "dream of musing," loss of consciousness, and distraught retellings also recall Utterson's nightmares and his efforts to regain control. In these repetitions the tale seems to be retelling the story of its own oneiric origins, retracing the links between its active and passive voices or the suffering and infliction of narrative violence. Stevenson tells of the dreams that inspired *Dr. Jekyll and Mr. Hyde* in "A Chapter on Dreams," in *Across the Plains* (London: Chatto and Windus, 1892), pp. 249–51.

nausea and distaste of life" (41), and this effect is carried further in the mortally shaken Lanyon. "'I have had a shock,' he said, 'and I shall never recover. It is a question of weeks. Well, life has been pleasant; I liked it; yes sir, I used to like it. I sometimes think if we knew all, we should be more glad to get away'" (57). The implied reader's position is less clearly marked here. We may only register the excitement of increasing threat and mystery, but we may also anticipate the savage pleasure of sharing in dark knowledge that the mystery plot promises. As the repeated pattern of devastating experiences allows us to assume a privileged detachment instead of sharing shock and nausea, the narrative drive to destroy complacency again proposes a conspiracy of aggression.

It may seem that this violence is contained and redefined within the tale's larger moral purpose, in which the insistence on evil and its inseparability from human existence opposes Jekyll's mistaken project of purification. His own scientific optimism has been harshly refuted. "I have been made to learn that the doom and burthen of our life is bound forever on man's shoulders, and when the attempt is made to cast it off, it but returns upon us with more unfamiliar and more awful pressure" (83). But the logic of the cautionary tale, with its insistence on the appropriateness of the retribution that overtakes him ("If I am the chief of sinners, I am the chief of sufferers also. I could not think that this earth contained a place for sufferings and terrors so unmanning" [58]), is produced by a punitive impulse that is the respectable double of Hyde's pleasure from torture to another. The tale provides no position, no point of identification, that is not implicated in some form of victimization and violence.

In *Dr. Jekyll and Mr. Hyde,* as in many other Gothic tales, we are confronted with troubling reflections of our own demand for narrative intelligibility, reflections that should lead us to question the ways Stevenson's tale has usually been read and retold. The most common procedure has been to extend the logic of the hermeneutic code or mystery plot, to name the tale's secret or say what Hyde hides, and the most common answer for more than a century has been sex. Both ordinary and more sophisticated contemporary readers readily assumed that the details of Hyde's infamy that Jekyll withholds are sexual and that, as James puts it, though Stevenson "achieves his best effects without the aid of the ladies," who play only a minor part in the tale, "it is very obvious . . . that they must have played an important part in [Hyde's] development."[17] Popular stage and film versions have

---

[17] Maixner, *Critical Heritage,* p. 308. Compare Hopkins's comments cited in the previous note. Stevenson betrays some exasperation with readings that equate "immorality" with sexuality. "The harm was in Jekyll because he was a hypocrite—not because he was fond of

remedied this omission by introducing several women's roles, typically an upper-class fiancée for Jekyll and a lower-class mistress for Hyde, so that the divided protagonist can be conventionally torn between sanctioned and illicit desires.[18] More recent interpretations have taken the marginal role of women as a sign that Jekyll's illicit desires are instead homosexual, and *Dr. Jekyll and Mr. Hyde,* often paired with *The Picture of Dorian Gray,* is now becoming established as a classic of fin-de-siècle "Gay Gothic."[19] Changing the gender of Jekyll/Hyde's object choice, however, does not change the assumption that the key to understanding the tale is to uncover its sexual secrets, that the aim of reading should be some final nomination of a love that presumably dare not speak its own name.

Such readings also entail a certain refusal to read, to accept the tale's repeated insistence on Hyde's cruelty and malice as the essence of his evil. It is his capacity for drinking pleasure from any degree of torture to another that makes him seem monstrous to the wondering Jekyll, a desire to dominate whose drive toward death emerges as a primary force, not the disguised expression of some deeper impulse. And what is most disturbing, as we have seen, is that this savage will to power cannot be contained within the figure of Hyde or exorcized by Jekyll/Hyde's final self-destruction; it becomes truly monstrous in becoming mingled with the motives of the other characters, the narrative, and its readers—precisely as they seek the solution to a mystery or a responsible moral message. Like Jekyll, the tale releases a force that cannot be mastered—not because it simply overwhelms all resistance but because all efforts to resist or contain it seem to become further instances of its cruel logic. As the violence of anarchic desire and the violence of moral order threaten to become indistinguishable, we again confront the darkest Gothic vision, the reduction of all values to common terms of power.

women; he says so himself; but people are so filled full of folly and inverted lust, that they can think of nothing but sexuality. The hypocrite let out the beast Hyde—who is no more sensual than another, but who is the essence of cruelty and malice, and selfishness and cowardice: and these are the diabolic in man—not this poor wish to have a woman, that they make such a cry about." Maixner, *Critical Heritage,* p. 231.

[18] See Harry M. Geduld, *The Definitive Dr. Jekyll and Mr. Hyde Companion* (New York: Garland, 1983).

[19] The phrase is Elaine Showalter's, who claims that the tale "can most persuasively be read as a fable of fin-de-siècle homosexual panic." *Sexual Anarchy: Gender and Culture at the Fin de Siècle* (New York: Viking, 1990), p. 107. For Judith Halberstam too, "the Gothic monstrosity of Dorian and definitely of Mr. Hyde have everything to do with the sexual secrets the represent." *Skin Shows: Gothic Horror and the Technology of Monsters* (Durham: Duke University Press, 1995), p. 71. See also William Veeder, "Children of the Night: Stevenson and Patriarchy," in Veeder and Hirsch, *Dr. Jekyll and Mr. Hyde after One Hundred Years,* pp. 107–160, for a detailed psychoanalytic reading of the tale's homosocial and homosexual implications.

Yet such a constricted single logic looks too much like the other hermeneutic finalities we have encountered. We need to recall the narrative dialogism that, as in earlier Gothic fictions, cannot be so reduced, the impurities of Stevenson's tale that both contaminate every position it offers and preserve what James calls its "stamp of a really imaginative production, that we may take it in different ways." Those ways are not directly represented by competing narrative voices but insinuated through the inner differences that animate each voice, like Jekyll's continually changing versions of his relation to Hyde. The drama of his account clearly arises from its compelling story, the trajectory that leads from his triumphant discovery of a new province of knowledge and new avenues to fame and power to his utter and terrifying loss of control, from his initial leap of welcome to his new self to his desperate sense of being possessed by something not only hellish but inorganic. But it also arises from his struggle to make sense of his experience by telling his story to another, to relieve his terrible isolation by addressing his confession to his closest friend. We can respect the need that impels his account without accepting the oppositions that frame it.

The need for narrative communication and the forces that block it lie as deep in the conception of *Dr. Jekyll and Mr. Hyde* as the more prominent notion of human duality. The second of the two scenes Stevenson attributes to his dreams, "afterward split in two," was one "in which Hyde, pursued for some crime, took the powder and underwent the change in the presence of his pursuers."[20] The first, and the only one that appears unaltered in the tale, forms its shortest chapter, "Incident at the Window." Here, recalling the beginning of the narrative, Utterson and Enfield are again on one of their regular Sunday walks and again stop before the door whose story set the mystery plot in motion. Now they enter the court. "I am uneasy about poor Jekyll," Utterson explains, "and even outside, I feel as if the presence of a friend might do him good" (60). They find him sitting "like some disconsolate prisoner" at a window, and, since he says he can neither go out with them nor invite them in, they offer to "stay down here, and speak with you from where we are."

"That is just what I was about to venture to propose," returned the doctor, with a smile. But the words were hardly uttered, before the smile was struck out of his face and succeeded by an expression of such abject terror and despair, as froze the very blood of the two gentlemen below. They saw it but for a glimpse, for the window was instantly thrust down; but that glimpse had been sufficient, and they turned and left the court without a word. (61)

[20] Stevenson, "Chapter on Dreams," p. 250.

Although Jekyll's "Statement" refers to this moment only indirectly in recounting the child-trampling incident, mentioning Enfield as "a passerby, whom I recognized the other day in the person of your kinsman" (87), we can easily infer that he has been seized by one of the sudden transformations that have been overtaking him more and more frequently. Together, the two dream scenes represent, as Stevenson says, "the central idea of a voluntary change becoming involuntary,"[21] as well as the contrary movement involved in composing the tale, but we can also observe how the incident at the window links Jekyll's loss of control with the violent disruption of dialogue. Not only must Jekyll withdraw in terror and despair, but Utterson and Enfield are also silenced.

> In silence, too, they traversed the by street; and it was not until they had come into a neighbouring thoroughfare, where even upon a Sunday there were still some stirrings of life, that Mr. Utterson at last turned and looked at his companion. They were both pale; and there was an answering horror in their eyes.
> "God forgive us! God forgive us!" said Mr. Utterson.
> But Mr. Enfield only nodded his head very seriously, and walked on once more in silence. (61)

Walking in silence is the usual way this odd couple spend their time together. "It was a nut to crack for many, what these two could see in each other, or what subject they could find in common. It was reported by those who encountered them in their Sunday walks, that they said nothing, looked singularly dull, and would hail with obvious relief the appearance of a friend" (29–30). Jekyll and Hyde represent a potential subject in common that prompts speech between Utterson and Enfield, but their exchanges are repeatedly cut off. Discretion prevents Enfield from giving Hyde's name till Utterson asks for it, and neither names Jekyll, though Utterson explains that "if I do not ask you the name of the other party, it is because I know it already." Disturbed at having opened an apparently scandalous hidden story, they pledge to return to silence. "Here is another lesson to say nothing," says Enfield. "Let us make a bargain never to refer to this again" (34). When they again find themselves before the door, Enfield allows himself to break their bargain because he believes "that story's at an end, at least. We shall never see more of Mr. Hyde," and he adds that

---

[21] Stevenson, "Chapter on Dreams," p. 251. The recurrent Gothic trope of dream origins, already present in Walpole's account of his inspiration for *The Castle of Otranto* and elaborated in Shelley's 1831 introduction to *Frankenstein*, here turns from the Romantic conception of inward, unconscious inspiration toward the desire for dialogic exchange.

he now realizes the door is "a back way to Dr. Jekyll's," allowing Utterson to propose the visit that leads to the aborted dialogue at the window (60). Between these two episodes, there are several other untold or uncompleted stories, such as when Utterson invites Jekyll to "make a clean breast of this in confidence" and Jekyll declines: "It is one of those affairs that cannot be mended by talking" (44), or when the devastated Lanyon refuses to explain his break with Jekyll. "Some day, Utterson, after I am dead, you may perhaps come to learn the right and wrong of this. I cannot tell you" (57). All these stories that are broken off or left untold are of course functional parts of the mystery plot, enigmas, snares, and blockages that heighten and prolong suspense before Lanyon's and Jekyll's narratives resolve it. But besides helping to constitute hermeneutic truth by delaying its final naming, these moments also express a thwarted urge to give and receive help and understanding that can neither be reduced to nor securely separated from the will to knowledge and power. Narrative figures here as both an effort to master disturbance and a tenuous bond between isolated individuals.

The most important story that remains untold to the end is Edward Hyde's. The absence of an account that, like the creature's in *Frankenstein*, would present Hyde's own version perturbs the development of the whole narrative, like a dark star in a binary system. We get only glimpses of how the strange case appears from his perspective, always mediated through Jekyll's account and mostly in the form of summaries. If we suppose that this mediation conceals a hidden truth, we are likely to set off on the sort of interpretive quest that has led so many readers to claim discovery of the tale's sexual secrets, but if we consider the interplay of communication and silence, telling and withholding that runs through the tale, we can also recognize another explanation. Hyde's story remains untold, not just because its scandalous content demands the sort of culturally determined reticence that Enfield, Utterson, Lanyon, and Jekyll display, but more fundamentally because he would never tell it. Frankenstein's creature actively seeks the chance to tell his story and unfolds it with all his formidable eloquence because he wants to become linked with the chain of existence and events, and though his other desires are all thwarted, this one is fulfilled in the act of narration itself, which necessarily links him with others in a dense network of shared and contested meanings. Hyde has nothing to gain, nothing to explain, no interest in forming such links. The potion that brings him to life produces the exhilarating sense of "a solution of the bonds of obligation" (83), a release that not only undoes all moral restraints but also removes any obligation or motive to account for oneself. His untold story figures as a negative space in the composition of the tale that, by marking the limits of narrative, reaffirms its dialogical conditions. Once freed from the chafing bonds of obligation, narrative disappears.[22]

Through the question of narrative accountability we have encountered again the effects of impurity that mark every aspect of *Dr. Jekyll and Mr. Hyde*. The absence of Hyde's version may seem to serve the aim of excluding his monstrous otherness, but it finally works to reassert his inseparability from the other characters and ourselves. As a closing emblem of this mutual implication, we could consider the story that remains untold when we leave Utterson as he "trudged back to his office to read the two narratives in which this mystery was now to be explained" (73). That unrecorded reading is replaced by our own, since we never return to Utterson or learn what he makes of those two narratives. Would he have recognized his own role in the destruction of his friend, the way he had become identified with what he opposed, and the violence produced by his demand for explanation? If we feel no desire to be shown Utterson's response to what he has read, it may be because we prefer not to reflect any further on our own complicity. That, perhaps, would be too cruel.

---

[22] Compare James on both *Dr. Jekyll and Mr. Hyde* and "The Turn of the Screw" as "irresponsible" fictions. See n. 2, above.

6

Dracula

The search for Mr. Hyde turns reflexively back on itself: instead of uncovering the secrets of a monstrous other, we confront a disturbing image of ourselves in the very act of solving the tale's mysteries. Something similar happens in *Dracula*, but in this last and most popular of the great nineteenth-century monster stories there appears to be no mystery about the source of disturbance or any doubt about the critical role of narrative in containing it. Here the threat is emphatically external; the monster is not created by or from the protagonist but comes as an alien invader from a distant time and place. Frankenstein considers "the being whom I had cast among mankind, and endowed with the will and power to effect purposes of horror . . . nearly in the light of my own vampire, my own spirit let loose from the grave, and forced to destroy all that was dear to me,"[1] and Jekyll calls Hyde "this familiar that I called out of my own soul, and sent forth alone to do his good pleasure." In *Dracula*'s autonomous monster these preternatural figures become literal again, and crediting superstitious beliefs about vampires or familiars becomes a crucial requirement ("to superstition must we trust at the first," Dr. Van Helsing tells the other vampire hunters) in the concerted effort to objectify and eliminate Dracula's menace.[2] Yet as in its predecessors, the crucial issue here is not the preternatural but the unnatural, the boundaries of the human that the monster seems to lie outside.

The question of belief and its relation to the source and status of the nar-

[1] Mary Wollstonecraft Shelley, *Frankenstein; or, The Modern Prometheus*, ed. James Rieger (Chicago: University of Chicago Press, 1982), p. 72.
[2] Bram Stoker, *Dracula* (New York: Bantam, 1981), p. 346.

rative frames the whole book, which begins with a note on the text: "How these papers have been placed in sequence will be made more manifest in the reading of them. All needless matters have been eliminated, so that a history almost at variance with the possibilities of latter-day belief may stand forth as simple fact." The question returns in the final note, as Jonathan Harker tells how, seven years after the story's conclusion, he and the other survivors reviewed the papers that constitute the narrative. "We were struck with the fact, that in all the mass of material of which the record is composed, there is hardly one authentic document. . . . We could hardly ask any one, even did we wish to, to accept these as proofs of so wild a story." "We want no proofs," Van Helsing declares; "we ask none to believe us!" (400), making their shared belief a bond that unites their "little band." Whether other readers join them or keep some distance from their beliefs is a crucial question from beginning to end.

The reason hardly one authentic document remains is of course that Dracula, in his invasion of Dr. Seward's asylum, has destroyed all the original manuscript versions of the various journals and letters, as well as the phonograph cylinders on which Seward kept his diary. Both the vampire and his opponents clearly place great importance on these records. "Thank God there is the other copy in the safe!" Seward exclaims (301), and it is largely this copy, "nothing but a mass of typewriting" (400), that makes up the wild story we read. Most commentaries on *Dracula* understandably concentrate on its wild content, especially the luxuriant growth of polymorphous sexuality that vampirism can represent, but to appreciate its relation to earlier monster stories and Gothic reflexivity we also need to consider how and why the novel repeatedly draws our attention to its emerging form, the production and reproduction of its narrative.

We can begin to read the relation between *Dracula*'s sensationalism and self-consciousness by looking at the way they appear together in the first of the novel's spectacular sex scenes, Jonathan's encounter with the vampire women. The scene is framed by two passages of reflections on his shorthand journal, composed just before and after it takes place. The first is written as he feels "a soft quietude come over me" in the newly discovered rooms that are "evidently the portion of the castle occupied by the ladies in bygone days. . . . Here I am, sitting at a little oak table where in old times possibly some fair lady sat to pen, with much thought and many blushes, her ill-spelt love-letter, and writing in my diary in shorthand all that has happened since I closed it last. It is nineteenth century up-to-date with a vengeance. And yet, unless my senses deceive me, the old centuries had, and have, powers of their own which mere 'modernity' cannot kill" (37). Placing himself in the position of the imagined fair lady begins the feminization that will mark his part

in the scene that follows and that contributes greatly to its disturbing eroti-
cism as he lies motionless in the grip of "some longing and at the same time
some deadly fear" (39).[3] The affinities between the lady's blushes and his
arousal are clear, those between her ill-spelt love letter and his shorthand
more obscure, but the insistence of a desire that reveals itself despite its unorthodox or coded inscription will also run through the scene. As Jonathan
turns his attention toward his writing, the relation of past and present begins to shift, anticipating the replacement of the romanticized fair lady by
the sexually aggressive "fair girl" whose "deliberate voluptuousness" he will
find "both thrilling and repulsive" (39). His last sentence offers the sharpest
formulation of the novel's organizing opposition between modernity and the
archaic powers of the old centuries whose greatest threat may lie in their se-
ductive appeal, and it is telling (and foretelling) that the modern is represented here by a technique of writing, that writing is considered as itself a
kind of power, and that modernity will evidently require the aid of something not merely modern to combat what threatens it.

The second passage immediately follows the first but is written after
Jonathan has nearly succumbed to the centuries-old power of the vampire
women and been rescued only by the greater power of Dracula. "God preserve my sanity, for to this am I reduced. Safety and the assurance of safety
are things of the past. Whilst I live on here there is but one thing to hope
for, that I may not go mad, if, indeed, I be not mad already. If I be sane,
then surely it is maddening to think that of all the foul things that lurk in
this dreadful place the Count is the least dreadful to me; that to him alone
I can look for safety" (37). Dracula is less dreadful because Jonathan views
him only with fear and repulsion that are not monstrously mixed with the
longing and thrill the women inspire, the "wicked, burning desire that they
would kiss me with those red lips" (39). His account of his experience is as
close as we get to being told what it feels like to yield to the vampire's
spell—any further and the experience would become untellable. Lucy in
her waking phase can speak only vaguely of "something very sweet and
very bitter all around me" (104) and "the pain of the fear of sleep, with
such unknown horrors as it has for me" (140);[4] Mina can at least recall her

---

[3] For a reading of the reversal of conventional gender roles here as disguised homoeroticism,
see Christopher Craft, "'Kiss Me with Those Red Lips': Gender and Inversion in Bram Stoker's
Dracula," in *Dracula: The Vampire and the Critics*, ed. Margaret L. Carter (Ann Arbor: UMI
Research Press, 1988), pp. 167–94. "Virile Jonathan Harker enjoys a 'feminine' passivity and
awaits a delicious penetration from a woman whose demonism is figured as the power to penetrate" (169).
[4] In her unconscious, increasingly vampiric phase, Lucy also tries to destroy the memorandum she has written telling of her mother's death and Dracula's approach (160).

encounter with Dracula and resolutely struggles "to tell of this fearful thing," but of her feelings as he prepares to drink her blood (for the third time) she can only say, "I was bewildered, and strangely enough, I did not want to hinder him" (303–4). Only in Jonathan's unconsummated passion can the novel clearly acknowledge the answering desire that is the most disturbing part of vampirism, that makes it more than an external threat.[5]

The knowledge of this desire, in addition to the terrifying danger of "those awful women, who were—who are—waiting to suck my blood" (42), is what jeopardizes Jonathan's sanity and impels him, like Hamlet, to take up his (slightly misquoted) "tablets." "Feeling as though my own brain must end in its undoing, I turn to my diary for repose. The habit of entering accurately must help to soothe me" (37–38). Like so many other points where characters refer to their motives for scrupulously recording their experiences, this can be read functionally as reinforcing the narrative's claims to reliability, but it also takes up the earlier association of writing with power and clearly presents narrative as a struggle to control disturbance. We will need to follow that struggle as it develops throughout the novel, but it is worthwhile to dwell a little longer on the relation of this self-conscious frame to the sensational scene that follows.

We can see how the therapeutic need for accurate representation licenses erotic detail. When Jonathan describes his desire for the vampires' kisses, he adds, "It is not good to note this down, lest some day it should meet Mina's eyes and cause her pain, but it is the truth" (39). It would be interesting to know what Mina does make of this passage when she reads it, since all she confides to *her* shorthand journal is pity for her husband's suffering and uncertainty "whether it be true or only imagination" (188), but there are further implications for writing and reading here. The invitation to vicarious passive surrender ("I closed my eyes in a languorous ecstasy and waited—waited with beating heart" [39]) works together with the deliberate voluptuousness of the description that exercises manipulative control, just as the demands of honest self-exposure permit the indulgence of renewed arousal. Rather than soothing, Jonathan's account recreates his disturbance, but it does allow him to regain control by taking over in the act of telling the vampires' ability to regulate the pace of events in both the girl's achingly slow approach and Dracula's sudden intervention. In this shift from passivity to action, narrative offers a power that has been appropriated from the monstrous forces it works to contain.

[5] Compare the motif of seduction we considered earlier in "The Turn of the Screw," a contemporary text that also self-consciously reworks Radcliffean conventions, where seduction is a figure for narrative transactions and the reader's cooperating desire.

Jonathan's fears for his sanity, reprised in Mina's later doubts when she reads his journal ("Did he get his brain fever, and then write all those terrible things, or had he some cause for it all?" [188]), return us to the questions of belief and narrative reliability. The first four chapters, presenting Jonathan's Transylvanian experiences through his journal, draw on Gothic conventions that were well established a hundred years before *Dracula*, including the exotic setting of a remote castle in the mountains occupied by a mysterious, sinister aristocrat who fascinates and menaces the naive protagonist.[6] The most important role of these conventions is to pose the problem of isolated subjectivity under the assault of experiences that defy rational explanation. There is, however, little question here of our doubting Jonathan's account or constructing an alternative version; the issue is rather his own and other characters' belief in its reliability. He can escape from the castle but not from the private nightmare of his experience, which leads to mental breakdown and the effort to repress the memories contained in his diary. He gives the book to Mina: "The secret is here, and I do not want to know it" (110), and she wraps and seals it as "an outward and visible sign for us all our lives that we trusted each other" (112). But this pact of ignorance cannot last. The sight of Dracula in London revives his torment ("If only I knew! If only I knew!" [181]), from which only Van Helsing, having read Mina's transcript of the diary, can release him: "Strange and terrible as it is, it is *true!*" (196). The confirmation, Jonathan writes as he now resumes his journal, "seems to have made a new man of me. It was the doubt as to the reality of the whole thing that knocked me over. I felt impotent, and in the dark, and distrustful. But now that I *know*, I am not afraid, even of the Count" (197).

This movement from the isolation and uncertainty of individual accounts to the mutual support and assurance of shared knowledge and beliefs drives the development of the whole narrative. It begins with the shift in chapter 5 to the exchange of letters between Mina and Lucy, soon followed by Seward's diary and Mina's journal, offering multiple, partial accounts that the reader must try to integrate. Mina provides a figure for this work when she records her observations from the elevated viewpoint of the cliffs overlooking Whitby. "The band on the pier is playing a harsh waltz in good time, and further along the quay there is a Salvation Army meeting in a

6 As David Seed observes, "the first four chapters seem to present a miniature pastiche-Gothic novel." See "The Narrative Method of *Dracula*," in Carter, *Dracula: The Vampire and the Critics*, p. 200. Harker's assuming the position of Emily in *The Mysteries of Udolpho*, like his taking the place of the "fair lady" writing her love letter, is an instance of the inversions to which he seems especially liable, alternating between moments of assertive action and passive collapse.

back street. Neither of the bands hears the other, but up here I hear and see them both" (72). Our sense of occupying a detached, superior position grows as we infer the hidden action of Dracula's arrival in England and his repeated draining of Lucy's blood. The gap between the reader's and the characters' understanding creates increasing tension here, and in opening and closing this gap *Dracula* works out its distinctive formal drama. The shifts from single to multiple narration and from the exotic otherness of Transylvania to the domestic familiarity of contemporary England produce a modulation from the older Gothic mode to that of Victorian sensation fiction, up-to-date with a vengeance, where the initial relation of modernity and the powers of the old centuries is inverted. Several commentators have noted Stoker's debt to Wilkie Collins both in composing his narrative from diaries, letters, and other documents and in insinuating mystery and terror into familiar settings.[7] Stoker, however, is writing not a mystery but a monster story where deferred explanation is subordinated to creating consensus. In contrast to *The Woman in White* or *Dr. Jekyll and Mr. Hyde,* with their hermeneutic structures in which "truth is what completes, what closes,"[8] *Dracula* makes discovering the truth of vampirism the pivot of its action, the crucial central stage that, as Van Helsing says of Mina's diary, "opens the gate" to everything that follows (193).

It opens the way not only to knowledge but to action, for it is only after he has read Mina's and Jonathan's journals that Van Helsing begins to organize the counterattack that eventually destroys Dracula. Most remarkably, it opens one of the longest sustained reflexive sequences in Gothic fiction, as the assembly and reproduction of the narrative itself takes over the action of the novel. Mina's privileged vision from the cliffs becomes a prefiguration of her role in bringing the separate accounts together, making private experience publicly available. Jonathan's diary and her own, written in the shorthand code they share, become accessible to others through her typed transcriptions, as does Seward's phonograph diary. Much is made of the way these texts reach a destination their writers never anticipated.[9] Jonathan's begins as a travel diary and intensifies into a des-

---

[7] See, for example, Seed, "Narrative Method of *Dracula*," pp. 199–201.

[8] Roland Barthes, *S/Z*, trans. Richard Miller (New York: Hill and Wang, 1974), p. 76.

[9] Much is also made of the material processes of transforming the diaries into multiple typescripts, and there are several reflections on the power and restrictions of different media. Shorthand protects privacy when Dracula intercepts Harker's letter to Mina, which he denounces as "a vile thing, an outrage upon friendship and hospitality" (44); it signifies a different kind of exclusion when Mina, who "could not resist the temptation of mystifying him a bit—I suppose it is some of the taste of the original apple that remains still in our mouths," first offers Van Helsing the original shorthand version of her diary (192). When Seward later shows her his phonograph, she exclaims, "Why, this beats even shorthand!" (233), but he

perate effort to keep his mental balance; Mina's begins as an exercise, practicing secretarial skills "to be useful to Jonathan. . . . I do not suppose there
will be much of interest to other people; but it is not intended for them"
(57); Seward's begins as a record of clinical observations on his patient Renfield and grows into his account of Lucy's mysterious decline and apparent
and "true" death. In narrating the process of opening these private narratives to the eyes of others, the novel not only allows us to reflect on our position as readers but proposes a new way of understanding it. Instead of the
detached or voyeuristic stance implied in reading others' diaries and letters
without their knowledge, we come to take up the collective position of the
little band of vampire hunters for whom these texts, as well as such previously unaccountable documents as business correspondence and newspa-
per cuttings, have been assembled. Mina's and Jonathan's joint efforts in
"knitting together in chronological order every scrap of evidence they
have" (238) continue until "the whole story is put together in such a way
that every point tells" (261), closing the gap between us and Dracula's opponents by making them readers of the same text we have been reading and
arming them with its knowledge for the coming struggle. Fulfilling the
promise of the opening note ("How these papers have been placed in
sequence will be made manifest in the reading of them"), this reflexive in-
terlude also works to consolidate both the little band and our own involvement.

The process of narrative integration thus both represents and enacts the
integration of the group, incorporating their fragmentary accounts in a unified sequence and their uncertain perceptions in a framework of shared
belief. Narrative figures here as an instrument of order and knowledge, con-
ferring a power whose importance Dracula himself confirms when he destroys the "authentic" materials from which the tale has been composed.
In producing their collaborative account, the little band exercises the
"power of combination—a power denied to the vampire kind" (251) that
is their greatest source of strength, but to gain it they must also make themselves vulnerable by revealing their private lives. The narrative seldom
dwells on the sudden intimacy produced by reading one another's diaries,
but its disturbing intensity is indicated in Mina's response to Seward's
recordings. "That is a wonderful machine, but it is cruelly true. It told me,
in its very tones, the anguish of your heart" (235). Writing mediates this

---

soon realizes he has no way to locate any particular part of his diary, which becomes possible only after she has typed out a transcript. In all these cases the private, "authentic" quality of the documents must be sacrificed in their transformation into a publicly readable "mass
of typewriting." For a reading that focuses on some of these writing technologies, see Jennifer
Wicke, "Vampiric Typewriting: *Dracula* and Its Media," *ELH* 59 (1992): 467–93.

physical intimacy ("I have copied out the words on my typewriter, and none other need now hear your heart beat, as I did" [235]), but it also exposes the most private experience.[10] "No one need ever know," Seward says, but Mina insists "they must!" and reassures him, "We need have no secrets among us; working together and with absolute trust, we can surely be stronger than if some of us were in the dark" (235). This becomes the rule for the whole group: those who do not write also become included in the confessional process as their most unguarded moments are revealed through others' accounts, Van Helsing's hysterical surrender to "King Laugh" through Seward's diary and Arthur's and Quincey's cathartic interviews with Mina through hers. She suggests withholding this purely "personal" material from the shared record, but Van Helsing urges her to include it: "We have told our secrets, and yet no one who has told is the worse for it" (249). Quite as much as the information they share, this full mutual exposure forges the group's power of combination.

The thrust of this narrative collaboration marshals the solidarity of the group against the solitary predator, but in demanding the surrender of privacy it also mirrors (reflects and reverses) the obscene intimacies of vampirism. The exchange and mingling of personal accounts, presented with an insistent emphasis on the material processes of narrative production and reproduction, develop in close counterpoint with the sustaining and contaminating corporeality of transfusion and bloodsucking.[11] These correspondences take their place in a wider network of parallels between the novel's forces of light and darkness that develop as the narrative expands into multiple voices. Lucy's three suitors recall the three vampires that hunger for Jonathan, and the proposals she receives from each of them are later matched by the intimate emotional revelations each makes to Mina. Like several other parallels and counterpoints, such as the physical resemblances between Dracula and Van Helsing or the chiasmic exchange of youth and age between Dracula and Jonathan, these doublings can be read

[10] Something of the physical intimacy of voice is transferred to writing when Seward emotionally records the reading of the burial service over Mina. "I—I cannot go on—words—and—v-voice—f-fail m-me!" (352). Even as voice "fails," it (improbably) predominates by making writing stammer. Compare Mina's journal entry written under Dracula's influence about "the . . . the . . . the . . . Vampire. (Why did I hesitate to write the word?)" (375).

[11] Other cases of insistent materiality include Van Helsing's use of the host to seal Lucy's tomb or form a "Holy circle" around Mina, in which the mystic body of Christ assumes the same powers of metamorphosis vampire bodies have. Compare also the repeated emphasis on food, especially when the vampire hunters urge each other to eat. Thus Seward interrupts his work with Mina on exchanging and comparing their diaries: "Come, there is dinner. We must keep one another strong for what is before us" (236). Here narrative and food provide alternate forms of sustenance.

through the logic of inversion, in which mirroring images are assigned opposite values. But we can also begin to recognize that for Dracula's opponents to "become as him" is not only a danger but a necessity, and that, as we saw in our reading of Jonathan's journal, the power they seek shares its roots with the monstrosity they struggle to destroy.[12]

To understand that necessity and expose those common roots, we need to consider both the overt rhetorical aims and the covert psychosocial impulses that animate the novel's narrative strategy. As we move from *Frankenstein* to *Dr. Jekyll and Mr. Hyde* and *Dracula,* the perspective increasingly shifts from the isolated monster to his collective antagonists. It is as if Shelley's monster story were revised so that Frankenstein succeeded in enlisting Walton and his crew (as well as the reader) in the effort to destroy the creature,[13] or as if we were firmly positioned among the "circle of hateful faces" that surround Hyde. In *Dracula* the force of the developing narrative clearly aims at drawing us into the vampire hunters' orgy of righteous violence, and it is the orgiastic features of merging and release in their joint actions that link the novel's drama of narrative production with its strongest fears and fascinations. The forces that forge private accounts by isolated individuals into a coherent collective narrative reflect those that drive its underlying fantasies, which are preoccupied with transforming sexuality from a private to a collective bond. Throughout all the sexual aims and practices we may find figured in vampirism and the fight against it, the novel displays a persistent, even obsessive interest in group sex. From Jonathan's encounter with the vampire women, to Lucy's multiple suitors ("Why can't they let a girl marry three men, or as many as want her?" she asks [62]), to the transfusions by which they all (as well as van Helsing) become married to her, to the final consummation of their jointly driving a stake through her heart, sharing among multiple partners is a consistent source of sexual excitement. After Lucy's "true" death, the interest transfers to Mina as the three grief-stricken men each get emotional release and solace from her powerful "mother-spirit." The idealized image of Mina taking Arthur in her comforting arms ("I felt this big man's sorrowing head resting on me, as though it were that of the baby that some day may lie on my bosom, and I stroked his hair as though he were my own child" [243]) becomes demoniacally inverted later when she is forced to drink blood from Dracula's breast as her husband sleeps and the four others watch in

---

[12] Van Helsing admits as much, in inverted form, when he says of the vampire's need to sleep in consecrated earth, "it is not the least of its terrors that this evil thing is rooted deep in all good" (254).

[13] Compare the ending of Whale's film, in which the creature is destroyed by a mob of enraged villagers.

the novel's largest and most voyeuristic group scene. By the end, Mina's purity is restored and her maternal image secured by the birth of her son, who is symbolically fathered by the whole group. "His bundle of names links all our little band of men together" (400).

In all these versions of group sex, as in the collective production of the narrative, there is an insistence on breaking down privacy, whether its loss is represented as violation or voluntary sacrifice. This pressure is exerted on both sides of the novel's moral opposition between Dracula and his opponents, on both sides of that crucial emblem of privacy, the bedroom door. Dracula can slip past it in the form of a mist as he enters to drink Mina's blood and make her drink his while her husband sleeps; Van Helsing and the three others hesitate only a moment before making their own violent entrance. "Should we disturb her?" Quincey Morris asks. "May it not frighten her terribly?" Arthur adds. "It is unusual to break into a lady's room!" But Van Helsing dismisses such prohibitions: "All chambers are alike to the doctor; and even were they not they are all as one to me tonight" (297–98). "All as one" could be the motto for the whole narrative as it works toward its crisis and resolution. Earlier, Van Helsing has urged Seward, "Let us not be two, but one" (174); now the merging goes much further. Dracula boasts, "Your girls that you all love are mine already; and through them you and others shall yet be mine" (324), but neither he nor anyone else can exercise exclusive ownership and control through the bonds that join them. Mina becomes joined to Dracula through their exchange of blood, but that bond allows Van Helsing and the others to track him as he attempts to escape, tapping into his mental link with her through hypnotism.

In those hypnotic sessions, working in the border zone between night and day, unconscious and conscious, the novel extends its reflections on its narrative production. Earlier, as Seward struggles to make sense of Renfield's obsession both with keeping flies and spiders as "pets" and with keeping detailed accounts of his activities, he invokes this opposition. "There is a method in his madness, and the rudimentary idea in my mind is growing. It will be a whole idea soon, and then, oh unconscious cerebration! you will have to give the wall to your conscious brother" (73). Here, while he overlooks the correlation between his patient's accounts and his own, Seward locates the boundary between unconscious and conscious within his private cerebrations. When the topic reappears in the context of Van Helsing and Mina's publicly staged hypnotic sessions, however, the unconscious no longer figures as just a private, inward space but circulates between individuals as they work together to articulate an account. Van Helsing announces to Seward and Mina that "a half-thought has been buzzing often in my brain," whose growth is fostered by rereading the part of Jonathan's journal where Dracula tells the history of his "house" and "blood" (29–31), especially the deeds attributed to "that other of his race" in a border war with the Turks, one who, "when he was beaten back, came again, and again, and again, though he had to come alone from the bloody field where his troops were being slaughtered, since he knew that he alone could ultimately triumph" (360). Now they understand that this is Dracula's own story, and that, supplemented with "the philosophy of crime," it can be used to predict his actions. Van Helsing sets out the "elements" that, when brought together, produce "a flash of light . . . that show up all the earth below for leagues and leagues," but then he delegates the illuminating insight itself to Mina. "I see that your eyes are opened, and that to you the lightning flash show all the leagues. . . . Now you shall speak. Tell us two dry men of science what you see with those so bright eyes" (360–61). What she tells is a story that presents Dracula's actions as psychologically determined ("as he is criminal he is selfish; and as his intellect is small and his action is based on selfishness, he confines himself to one purpose") while it explains why her own "soul" feels "freer than it has since that awful hour" when he gained power over her (362). The passage from unconscious to conscious thought that confers a measure of freedom and control works here through transference and narrative collaboration, the basis of the talking cure.[14]

Unlike psychoanalysis, however, this version of the emergence of narrative from the unconscious does not stress the role of repression.[15] Like the accounts of the dream origins of *Frankenstein* and *Dr. Jekyll and Mr. Hyde*, a motif that goes back to the beginnings of the Gothic in Walpole's *Castle of Otranto*, it traces a movement outward from private to shared experience that leads to the publication of *Dracula* itself. As the focus shifts from isolated criminals, madmen, or monsters to the social group, this vector of narrative force gains prominence and becomes the main subject of reflection. The last quarter of *Dracula* develops those reflections at the same time that its action drives toward the conclusion. Once both the band of vampire hunters and their collective narrative have been assembled and they begin their counterattack, there is no clear need for them to continue their accounts, yet we

[14] On psychoanalysis as narrative collaboration, see Roy Schafer, "Narration in the Psychoanalytic Dialogue," *Critical Inquiry* 7 (1980): 29–53.

[15] Although *Dracula* is contemporary with the beginnings of psychoanalysis and invokes Charcot, its concept of "unconscious cerebration" is, as David Glover explains, taken from W. B. Carpenter's *Principles of Mental Physiology* (1874), where there is no theory of repression. See *Vampires, Mummies, and Liberals: Bram Stoker and the Politics of Popular Fiction* (Durham: Duke University Press, 1996), pp. 76–79.

are reminded at several points that they do manage to keep recording what happens as they pursue Dracula.[16] These many references to writing clearly serve as realistic motivation, but the importance of the collective narrative as a resource is also stressed at crucial moments in the action. Just as Van Helsing's half-thought that Mina completes draws on a rereading of the opening section of Jonathan's journal to predict Dracula's retreat to Transylvania, Mina's later review of the previous accounts, supplemented by reading "all the papers that I have not yet seen," leads to a new insight ("I do believe that under God's providence I have made a discovery" [371]) that identifies his precise route and enables the pursuers to intercept him.

Mina's discovery, elaborated in her cogently argued "Memorandum" (371–74), becomes possible only when the baffled men, having lost track of Dracula, decide to take her into their confidence again. It was their patronizing desire to protect her from further involvement once her work in assembling the narrative was done that left her isolated and vulnerable to Dracula, and after she has been contaminated the fear that he will learn their plans through her leads them once more to keep her in the dark. Allowing her full access to the others' recent accounts, including those of her hypnotic trances, enables her to show them the way again. "Our dear Madam Mina is once more our teacher," Van Helsing exclaims. "Her eyes have been where we were blinded. Now we are on the track once again, and this time we may succeed" (374). These moments show not just the reflexivity of *Dracula* but its remarkable recursiveness, repeatedly turning back to review earlier portions of its narrative in order to advance, and in each case the basis for moving forward is a shift from concealment to openness, from privacy toward publication.[17]

From its account of collective action to its staging of narrative production and exchange to its fantasies of group sex, *Dracula* insistently imagines community as assimilation, breaching the boundaries that separate individuals while it purges difference in the form of monstrous otherness. This is but one, extremely skewed version of a tension we can recognize in its nineteenth-century predecessors as well. In their tales of solitary, deviant figures all three monster stories necessarily also offer an account of social-

---

[16] Seward complains about having to change his mode of recording: "How I miss my phonograph! To write diary with a pen is irksome to me; but Van Helsing says I must" (354). Mina not only keeps her journal (presumably in shorthand) but also continues to type transcripts for the others with her "Traveller's" typewriter (370).

[17] The continued recording during the final chase sequence also provides the only remaining "authentic" documents. As Jonathan observes, there is "nothing but a mass of typewriting, except the later note-books of Mina and Seward and myself, and Van Helsing's memorandum" (400).

ity, and in each the isolated reprobate is not only opposed to others but linked with them through the dynamics of doubling. Frankenstein, having cut himself off from his family and friends to pursue his unlawful studies, is confronted with a terrible enactment of the same impulse as his creature destroys those he loves, while the violence of those murders is echoed in the madness and passion with which Frankenstein destroys the female companion. In that pivotal event the individuating impulse of separation, the assertion of autonomy, and the contrary desire for relation, for inclusion in the chain of existence and events, meet in reciprocating destruction. In *Dr. Jekyll and Mr. Hyde* the doubling between the monster and his antagonists is more extensive but also focused in a moment of righteous violence when Utterson breaks down the door of Jekyll's room. As we belatedly recognize how not only Hyde's pursuers but we as readers have become implicated in the aggressive self-assertion he embodies, we can sense how social solidarity may depend on the binding force of exclusionary violence.

Dracula makes the forging of social bonds its central action. The joining together of the little band under Van Helsing's leadership draws on the resources each can bring to the common cause, requiring mutual trust, self-sacrifice, and resolution in the face of terror. Their united and successful struggle clearly shows not only the power of combination but the possibility of creating community. At the same time, it also clearly shows how this unity entails a violent reduction of indeterminacy, embodied in the ambiguous condition of the Un-Dead. Dracula concentrates such ambiguity: he is both outside and inside, an alien invader from a remote time and place yet also strangely familiar, a figure of unacknowledged fantasies; he violates the privacy and autonomy of the self yet enters only where invited.[18] The violence required to resolve such ambiguities and make the vampire be "true dead" runs throughout the narrative, but it is most powerfully rendered in the scene of Lucy's staking, which contains its own horrific ambiguity as both a holy rite and a group rape, in which the chorus of prayer that rings through the vault sanctions the most extreme brutality.

Yet that searing moment of group fusion does not eliminate the threat of ambiguity. Instead, the parallel sequence in which the group must deal with Mina's contamination by Dracula requires them to negotiate much more difficult uncertainties. Just as she provides crucial guidance in their pursuit, Mina leads the little band into uncharted ideological territory. Her own guilty sense of being "unclean" (300) seems to be confirmed when the

---

[18] Compare Jonathan on the strange familiarity of the fair vampire woman: "I seemed somehow to know her face, and to know it in connection with some dreamy fear, but I could not recollect at the moment how or where" (38).

consecrated wafer burns her forehead, leaving her with a red mark that matches Dracula's scar. "Pulling her beautiful hair over her face, as the leper of old his mantle, she wailed out:—'Unclean! Unclean! Even the Almighty shuns my polluted flesh! I must bear this mark of shame upon my forehead until the Judgment Day'" (314). Yet instead of falling into despair or resentment, she rises to an affirmation of faith and an insistence on regarding even Dracula with pity that confronts the others with what Seward describes as a wrenching paradox. "Oh, that I could give any idea of the scene of that sweet, sweet, good, good woman in all the radiant beauty of her youth and animation, with the red scar on her forehead, of which she was conscious, and which we saw with grinding of our teeth—remembering whence and how it came; her loving kindness against our grim hate; her tender faith against all our fears and doubting; and we, knowing that so far as symbols went, she with all her goodness and purity and faith, was outcast from God" (326). His murky qualification ("so far as symbols went") fails to reduce the tension here. Mina's guilt is not merely arbitrary but motivated by her acquiescence: "Strangely enough, I did not want to hinder him." She is both pure and contaminated, both Dracula's bride ("flesh of my flesh, blood of my blood") and the cause for which the little band desperately fights.[19]

Mina's heterogeneity implicates her in monstrosity and makes it impossible to represent Dracula's threat as wholly alien.[20] Her mixed condition is dramatically rendered in the scene that parallels the violent ritual of Lucy's staking, where at her request the others read the burial service over her. It is a moment whose "bizarre" mixture, in Seward's faltering words, resists representation. "How can I—how could any one—tell of that strange scene, its solemnity, its gloom, its sadness, its horror; and withal, its sweetness" (351). In place of the earlier effort to exorcize difference, this unorthodox religious ritual confirms Mina's ambiguous condition as undead—still alive yet "deeper in death . . . than if the weight of an earthly grave lay heavy upon me" (351).

[19] The novel's closing words stress this role in Van Helsing's final declaration of the group's shared belief and their devotion to Mina. "We want no proofs; we ask none to believe us! This boy will some day know what a brave and gallant woman his mother is. Already he knows her sweetness and loving care; later on he will understand how some men so loved her, that they did dare much for her sake" (400).

[20] Compare Van Helsing's praise: "Ah, that wonderful Madam Mina! She has man's brain—a brain that a man should have if he were much gifted—and a woman's heart" (248). Further, more disturbing indications of her mixed or shifting nature come when he must admit that "our poor, dear Madam Mina is changing" (341), and although Jonathan earlier declared "there is nought in common" between Mina and the vampire women (55), when they reappear near the end they call to her, "Come, sister. Come to us" (388).

In the end, of course, Mina's purity is unambiguously restored and all the vampires destroyed. Compared with the earlier nineteenth-century monster stories, *Dracula* may seem least tolerant of ambiguity, least open to alternative versions, yet in Mina, the figure most responsible for the existence of its narrative, it not only admits but honors a version of impurity that confounds its mutually exclusive categories. And as a story-monster it has become the most fecund source of alternatives, engendering not only numerous versions and derivatives but literally Countless narratives in which Stoker's Transylvanian aristocrat is replaced by a swarm of modern vampire figures, fulfilling his ambition to be "the father or furtherer of a new order of beings" (320). Dracula remains undead in precisely the role the novel tries to deny him, as a site of identification and resistance to forces of righteous orthodoxy.[21] Stoker's monster story, like its predecessors, continues to let us play out the unstable, shifting relations of narrative power that Gothic fiction has exercised and explored from its inception.

[21] Nina Auerbach offers a survey and instance of such appropriations in *Our Vampires, Ourselves* (Chicago: University of Chicago Press, 1995).

Part III

The Language of Destiny

7

Dickens

Our readings of Gothic reflexivity and monstrosity in the previous chapters have at several points challenged the common external opposition between Gothic and the norms of realism, relocating it within the dialogue of perspectives and versions that Gothic fictions typically stage. The following chapters address that opposition from the other side, focusing on Gothic elements in the fiction of three major nineteenth-century realists (more precisely, in three versions, developed in successive generations, of the realist project of social representation) and tracing the narrative reflections they generate. In making this move, we will be crossing and redrawing boundaries that have till now marked the horizon of our studies. The fiction of Poe and his predecessors, as well as the great nineteenth-century monster stories, are commonly considered Gothic, but not *Little Dorrit, Daniel Deronda,* or *The Ambassadors.* As we shall see, however, they are linked through Gothic motifs such as ghosts and visions, through affinities with Gothic tales by the same authors, and through their self-conscious use of plots driven by the force of destiny. Pursuing the implications of these links will both extend and complicate our understanding of Gothic reflections.

Dickens provides the best starting point for this investigation, both because of his central position and because of the prominence of Gothic motifs in his fiction. From the interpolated "Madman's Manuscript" in *The Pickwick Papers* to *The Mystery of Edwin Drood,* he draws on Gothic conventions and rhetoric to develop many of his strongest concerns and effects, not only in narratives that, like these two, clearly work within Gothic genres but also at many other points where Gothic figures infiltrate and intensify scenes of domestic realism. Here, for instance, is a characteristic moment in *Bleak House.* The congenitally unsettled Richard Carstone, having abandoned medicine and the law, has now spent the last of his modest inheritance to purchase an army commission. Esther Summerson recounts the scene where John Jarndyce explains that with this move,

> "Rick has now chosen his profession for the last time. All that he has of certainty will be expended when he is fully equipped. He has exhausted his resources, and is bound henceforth to the tree he has planted."
>
> "Quite true that I have exhausted my present resources, and I am quite content to know it. But what I have for a certainty, sir," said Richard, "is not all I have."
>
> "Rick, Rick!" cried my guardian, with a sudden terror in his manner, and in an altered voice, and putting up his hands as if he would have stopped his ears, "for the love of God, don't found a hope of expectation on the family curse! Whatever you do on this side the grave, never give one lingering glance towards the horrible phantom that has haunted us so many years. Better to borrow, better to beg, better to die!"[1]

Figuring the Chancery suit as a family curse and haunting phantom strikingly articulates Jarndyce's terror and enforces "the fervour of this warning." The sudden irruption of Gothic here is more than a local effect, however: it taps into the novel's deepest narrative paradigms and thematic tensions.

The Jarndyce and Jarndyce suit does indeed work like an inherited curse in *Bleak House,* a fate arbitrarily imposed on those "born into the cause" like Richard (52), who will become its most prominent victim. Fatality and haunting permeate the novel's plotting, both in the Chancery sequences and in those where Lady Dedlock's secret past overtakes and destroys her and where Esther, in learning Lady Dedlock is her mother, is overwhelmed with the sense that, as she was told in her childhood, she is "set apart" (65), marked by a curse. The Gothic motif of the Ghost's Walk at Chesney Wold links these complementary sequences. According to the Dedlock family legend, its persistent echo, like a halting step, is a portent of calamity or disgrace (141), and it sounds a recurrent accompaniment to the advance of Lady Dedlock's doom. This atmospheric device gets an intensifying twist after Esther's disturbing interview with Lady Dedlock, as she is drawn toward Chesney Wold and finds herself on the terrace, approaching the window that might be her mother's, "when my echoing footsteps brought it

---

[1] Charles Dickens, *Bleak House* (Harmondsworth: Penguin, 1971), p. 393. All further references are to this edition.

suddenly into my mind that there was a dreadful truth in the legend of the Ghost's Walk; that it was I, who was to bring calamity upon the stately house; and that my warning feet were haunting it even then. Seized with an augmented terror of myself that turned me cold, I ran from myself and everything" (571).

In both these versions of a family curse we can see how Dickens uses Gothic to figure both the most inward private experience and the social forces or shared destinies of institutions and groups. The widespread blighting effects of Chancery and the humbling of the Dedlocks both work out their social symbolism through the fatal power of the past that also seizes individuals in moments of private terror when a haunting phantom suddenly reappears. The icy Lady Dedlock betrays her disturbance at recognizing the handwriting of her former lover on a legal document, as if a ghost had invaded her fashionable London drawing room. The revelation of Esther's birth brings back her wounding childhood experience, giving "new and terrible meaning [to] the old words, now moaning in my ear like a surge upon the shore, 'Your mother, Esther, was your disgrace, and you are hers. . . . Pray daily that the sins of others be not visited upon your head.' I could not disentangle all that was about me; and I felt as if the blame and the shame were all in me, and the visitation had come down" (569–70).

Gothic deeply informs the multiple plots and themes of *Bleak House,* but these fatal designs become occasions for narrative reflection only when exposed to the challenge of alternative versions. Such an alternative is clearly at work in the scene of Jarndyce's warning: if the suit is an implacable fate, the delusive hope it offers is also a temptation to be avoided, a phantom one must refuse to look at. In this version, Richard's fate is the consequence of his own errors and weakness, not the destruction of a helpless victim. That is the prevailing view we get through Esther's account, reinforced by Richard on his deathbed as he blames himself and resolves to "begin the world" again (927). The story of individual moral failure does not simply correct and replace that of Gothic fatality, however. The novel's indictment of Chancery requires that this corrupt and corrupting institution act as an impersonal, fatal force, and this version of events persists to the end, but we can also recognize it as a version, one that can allow the evasion of personal responsibility, as when Richard claims that the unsettled suit prevents him from settling down in life: "I was born into this unfinished contention with all its chances and changes, and it began to unsettle me before I quite knew the difference between a suit at law and a suit of clothes; and it has gone on unsettling me ever since" (376).

The same double logic informs Esther's pursuing past, the damaging account of herself as cursed that seems to be confirmed by Lady Dedlock's revelations. Overwhelmed by the force of this version, she thinks "that it was right, and had been intended, that I should die in my birth; and that it was wrong, and not intended, that I should be then alive" (569). Soon, however, she manages to replace this devastating narrative.

> I saw very well that I could not have been intended to die, or I should never have lived; not to say should never have been reserved for such a happy life. I saw very well how many things had worked together, for my welfare; and that if the sins of the fathers were sometimes visited upon the children, the phrase did not mean what I had in the morning feared it meant. I knew I was as innocent of my birth as a queen of hers; and that before my Heavenly Father I should not be punished for birth, nor a queen rewarded for it. (571)

This is a story she can live with, but we can see that it shares the logic of a comprehensive design with the dark tale it replaces. The difference between them could be called a shift from fate to destiny, from a narrative whose course is determined by its origin and whose protagonist is helplessly subjected to the oppressive power of the past to one directed toward an ultimate goal that offers a sustaining meaning and promises personal fulfillment. Fate is a familiar mainstay of Gothic plotting from *The Castle of Otranto* onward, as Manfred and his successors are repeatedly pursued by their various curses and phantoms to their inevitable dooms. The more hopeful, forward-looking pattern of destiny may seem to have an entirely different provenance, indicated in the religious language of Esther's affirmation, but because it is also a narrative whose outcome and meaning are determined in advance, it is actually quite close. The providential design is an inverted image of malign fatality, and the precariousness of the distinction between fate and destiny, between a feared and a desired narrative coherence, troubles not only *Bleak House* and several other Victorian novels but the logic and authority of narrative in general.[2]

---

[2] The difficulty of separating these terms is reflected in their interchangeable usage: a happy fate, a miserable destiny. Christopher Bolas tries to establish the distinction in psychoanalytic terms: "The person who is ill and comes to analysis . . . can be described as a fated person. . . . And we could say that the classical symptom is a kind of oracle: figure it out, unravel it through associations and the discovery of its latent meaning, and one can be free of that curse which its unknownness has sponsored. But along with the fate a person brings to analysis is a destiny which can only be a potential whose actualization depends less on the sleuth-like unraveling of the oracular symptomatology or the dream, than it does on the movement into the future through the usage of the object, a development that psychoanalysts term the transference." *Forces of Destiny: Psychoanalysis and the Human Idiom* (London: Free Association

We have already encountered a version of this issue in Barthes's challenge to the authority of narrative representation. "Everything suggests, indeed, that the mainspring of narrative is precisely the confusion of consecution and consequence, what comes *after* being read in narrative as what is *caused by;* in which case narrative would be a systematic application of the logical fallacy denounced by Scholasticism in the formula *post hoc, ergo propter hoc*—a good motto for Destiny, of which narrative all things considered is no more than the 'language.'"[3] Recalling the many narratives we have now read, we can recognize more clearly how much is at stake here: not just the structural articulations that bind each event to the next but the larger designs that confer a meaningful shape on individual and collective histories. Gothic protagonists from Caleb Williams to Victor Frankenstein and William Wilson insist on the fatality that determines their lives: "Destiny was too potent," Frankenstein declares, "and her immutable laws had decreed my utter and terrible destruction." As their narratives arouse our suspicions of bad faith and prompt alternative versions, however, they allow us to consider the inevitability of their fates as fictive constructions, articulations of the language of destiny. Similar suspicions may trouble any sense of narrative inevitability. When Godwin and Poe claim to have written *Caleb Williams* and "The Raven" "backwards," they point to the formal basis of these effects: not individual authorial forethought but the general retrograde logic the Russian Formalists called "motivation." From this functional perspective, narrative events are determined as means to an end, causes determined by their effects, and it is the ending, motivating everything that precedes it but followed by nothing more, that, as Gérard Genette observes, discloses the arbitrariness of narrative.[4] Beyond the play of alternating perspectives on characters' invocations of destiny lies the double logic that makes every narrative both motivated and arbitrary, a doubling that Gothic fatality exposes to our reflections in several Victorian fictions. We should also recall another doubling we have repeatedly found in Gothic fiction, that of destiny and destination, of narrative as a plotted story moving toward an end that will confer meaning on the whole and as a repeatedly renewed transaction, a discourse that can never reach a final point of arrival. It is this double force that, as we return to Dickens, can

---

Books, 1989), pp. 32–33. I will mark the sense of a more open process of actualization with the notion of destination, which includes not only characters' but narratives' movement into the future.

[3] Roland Barthes, "Introduction to the Structural Analysis of Narratives," in *Image, Music, Text,* trans. Stephen Heath (New York: Hill and Wang, 1977), p. 94.

[4] Gérard Genette, "Vraisemblance et motivation," *Communications* 11 (1968): 5–21.

help us see how the figure of destiny links the grasp (comprehension) of narrative form with the ideological grasp it exerts on its readers.

Destinies shape not only the course of individual lives but collective identities by naturalizing social roles, positing them as the inevitable or proper goal of development. The happy life for which Esther Summerson believes herself to have been reserved, the welfare for which so many things have providentially worked together, is a particularly restricted version of domestic duty. Insofar as the novel idealizes her role as "little old woman," the housekeeper of the old Bleak House and eventually housewife and mother in the new (both arranged for her by the paternal Jarndyce), it proposes her as a model of feminine fulfillment, where happiness is found not by pursuing personal desires or ambitions but by self-effacing devotion to others. Lady Dedlock's fate could then be seen as the punishment precisely for indulging desire and ambition, a punishment felt most painfully in the lack of any outlet for her maternal nature. Readers who register the persuasive force of this account occupy one possible destination for the cultural messages *Bleak House* transmits, but there are others. From a perspective less closely aligned with Esther's and more alert to the shared logic of providential design and family curse, her happy destiny seems to be inseparable from the oppressive fate she struggles against. Her own account betrays this connection at several points, as when she feels "a burst of gratitude to the providence of God" that she has been so disfigured by her illness that no one will be able to recognize her resemblance to her mother (565), or when she persuades herself that she should accept Jarndyce's proposal of marriage as her destiny: "It came upon me as the close of the benignant history I had been pursuing, and I felt that I had but one thing to do" (667). In these impulses of self-effacement, which the novel invites us to see as excessive or mistaken, we can read a different story. Bowing to her Calvinist aunt's sentence of doom, accepting the damaging premise that she is "set apart" and not destined for the fulfillment of romantic love (a possibility her aunt also renounced because of the "disgrace" of Esther's birth), she allows us to see the fate she embraces as the sign of unhealed wounds rather than an idealized destiny.

The power of such plotting both to articulate individual destinies and to incorporate them in inclusive social representations makes it a central narrative paradigm in Dickens and a major resource for later novelists like Eliot and James. The possibility of alternative versions, however, leaves an opening for suspicion of this power, a sense of its coercive force. We have traced the effects of such alternatives and the narrative reflections they enable through nineteenth-century Gothic fiction, and we can now begin to see how they also figure in Dickens's use of Gothic. In his case, though, there is also a distinctive covert motivation for plots of fate and destiny.

At the same time that alternative versions of his characters' destinies play out a social drama of conflicting values, we can also read them as figurations of Dickens's own story. In *The Personal History of David Copperfield,* as we know from the autobiographical fragment he wrote a few years before, he had written a disguised version of his early life in which his youthful sense of abandonment and degradation in the blacking warehouse is reproduced in David's ordeal. David presents his experience as a secret and intensely painful part of his life, but also as a closed episode. After he has been adopted by his aunt, he feels that "a curtain had for ever fallen on my life at Murdstone and Grinby's," and its memory seems to play no part in his progress onward toward fulfillment in work and love, becoming a successful author and marrying Agnes.[5] John Forster, in disclosing Dickens's story, presents him as more deeply marked by "a time of which he never could lose the remembrance while he remembered anything, and the recollection of which, at intervals, haunted him and made him miserable even to that hour," and Dickens's own account powerfully renders this effect of haunting. "My whole nature was so penetrated with the grief and humiliation of such considerations, that even now, famous and caressed and happy, I often forget in my dreams that I have a dear wife and children; even that I am a man; and wander desolately back to that time of my life."[6] Instead of making David such a haunted man, however, Dickens defers exploring the continuing effects of early traumatic experience to later novels and, notably, displaces it onto female figures like Esther.

We should bear in mind that these accounts, including the autobiographical passages Forster published, are all versions, variations on themes of childhood deprivation and its consequences for which there is no single original story. Forster was the first critic in a position to read Dickens in the light of his secret past, an interpretive strategy whose power has since been repeatedly demonstrated but that always runs the risk of reducing the complex social panoramas of his novels to the privacy of encrypted autobiography.[7] That, as we shall soon see, is a problem with which the novels

---

[5] Charles Dickens, *David Copperfield* (Penguin: Harmondsworth, 1966), p. 272. In retrospect, having at last exchanged declarations of love with Agnes, David links his earlier suffering with his present happiness in a story of destiny. As he stands with her and looks out the window, "long miles of road then opened out before my mind; and, toiling on, I saw a ragged way-worn boy, forsaken and neglected, who should come to call even the heart now beating against mine, his own" (937).

[6] John Forster, *The Life of Charles Dickens* (London: Dent, 1966), 1:19, 23.

[7] At the same time that it seems to confer interpretive power, the secret of Dickens's past exercises its own remarkable narrative force. Not only does Dickens himself seem compelled to retell it over and over, but so do his many interpreters. Any criticism that engages with his biography registers its force by either repetition or deliberate resistance.

themselves struggle, but we can also see in Forster's version a range of developmental possibilities that are both distinctively personal and culturally coded. In his account of how "these strange experiences of his boyhood affected him afterwards," for example, he stresses qualities that are not prominent in the characters who suffer comparable afflictions. Forster emphasizes the young Dickens's "passionate resolve, even while he was yielding to circumstances, *not to be* what circumstances were conspiring to make him," generating "the fixed and eager determination, the restless and resistless energy, which opened to him opportunities of escape from many mean environments." Forster observes that Dickens was aware of the disadvantages of this tendency, "but not to the full extent."

> What it was that in society made him often uneasy, shrinking, and over-sensitive, he knew; but all the danger he ran in bearing down and over-mastering the feeling, he did not know. A too great confidence in himself, a sense that everything was possible to the will that would make it so, laid occasionally upon him self-imposed burdens greater than might be borne by anyone with safety. In that direction there was in him, at such times, something even hard and aggressive; in his determinations a something that had almost the tone of fierceness; something in his nature that made his resolves insuperable, however hasty the opinions on which they had been formed.

These "hard" qualities, Forster adds, were only rarely manifested, "but there they were; and when I have seen strangely present, at such chance intervals, a stern and even cold isolation of self-reliance side by side with a susceptivity almost feminine and the most eager craving for sympathy, it has seemed to me as though his habitual impulses for everything kind and gentle had sunk, for the time, under a sudden hard and inexorable sense of what Fate had dealt to him in those early years."[8] The gendered opposition between hard and soft in this account of inexorable fate can help us understand the role of figures like Esther in working out different possible destinies for lives shaped by such influences. She too resolves not to be what circumstances conspire to make her, but in the feminine mode of devotion, determining "that I would try, as hard as ever I could, to repair the fault I had been born with (of which I confessedly felt guilty and yet innocent), and would strive as I grew up to be industrious, contented, and kind-hearted, and to do some good to some one, and win some love to myself if I could" (65). To read such humble dedication as both the elected opposite

[8] Forster, *Life of Dickens,* 1:34–35.

and secret counterpart of cold isolation allows us to recognize how deeply the Gothic problematic of fate and destiny informs Dickens's fiction.

The doubleness of Dickens's fate, registered both in stories of victimization and in struggles to convert trauma into sustaining value, also appears in the narrative power Gothic offers, whether in the comic grotesque of the Fat Boy in *Pickwick*[9] or in the appalling spectacle of the compulsively repeated readings of Sikes's murder of Nancy that hastened Dickens's death, in which he both displayed the fierceness of his will and played the role of its ultimate victim. Gothic also offered Dickens more specialized plot and character conventions for elaborating the guilty and yet innocent condition of being haunted by a secret past, as well as a narrative form for producing concentrated representations of isolated subjectivity in first-person tales of madness, crime, and victimization. "A Madman's Manuscript" and "A Confession Found in a Prison in the Time of Charles the Second," tales that Poe singled out from Dickens's early work and may well have copied, are strong, clear instances of the genre, in which the rising pressure of self-enclosed alienation and guilt culminates in violent explosions of confession and exposure.[10] More significant for our concerns here, however, are the ways such motifs enter narratives that mix Gothic with other modes to produce versions of isolation and estrangement. Murder is one occasion for drawing on these resources, not so much in presenting the preparation or commission of the crime as in rendering the isolated and intensified consciousness of the murderer afterward. Sikes fleeing after having killed Nancy is a brute suddenly stricken by consciousness, cut off from others and pursued by the figure of his victim, a "phantom . . . a living gravestone, with its epitaph in blood," and worst of all, with its staring eyes that follow him everywhere and at last drive him to his doom.[11] Jonas Chuzzlewit fleeing after having killed Tigg is also tormented, by thoughts not of his victim but of the locked room in which he himself is supposed to be sleeping.

---

[9] See Julian Wolfreys, "'I wants to make your flesh creep': Notes toward a Reading of the Comic-Gothic in Dickens," in *Victorian Gothic: Literary and Cultural Manifestations in the Nineteenth Century,* ed. Ruth Robbins and Julian Wolfreys (New York: Palgrave, 2000), pp. 31–59.

[10] On Poe's criticisms and appropriations of Dickens, see chapter 1.

[11] Charles Dickens, *Oliver Twist* (Harmondsworth: Penguin, 1966), p. 428. Though Dickens brings Sikes to poetic justice by having him accidentally hang himself when spooked once more by what he takes to be the pursuing phantom ("'The eyes again!' he cried in an unearthly screech" [454]), he also insists on the retribution of his inward torments. "Let no man talk of murderers escaping justice, and hint that Providence must sleep. There were twenty score of violent deaths in one long minute of that agony of fear" (428).

Dread and fear were upon him, to an extent he had never counted on, and could not manage in the least degree. He was so horribly afraid of that infernal room at home. This made him, in a gloomy, murderous, mad way, not only fearful *for* himself, but *of* himself; for being, as it were, a part of the room: he invested himself with its mysterious terrors; and when he pictured in his mind the ugly chamber, false and quiet, false and quiet, through the dark hours of two nights; and the tumbled bed, and he not in it, though believed to be; he became in a manner his own ghost and phantom, and was at once the haunting spirit and the haunted man.[12]

Those last phrases can remind us that Dickens found other uses for Gothic motifs and the self-enclosure of the tale. Murder isolates and intensifies consciousness but in sequences that lead only to self-destruction; the supernatural machinery of the first and last Christmas books works to bring their protagonists out of cold isolation into community. Between *A Christmas Carol* (1843) and *The Haunted Man and the Ghost's Bargain* (1848), Dickens had written the account of his early hardships, of which we can find versions in both. When the Ghost of Christmas Past takes Scrooge to visit scenes of his earlier life, the first is the school in which he was "a solitary child, neglected by his friends," a sight that exerts "a softening influence."[13] Here the emphasis is not on the effects of his injuries but on dissolving the hardness he has developed in overcoming his early vulnerability. With Redlaw, the emphasis is instead on the wrongs he has suffered, and the bargain offered by the ghost who is his spectral double is not the recovery of the past but the erasure of its haunting memory. That, however, turns out to be the true curse, depriving him and those he encounters of all compassion. The rather strained lesson of his experience is that it is "a good thing for us, to remember wrong that has been done to us. . . . That we may forgive it."[14] These didactic ghost stories imagine a beneficent haunting and a reprieve from fate, hopeful possibilities that, like all the other Gothic strands we have been tracing, are interwoven in Dickens's most complex narratives.[15]

[12] Charles Dickens, *Martin Chuzzlewit* (Harmondsworth: Penguin, 1968), p. 804.
[13] Charles Dickens, *The Christmas Books* (Harmondsworth: Penguin, 1971), 1:71, 72.
[14] Dickens, *Christmas Books*, 2:347. The saintly Milly Swidger, who expounds this lesson, is a paragon of the feminine capacity for drawing strength from injury that Dickens elaborates in the more complex figures of Florence Dombey, Esther Summerson, and Amy Dorrit.
[15] Dickens can invoke didactic ghosts and beneficent spirits to intervene in public as well as private destinies, like the "good spirit" in *Dombey and Son* who would "take the house-tops off . . . and show a Christian people what dark shapes issue from amidst their homes." Charles Dickens, *Dombey and Son* (Harmondsworth: Penguin, 1970), p. 738. The project of deploying narrative omniscience and multiple plotting to represent social interconnections in his most ambitious novels can thus be seen as a transfiguration of Gothic.

Nowhere are they more densely interwoven than in his darkest novel, *Little Dorrit*. Secrets, mysteries, injuries, crimes, and their haunting consequences appear in most of the story lines. The effects of Arthur Clennam's oppressive childhood and lost youth are echoed in the various shadows the Marshalsea casts on the lives of the Dorrit family in both poverty and riches; Mrs. Clennam's secrets and suppressions are echoed in Mr. Merdle's mysterious complaint, and their self-inflicted injuries in the torments of Tattycoram and Miss Wade, whose confessional "History of a Self-Tormentor" incorporates the monological form of the Gothic tale in the novel's polyphonic composition. All these, and many others, are joined by multiple plotting figured as the intersecting paths of travelers seeking their different destinations yet sharing a common destiny. We will need to trace several of these paths and mark their intersections, but I want to begin with a much less prominent instance of the workings of destiny, almost imperceptible in its momentary appearance.

In chapter 12 of volume 1, "Bleeding Heart Yard," Arthur attempts to serve Amy Dorrit by getting her brother Tip released from imprisonment for debt. He has just tried to help her father by seeking information about his much more complicated affairs from the Circumlocution Office, and, thwarted there, has crossed paths again with Mr. Meagles and met Daniel Doyce. Since the inventor's factory is in Bleeding Heart Yard, where Arthur has been directed by Amy, he goes there with them to find Mr. Plornish, whose landlord turns out to be Mr. Casby, whom Arthur recalls as "an old acquaintance of mine, long ago."[16] All of these intersections are typical components of the novel's accumulating web, but what follows next obeys a different motivation that cannot be understood in strictly formal terms. Mr. Plornish takes Arthur to Tip's creditor, one Captain Maroon, "a gentleman with tight drab legs, a rather old hat, a little hooked stick, and a blue neckerchief," who after some skirmishing confirms Mr. Plornish's estimate "that ten shillings in the pound 'would settle him handsome,' and that more would be a waste of money" (182). As these two figures, the poor, kindly plasterer and the seedy horse dealer, perform a brief vignette of urban life such as Dickens had been writing since *Sketches by Boz*, they also encode a little secret message that only a few of his original readers would have been able to decipher.

Dickens's youngest child, Edward Bulwer Lytton Dickens, who had been born in 1852, received a series of playful nicknames. In later years he was known in the family as "Plorn," a contraction of the more elaborate form,

[16] Charles Dickens, *Little Dorrit* (Harmondsworth: Penguin, 1967), p. 181. All further references are to this edition.

current at the time Dickens was writing *Little Dorrit* (1855–57), "Plor-nishmaroontigoonter," and he is designated more than once in his proud father's letters as "The Plornish Maroon."[17] The conjunction of these two names would therefore seem to be a covert family joke: they are destined to meet here and form a message sent to a private destination.[18] Yet once received this meaning can hardly remain private and separated from the novel's formal and thematic structures. In a narrative so much concerned with family secrets and the relations of parents and children, as well as the destinies that bring so many other characters together, it becomes a sly, playful version of issues that elsewhere appear in much more troubled and painful forms. That context can also trouble the sense of inconsequential fun we might get from Dickens's slipping his son's nickname between the lines of his narrative. Nicknames and other such substitutions appear frequently in *Little Dorrit,* like Tip, for whose sake Plornish and Maroon are brought together, and whose given name, we might recall, is also Edward. Other instances include Amy's becoming Little Dorrit and Minnie's becoming Pet Meagles, as well as the rather different case of Rigaud's becoming first Lagnier and then Blandois, but the most striking is that of Tattycoram.

Mr. Meagles explains how after he and his wife had taken her from the Foundling Hospital "to be a little maid to Pet" they came to change her name.

> Why, she was called in the Institution, Harriet Beadle—an arbitrary name, of course. Now, Harriet we changed into Hattey, and then into Tatty, because, as practical people, we thought even a playful name might be a new thing to her and have a softening and affectionate kind of effect, don't you see? As to Beadle, that I needn't say was wholly out of the question. If there is anything that is not to be tolerated on any terms . . . it is a beadle. . . . The name of Beadle being out of the question, and the originator of the Institution for these poor foundlings having been a blessed creature of the name of Coram, we gave that name to Pet's little maid. At one time she was Tatty, and at one time she was Coram, until we got into a way of mixing the two names together, and now she is always Tattycoram. (57)

---

[17] "The Plornish Maroon is in a brilliant state; beating all former babies into what they call in America (I don't know why) sky-blue fits" (letter to Thomas Beard, September 23, 1854). "The Plornish-Maroon desires his duty. He had a fall yesterday, through overbalancing himself in kicking his nurse" (letter to Wilkie Collins, September 26, 1854). In *The Letters of Charles Dickens,* ed. Madeline House and Graham Storey (Oxford: Clarendon Press, 1993), 7:419, 425.

[18] Has anyone else noticed this, or bothered to mention it? Dickens's hidden inscription now has at least one known destination.

The process seems a close parallel to the one that yielded Plornish-Maroon, but this playful expression of family feeling fails to exert the desired softening and affectionate effect. In Meagles's account of the explosion of rage that leads to her running away, Tattycoram piles up a series of grievances that culminates in "the wretched name we gave her. . . . Who were we that we should have a right to name her like a dog or a cat?" (371–72). And when she has found refuge with Miss Wade, that formidable woman scornfully interprets Meagles's offer to take her back. "Here is your patron, your master. He is willing to take you back, my dear, if you are sensible of the favour and choose to go. You can be, again, a foil to his pretty daughter, a slave to her pleasant wilfulness, and a toy in the house showing the goodness of the family. You can have your droll name again, playfully pointing you out and setting you apart, as it is right that you should be pointed out and set apart. (Your birth, you know; you must not forget your birth)" (377). While this is presented as a perverted version of Meagles's good intentions, it also exposes the social psychology of such nicknames, which however affectionate always serve as emblems and reminders of subordination. Even Mr. Meagles more or less gets the point at last. "Perhaps, if I had thought twice about it, I might never have given her the jingling name. But, when one means to be good-natured and sportive with young people, one doesn't think twice" (878).

The question of names reaches deep into the novel's social and psychological concerns and probes further into the underlying logic of its narrative. Harriet Beadle is "an arbitrary name, of course," because as an illegitimate foundling she has no proper one, no patronymic; instead she has a patron and can be patronized. This is the basis for Miss Wade's powerful influence, "founded in a common cause. What your broken plaything is as to birth, I am. She has no name, I have no name. Her wrong is my wrong" (379). Arthur appears in this scene as Mr. Meagles's ally, ineffectually seconding his appeal ("Do not reject the hope, the certainty, this kind man offers you"), but in the end we will discover, though he does not, that he too shares in the common cause of these two angry women as to birth, that he is the illegitimate child of a woman who was also an orphan and bears no name at all in the novel. Though he is not aware of this common cause, Arthur takes great interest in them, and his path is destined to cross theirs again. The next time comes when he encounters them by chance in the street and follows them to Casby's house. By the time he manages to gain the Patriarch's presence, however, they have left.

"Pray, sir" demanded Clennam, anxiously, "is Miss Wade gone?"

"Miss ———? Oh, you call her Wade," returned Mr. Casby. "Highly proper."

Arthur quickly returned, "What do you call her?"
"Wade," said Mr. Casby. "Oh, always Wade." (592–93)

This reminds us that Wade is no more a "proper" name than Tattycoram, that as Pancks explains, telling Arthur all he can about her, "She is somebody's child—anybody's—nobody's" (595). We may remember here that "Nobody" has become a substitute for Arthur's name in the account of his disappointed love for Pet Meagles, and perhaps also that the whole novel was originally named "Nobody's Fault."[19]

The proper name, according to Barthes, plays a crucial role in the narrative construction of character in the classic realist text. "When identical semes traverse the same proper name several times and appear to settle upon it, a character is created." This means that "the person is no more than a collection of semes. . . . What gives the illusion that the sum is supplemented by a precious remainder (something like *individuality*, in that, qualitative and ineffable, it may escape the vulgar bookkeeping of compositional characters) is the Proper Name, the difference completed by what is *proper* to it."[20] Dickens's characters, with their many odd names and vividly distinctive, repeated traits would seem to obey this logic, their sharply defined "flat" contours bounded by firm outlines. But in questioning the propriety of names, *Little Dorrit* points toward effects that are equally characteristic: the variability and uncertainty of at least some names

---

[19] See Forster, *Life of Dickens,* 2:179. In another version of the arbitrariness of "proper" names, the Dorrits are suddenly catapulted from poverty to riches when it turns out that they are connected to "the Dorrits of Dorsetshire." The resonances of naming and renaming extend widely through Dickens's work, from *Oliver Twist,* whose protagonist is named by if not for a beadle, to *Great Expectations,* whose protagonist names himself: "My father's family name being Pirrip, and my christian name Philip, my infant tongue could make of both names nothing longer than Pip. So, I called myself Pip, and came to be called Pip." *Great Expectations* (Harmondsworth: Penguin, 1965), p. 35. The sense of autonomy here becomes compromised, however, when he accepts the control of a patron and the expectations for which one condition is that he "always bear the name of Pip" (165). His brutal double Orlick, who in attacking Mrs. Joe seems to act as Pip's proxy, also names himself: "He pretended that his christian name was Dolge—a clear impossibility" (139). The closest precedent for Tattycoram is Esther, who is also "set apart" by her illegitimate birth (her "real name," her aunt once disclosed, "was not Esther Summerson, but Esther Hawdon" [*Bleak House,* p. 464]), and who receives a series of affectionate nicknames when she becomes housekeeper at Bleak House: "This was the beginning of my being called Old Woman, and Little Old Woman, and Cobweb, and Mrs. Shipton, and Mother Hubbard, and Dame Durden, and so many names of that sort that my own name soon became quite lost among them" (148). Finally, we might recall that Dickens himself, beginning his career as Boz, took the family nickname of his younger brother Augustus as his pseudonym. "Boz was a very familiar household word to me, long before I was an author, and so I came to adopt it." Forster, *Life of Dickens,* 1:55.

[20] Roland Barthes, *S/Z,* trans. Richard Miller (New York: Hill and Wang, 1974), pp. 67, 191.

are accompanied by the displacement and exchange of traits that allow characters to become doubles, figures for each other. Their feelings do not remain their exclusive property but become embodied in others as well or instead. Tattycoram tells Miss Wade, "I am afraid of you. . . . You seem to come like my own anger, my own malice, my own—whatever it is—I don't know what it is" (65), and when she returns at the end as a penitent ("Dear Master, dear Mistress, take me back again, and give me back the dear old name!") she credits her double's negative example for her change of heart: "I am not so bad as I was. . . . I have had Miss Wade before me all this time, as if it was my own self grown ripe—turning everything the wrong way, and twisting all good into evil" (880).[21]

Such doublings may seem far removed from the conjunction of Plornish and Maroon, but they also are governed by the workings of destiny, producing a didactic message whose destination is quite overt. We saw in considering Gothic doubles how they can be derived from the logic of alternative narrative versions, just as here Miss Wade figures a possible destiny for Tattycoram that she averts by returning to the Meagleses. What I want to consider now, though, is an instance that is both more central and more obscure and that turns on the doubling of Miss Wade and Arthur. It is Miss Wade who, in the second chapter, introduces the theme of destiny. As the fellow travelers, released at last from quarantine, are taking leave of each other, Mr. Meagles comes round to Miss Wade.

> "Goodbye! We may never meet again."
> "In our course through life we shall meet the people who are coming to meet *us,* from many strange places and by many strange roads," was the composed reply; "and what it is set to us to do to them, and what it is set to them to do to us, will all be done." (63)

Her ominous, prophetic speech jars with the superficial cordiality of the social occasion. It sounds as if it came from some other, distanced position like that from which the narrator surveys the landscape in the opening and closing passages of the preceding chapter, and indeed at the end of this one, as the narrator resumes that position, he restates her vision. "The day passed on; and again the wide stare stared itself out; and the hot night was on Marseilles; and through it the caravan of the morning, all dispersed,

---

[21] The frequency and explicitness of such effects in *Little Dorrit* are implied in Brian Rosenberg's use of it as his principal text in his recent study, *Little Dorrit's Shadows: Character and Contradiction in Dickens* (Columbia: University of Missouri Press, 1996). See also Barbara Hardy on the role of "the moral double or opposite" in Dickens's narratives of "the change of heart," in *The Moral Art of Dickens* (London: Athlone Press, 1970), pp. 27–56.

went their appointed ways. And thus ever, by day and night, under the sun and under the stars, climbing the dusty hills and toiling along the weary plains, journeying by land and journeying by sea, coming and going so strangely, to meet and to act and react on one another, move all we restless travellers through the pilgrimage of life" (67). The symbolic patterns of the panoramic landscapes that frame the first chapter stress radical separations: the impassable "line of demarcation" between "the pure sea" and "the abominable pool" of the harbor (39), the "staring" sun and the darkness of the prison (40), the stars in the heavens and the fireflies that "mimicked them in the lower air" (53). Here, however, as we get anticipations of converging paths, there is a strange convergence between Miss Wade's voice and the narrator's. His version removes her implication "that what was to be done was necessarily evil" (64), and it does not present the travelers' anticipated actions and reactions as already "set." The "composed" Miss Wade seems to view the future as if it were a narrative already composed, determined in advance, while the narrator seems to leave it more open, but this difference between versions of fate and destiny is, here as elsewhere, uncertain.[22]

These reflections appear in the context of a previous exchange between Mr. Meagles and Miss Wade that suggests part of what is at stake here. He has been chafing violently under the confinement of quarantine, but once released he feels no more resentment. "I bear those monotonous walls no ill-will now. . . . One always begins to forgive a place as soon as it's left behind; I dare say a prisoner begins to relent towards his prison, after he is let out" (60). Miss Wade, introduced at this point, takes an opposing view. "If I had been shut up in any place to pine and suffer, I should always hate that place and wish to burn it down, or raze it to the ground" (61). The opposition between releasing and retaining resentment for past suffering certainly will be important for understanding Miss Wade, and it suggests one way of understanding the difference between closed and open versions of destiny, in which inability or refusal to let go of a sense of injury constricts possibilities into a bitter fate. But the most important and immediate bearing of these terms is their application to Arthur. He first presents himself, a page before the exchange about imprisonment, as having no sense of direction ("I am such a waif and stray everywhere, that I am liable to be drifted where any current may set"), no firm purpose. "I have no will. That is to say . . . next to none that I can put in action now. Trained by main

---

[22] Audrey Jaffe notes in Miss Wade's words the "resemblance to an authorial point of view" but not the narrator's revision of them. See *Vanishing Points: Dickens, Narrative, and the Subject of Omniscience* (Berkeley: University of California Press, 1991), p. 13.

force; broken, not bent; heavily ironed with an object on which I was never consulted and which was never mine; shipped away to the other end of the world before I was of age, and exiled there until my father's death there, a year ago; always grinding away in a mill I always hated; what is to be expected from *me* in middle life? Will, purpose, hope? All those lights were extinguished before I could sound the words" (59). He has clearly not forgotten these injuries, but neither does he acknowledge resentment. The place where he pined and suffered will eventually be razed to the ground, but not by his act or conscious wish, and we may suspect that his sense of having no will is the price he pays for not allowing himself to feel such hatred. Tattycoram can see in Miss Wade an embodiment of her own anger or malice, but Arthur seems to have none of his own, even where we would expect to find them. Instead, they appear through her shortly after his depressed account of himself, and by the time she stands watching the tormented Tattycoram, "as one afflicted with a diseased part might curiously watch the dissection and exposition of an analogous case" (65), they have been thoroughly displaced onto a pathologized female figure.

The narrative syntax that articulates the language of destiny at this first crossing point is not so much one of causality or the characters' interactions as the sort of covert association and complementarity that joins Plornish and Maroon. Arthur's subsequent encounters with Miss Wade continue to involve these secret linkages, elaborated through the developing family mystery introduced when he questions his mother about some possible past wrong for which reparation should be made and given sharper focus by his suspicions of some hidden connection between his family and the Dorrits. From the retrospective vantage point of the dénouement, the perspective of a completed destiny, these suspicions are confirmed, but the passages in which Arthur repeatedly ponders and probes the family mystery do not function as components of a conventional hermeneutic sequence. Instead, as in Radcliffe's extended deferrals, the long delay and lack of progress toward a solution shift the stress to his subjective state of painful obsession, in which concern with repairing some unspecified wrong to another offers oblique expression for his unacknowledged sense of the wrong done to himself. We find him deep in such thoughts at the opening of chapter 27. "A frequently recurring doubt, whether Mr Pancks's desire to collect information relative to the Dorrit family could have any possible bearing on the misgivings he had imparted to his mother on his return from his long exile, caused Arthur Clennam much uneasiness at this period" (367). A long iterative exposition of his troubled reflections follows, but it seems to lead nowhere: "Labouring in this sea, as all barks labour in cross seas, he tossed about and came to no haven" (368), a figure that internalizes the travel motif earlier linked with the theme of destiny. The outward events narrated in this chapter concern Tattycoram's flight and the futile visit Mr. Meagles and Arthur make to Miss Wade in seeking her, events with no apparent narrative connection to Arthur's family worries but linked to them by the secret logic we have been tracing.[23]

We can read these connections as projections of Arthur's unconscious: the narrative allows no direct expression of his anger but instead produces a sequence in which his troubled thoughts are directly followed by the account of Tattycoram's explosion and the confrontation with Miss Wade. We can also observe a motivating impulse at work here, however, that does not issue from a hidden private source but circulates through the narrative, an unconscious that is between rather than within the characters. Like the effects of contamination we traced in *Dr. Jekyll and Mr. Hyde* or the collective production of narrative in *Dracula*, these boundary crossings between subjectivities present a version of Gothic doubling as an entry into the social imaginary. Such an intersubjective source is suggested in Mr. Meagles's explanation of how he knows where to look for Miss Wade. "There is one of those odd impressions in my house, which do mysteriously get into houses sometimes, which nobody seems to have picked up in a distinct form from anybody, and yet which everybody seems to have got hold of loosely from somebody and let go again, that she lives, or was living, thereabouts" (372–73). This, we might quite reasonably say, is a rather transparent veil thrown over the absence of a realistic explanation, but it also accurately describes the sort of psychosocial forces that fuel the "epidemic" of enthusiastic belief in Merdle or foster the growth of "the great tree of the Circumlocution Office" (239). In *Little Dorrit* Dickens develops a narrative form that attempts to trace the production of the social from

---

[23] The linkage is further evidenced in the long account of Arthur's troubled thoughts. "The shadow of a supposed act of injustice, which had hung over him since his father's death, was so vague and formless that it might be the result of a reality widely remote from his idea of it. But, if his apprehensions should prove to be well founded, he was ready at any moment to lay down all he had and begin the world anew." The vague sense that his uneasiness arises from a source beyond his awareness leads to anticipations of renouncing what he has gained from the family business, in which he has already resigned his active share. Making restitution to someone else would offer an acceptable way of disinheriting himself. This is followed by the narrator's denial that his character has been shaped by his early experience: "As the fierce dark teaching of his childhood had never sunk into his heart . . ." The repeated observation that the effect of his early deprivation has been "to make him a dreamer, after all" (80), that he has "deep-rooted in his nature, a belief in all the gentle and good things his life had been without" (206), allows us to sense the hidden fierce dark feelings whose absence is so strenuously asserted.

the imaginary, the desires and disturbances that impel both private and public fantasies.[24]

As the complex plot advances and its various strands are drawn toward their destined intersections, the secret connections that have been intimated between these characters become objectified at the level of action. Their next encounter is introduced by a scene that recapitulates the themes of "odd impressions" in the Meagles house and emergence from unconsciousness. Arthur visits the house while the family are away and hears an elaborate account from Mrs. Tickett the housekeeper of how as she sat in a state hovering between dreaming and consciousness ("I was not sleeping, nor what a person would term correctly, dozing. I was more what a person would strictly call watching with my eyes closed"), she thought she saw Tattycoram (583). Arthur believes she was just dreaming, but then soon afterward finds himself in the Strand at nightfall, is suddenly diverted from his own "current of thought," and spots Tattycoram and Miss Wade nearby (585). He follows them to Casby's house where, as we have seen, he fails either to speak to them or to learn anything more about Miss Wade, but the most important event of the chapter has already taken place in his observing them with a man he has never seen before but whom we recognize as Blandois. This is a crossing of paths that have unfolded separately since the beginning of the novel, repeated in the next chapter when Arthur finds Blandois at his mother's house.

As he walks toward "that grim home of his youth," his thoughts fall under its old spell. "It always affected his imagination as wrathful, mysterious, and sad; and his imagination was sufficiently impressionable to see the whole neighborhood under some tinge of its dark shadow." The passage elaborates the motifs of "shadow" and "secrets," ending with a vision of Mrs. Clennam as their source and center. "At the heart of it his mother presided, inflexible of face, indomitable of will, firmly holding all the secrets of her own and his father's life, and austerely opposing herself, front to front, to the great final secret of all life" (596–97). Blandois suddenly emerges from this dark atmosphere of secrecy; he turns out to have the same destination, and by the time he and Arthur have been admitted together and Arthur has vainly protested the unsavory stranger's presence there, their mutual antipathy has been firmly established. Now linked with the

---

[24] More conscious instances can be found in the novel's thematization of fiction making, both in private versions such as Amy's figuration of her secret love for Arthur in her story of the "Princess" and the "tiny woman" (339–42) and in the social collaborations that produce and sustain the "genteel fiction" of the Dorrits' superiority (114), Mrs. Merdle's "Society," or the pretenses of the "gipsies of gentility" at Hampton Court (359–60). See Janice M. Carlisle, "*Little Dorrit*: Necessary Fictions," *Studies in the Novel* 7 (1975): 175–214.

Clennam family secrets as well as with Miss Wade, Blandois becomes a new focus for Arthur's obsessions, and the later stages of the Clennam mystery plot will play out this doubling.[25] Not only their paths but their roles cross as Arthur becomes the prisoner (the loss of all his money in Merdle's collapse replacing his previous plan of restitution) while Blandois takes on the role of exposing the family secrets.

Only by tracing such small links in its narrative sequences can we appreciate how extensively the force of destiny operates in *Little Dorrit*. At issue in each of these junctures are the novel's larger concerns with freedom and compulsion, the possibilities open to its characters and the coherence of its form. Destiny figures as a force when there is a sense of psychological bondage, as in the many characters imprisoned in or haunted by their past and thus fated to compulsive repetition or denial. It also appears, however, when the direction of the narrative itself seems set in advance by a necessity that has nothing to do with the characters' conscious or unconscious will. That is how the theme reappears when the narrator ponders the light shining from Mrs. Clennam's window.

> Strange, if the little sick-room fire were in effect a beacon fire, summoning some one, and that the most unlikely some one in the world, to the spot that *must* be come to. Strange, if the little sick-room light were in effect a watch-light, burning in that place every night until an appointed event should be watched out! Which of the vast multitude of travellers, under the sun and the stars, climbing the dusty hills and toiling along the weary plains, journeying by land and journeying by sea, coming and going so strangely, to meet and act and react on one another; which of the host may, with no suspicion of the journey's end, be travelling surely hither? (221)

With the privilege of narrative hindsight, the counterpart to the narrator's foresight here, we can answer his question quite precisely. The traveler summoned to this spot is Blandois, and the appointed event is his forcing Mrs. Clennam to confess the truth (or rather assert her version of it) about

---

[25] Several passages develop Arthur's obsessive interest in Blandois and his secret relation to the Clennams, of which the most remarkable reverses their positions, figuring Arthur as the guilty party: "As though a criminal should be chained in a stationary boat on a deep clear river, condemned, whatever countless leagues of water flowed past him, always to see the body of the fellow-creature he had drowned lying at the bottom, immovable, and unchangeable, except as the eddies made it broad or long, now expanding, now contracting its terrible lineaments, so Arthur, below the shifting current of transparent thoughts and fancies which were gone and succeeded by others as soon as come, saw, steady and dark, and not to be stirred from its place, the one subject that he endeavoured with all his might to rid himself of, and that he could not fly from" (742).

Arthur's birth and the suppressed codicil, followed by his death in the collapse of the house once the plot has no further use for him.

In anticipating this destiny, the narrator's version of the theme converges
with Miss Wade's: the actions of these characters are predetermined by the
form of a narrative conceived as a completed whole. If in her angry resentment Miss Wade serves as a double for the novel's protagonist, in her
fatalism she does the same for its narrator, offering a troubling reflection
on the coercive force of its teleology. Both are developed, in a way that also
foregrounds her own narrative destiny, when the novel incorporates her autobiographical account as "The History of a Self-Tormentor." Its inclusion
motivates (or receives a minimal realistic explanation from) Arthur's brief
excursion to Calais in hopes of gaining information about Blandois, whose
name he gives in place of his own. After frustrating that hope and taunting
him about his mother's mysterious connection with such a doubtful figure,
"that dark side of the case . . . of which there was a half-hidden shadow in
his own breast" (721) and about "your dear friend, Mr Gowan," whom
she knows to be his successful rival, she abruptly declares, "I hate his wife"
and adds,

> I hate him. . . . Worse than his wife, because I was once dupe enough, and
> false enough to myself, almost to love him. You have seen me, sir, only on
> common-place occasions, when I dare say you have thought me a com-
> mon-place woman, a little more self-willed than the generality. You don't
> know what I mean by hating, if you know me no better than that; you can't
> know, without knowing with what care I have studied myself and people
> about me. For this reason I have for some time inclined to tell you what
> my life has been—not to propitiate your opinion, for I set no value on it;
> but that you may comprehend, when you think of your dear friend and his
> dear wife, what I mean by hating. (722)

With this slender excuse, she hands him some papers. "Without any con-
ciliation of him, scarcely addressing him, rather speaking as if she were
speaking to her own looking-glass for the justification of her own stub-
bornness, she said, as she gave them to him: 'Now you may know what I
mean by hating!'" It is of course his own hating that Arthur has not wanted
to know about; here his mirroring double seems to be transmitting that
knowledge, but it does not register. We hear only that he reads her account
on his way back to England, not what he makes of it: for him, the looking
glass remains blank.[26]

---

[26] The text of her narrative makes it clear that it is not only delivered but addressed to Arthur,

Instead of reaching that destination, her narrative offers its reflections to the whole novel that tries to contain it. In its concentrated history of suspicion and resentment we are clearly meant to see a case of enclosed paranoid delusion, labeled in advance as self-torment and further glossed by running heads such as "Miseries of a Morbid Breast" and "Distorted Vision." Like Poe's and other Gothic tales, it foregrounds questions of narrative power by presenting an intense, singular account with which the reader struggles by constructing an alternative version. Where she detects hidden condescension in nearly everyone she encounters, we are to see her, as Tattycoram will say, "turning everything the wrong way, and twisting all good into evil" (880). But the concerted effort to refuse her any authority betrays a certain strain, as if, like Arthur, the novel needs to deny having anything in common with this perverse, fascinating figure.

Miss Wade's narrative tells of the same story happening over and over. The other girls among whom she is raised by her supposed grandmother, the young women she lives with next, and the successive families she serves as a governess all treat her with extreme consideration and forbearance, which she soon comes to perceive as patronage. Once she learns of her illegitimate birth, it provides the explanatory key. "I carried the light of that information both into my past and into my future. It showed me many new occasions on which people triumphed over me, when they made a pretense of treating me with consideration, or doing me a service" (728). In every instance, we are encouraged to regard her interpretations as baneful errors, based only on her peculiarly "unhappy temper," but we should also recall that the novel itself shares her genius for detecting patronage. Whether it is Rigaud or Mrs. Plornish patronizing Cavalletto, William Dorrit patronizing old Nandy, Mrs. Merdle patronizing Fanny Dorrit, or even Mr. Meagles patronizing Doyce, in which Arthur detects a "microscopic portion of the mustard-seed that had sprung up into the great tree of the Circumlocution Office" (238), *Little Dorrit* repeatedly tells the story of figures positioned up and down the social scale who establish their relative superiority by finding someone to whom they can condescend. Together with its indictment of gentility and the other flattering fictions in which its characters collaborate, the novel's variations on this theme strongly enforce its ironic psychosocial analysis, yet in Miss Wade a comparable sensitivity is marked as pathological deviance.

---

since it refers several times to Gowan as "your dear friend" (732–34). This confirms her description of her account when she delivers it as "something I have written and put by for your perusal" (722), so that we must suppose that without having any reason to expect his visit, she has composed it specifically for him. She may be concerned only with her self-justification, but like so many previous tellers of Gothic tales, she also needs an audience, and her choice of Arthur strengthens the sense of an unacknowledged bond between them.

However unjust her suspicions of others may be, in reading her narrative ironically and correcting her distorted vision from a superior position we inevitably confirm her belief that she is the object of condescension. This is the double bind that the struggle for narrative control in the Gothic tale typically imposes and that few readers of "The History of a Self-Tormentor" have escaped.[27] The unease it produces is registered in Trilling's attempt to put the best face on an apparent contradiction. "It is part of the complexity of this novel which deals so bitterly with society that those of its characters who share its social bitterness are by that very fact condemned."[28] To call Miss Wade's bitterness social, however, is already to reduce the tensions that her narrative produces. In adapting the form of the Gothic tale with its monological representation of the isolated, aberrant individual, Dickens develops the opposition between single and multiple voices, inwardness and social scope, that animates both the tale and the novel. It is not by the fact of her bitterness that Miss Wade is condemned but by her self-enclosure, which threatens to collapse that opposition and contract the novel's diverse social panorama into the private miseries of a morbid breast. To consider her tale as a looking glass for the whole novel would be to read *Little Dorrit* as an elaborately coded version of a secret history, the haunting story of childhood injuries and persisting resentments. Insisting on the perversity of her self-inflicted torment is a way of warding off that recognition.[29]

[27] Thus Carol A. Bock proposes, with no apparent discomfort, that "Miss Wade's tale can perhaps be best compared to the kind of dramatic monologue that Ralph Rader describes as evoking a posture of 'comic condescension' on the part of the reader." See "Miss Wade and George Silverman: The Forms of Fictional Monologue," *Dickens Studies Annual* 16 (1987): 118. The second tale Bock considers, one of the last works Dickens completed ("George Silverman's Explanation," 1868), is a remarkable inversion of Miss Wade's. Its pathologically self-effacing male protagonist repeatedly suffers from the unjust accusations of others, often echoed by his own guilty sense of being a "worldly little devil," but his explanatory narrative project, like hers, aims at self-justification. Bock considers this tale "ethically neutral," because unlike "The History of a Self-Tormentor" it offers no consistent cues for either sympathy or judgment. One could argue instead that neither allows its readers a consistent position. The insistent irony of Miss Wade's tale finally turns on those who most relish it; the grotesque pathos of Silverman's defeats any attempts to maintain a secure ironic distance.
[28] Lionel Trilling, "*Little Dorrit*," in *The Opposing Self* (New York: Viking, 1959), p. 58. The essay first appeared as the introduction to the New Oxford Illustrated Dickens edition in 1953.
[29] To readers today, the sexual component of her perversity is likely to seem the most striking. The passionate possessiveness of her love and the fierce jealousies it inflicts appear in her relations with both women and men, but it is her relations with the "stupid mite" she loves as a child and Tattycoram that are especially stigmatized. The first is marked as deadly ("often feeling as if, rather than suffer so [from her supposed infidelities], I could so hold her in my arms and plunge to the bottom of a river—where I would still hold her after we were both

This possibility of reducing broad social representations to the scale of individual subjectivity is not unique to Dickens, though the relative ease of reading his fiction autobiographically makes it yield more readily to such moves. The disturbance that possibility can produce, the anxious sense that despite their apparent realism fictional worlds may be no more than objectified fantasies or nightmares, can also account for the persistence of Gothic elements in the later writers we will be considering and may well be the most important way Gothic reflections work within realism. If in more obviously Gothic fictions, with their heavy stress on isolated subjectivity and extremity, Gothic reflections enforce the sense of narrative as a social transaction, here they draw our attention back toward the private origins and secret histories that lie behind and lurk within the expansive social landscapes.

Making Miss Wade a scapegoat of perversity is part of the novel's effort to control this disturbance, but stigmatizing her as illegitimate only justifies her resentment for being set apart and ratifies her role as a double. That role expands through the links between her narrative and the novel's earlier events, which shed a new light on the question of destiny. From her account of her affair with Gowan we learn that her initial presence among the group of travelers at Marseilles was no chance encounter. Seduced by the opportunity of for once inspiring jealousy and exercising condescending superiority instead of suffering them, she has sacrificed her prospects of a good marriage and secure social position. When Gowan abandons her to pursue just such prospects through courting Pet Meagles, she feels that observing her hated rival is "one of the few sources of entertainment left to me. I travelled a little: travelled until I found myself in her society, and in yours" (734). In this narrative context, her startling oracular pronouncements about inevitable meetings and what is "set" to be done, as well as their intimidating effect on Pet, disclose a secret meaning.[30] Instead of

---

dead" [727]), the second as already dead (or sterile) through the metonymy of her "dead sort of house, with a dead wall over the way and a dead gateway at the side," and so on (716). Despite her obvious interest as a proto-lesbian figure, however, it seems more appropriate to consider her sexuality as part of her condemnation rather than the reason for it. She poses a greater threat to the authority of the narrative as "a woman . . . shut up . . . devouring her own heart" (719) than as a figure of transgressive desire.

[30] Pet's fearful response to her words prompts her to expand. " 'Your pretty daughter,' she said [to Meagles], 'starts to think of such things. Yet,' looking full upon her, 'you may be sure that there are men and women already on their road, who have their business to do with *you*, and who will do it. Of a certainty they will do it. They may be coming hundreds, thousands, of miles over the sea there; they may be close at hand now; they may be coming, for anything you know or anything you can do to prevent it, from the vilest sweepings of this very town' " (64). Besides expressing her hostility toward her rival, these words also anticipate her later

seeming to come from a detached, superior position, they now reflect a private agenda and self-tormenting obsession. Again, the mirroring effect of doubling in this revised account allows her to figure as both inversion and counterpart of the narrator. We can oppose her distorted vision to his genuinely detached and comprehensive view, disentangling fate and destiny once more, but we can also suspect that his claims to grasp the form of the narrative as a completed whole produced by some impersonal necessity likewise mask more partial, private interests and that the workings of destiny in the novel serve hidden needs.

Both these perspectives bear strongly on the way *Little Dorrit* works out the destinies of its protagonists and on the role Miss Wade is made to play in that resolution. By at last joining Arthur and Amy in its one successful love story, the novel represents a hopeful release from secrecy and suppression, private obsession and bondage to the past. This is a different form of destiny, linked with liberation and fulfillment rather than compulsion, indicated in the different tone of the narrator's prolepsis at the outset: "How young she seemed to him, or how old he to her; or what a secret either to the other, in that beginning of the destined interweaving of their stories, matters not here" (140). The disparity between their ages and the difference in their social positions are only some of the obstacles to be overcome in bringing them together. Amy's hopeless love for Arthur becomes her great secret, the treasured "shadow" the "tiny woman" of her story keeps hidden (341), while Arthur, first trying to recapture his lost youth in loving Pet, then resigning himself to being "a very much older man who had done with that part of life" (383), continues to suffer from the lack of will he announced at the beginning. He can act on behalf of others, storming the Circumlocution Office with his persistent demand "I want to know" (154), and he broods obsessively and futilely about the Clennam family secret, but as we have seen he also avoids acknowledging the destructive anger figured in Miss Wade. Solving these problems requires interweaving not only stories but strands of knowledge and ignorance. Arthur must learn of Amy's love, which is accomplished through the generosity of his comic rival John Chivery, while he remains ignorant of the secrets revealed through the blackmailing scheme of his melodramatic antagonist Blandois. Spectacular effects of revelation, the explosive undoing of repression in Mrs. Clennam's confession, are closely joined with renewed suppression as Amy agrees to keep the truth from Arthur.

---

use of Blandois as her spy, in which another apparently chance encounter of travelers becomes part of her secret design. Such proleptic traces of a knowledge only the narrator could possess again mark their affinities.

The aim of these maneuvers, like that of Dickens's earlier Gothic parable in *The Haunted Man,* is release from the past through forgiving injuries, yet they also fulfill the desire for oblivion that was condemned in Redlaw. Here, as earlier, Arthur's emotional work gets done by female proxy. The bitter resentment of "a woman . . . shut up . . . devouring her own heart" (719) can be left behind, while Amy receives his mother's confession and grants her plea for forgiveness. Yet Miss Wade is not entirely forgotten in the final stages of the narrative. In escaping from her, Tattycoram brings back the box of papers left by Blandois, which forms the only plot connection between Miss Wade and Amy as the documents containing the Clennam family secrets pass from one to the other. This moment also provides the occasion for formulating the symbolic opposition between them, as Mr. Meagles points out in "that little, quiet, fragile figure" the alternative to Miss Wade's self-torment. "Duty, Tattycoram. Begin it early, and do it well; and there is no antecedent to it, in any origin or station, that will tell against us with the Almighty, or with ourselves" (881–82). This repeats the lesson Esther Summerson draws from her story, guiding the penitent away from resentment and toward a proper feminine destiny. Like Affery in rebelling at last against Mrs. Clennam and Flintwinch ("I have broke out now, and I can't go back" [835]), like Pancks in rebelling against Casby and exposing his imposture to all of Bleeding Heart Yard, Tattycoram is presented here as exercising her will and freeing herself from degrading subjection, but she is also submitting once more to her "dear Master" and "dear Mistress," to Duty, and to the demands of the plot. As in the case of Miss Wade's narrative, writing that has been hidden in her Calais retreat gets delivered to an unexpected destination by a figure of female resistance who is thereby conscripted to serve the novel's larger needs. And yet in both cases, the message does not quite arrive. "In Miss Wade," Dickens told Forster, "I had an idea . . . of making the introduced story so fit into surroundings impossible of separation from the main story, as to make the blood of the book circulate through both. But I can only suppose, from what you say, that I have not exactly succeeded in this."[31] Incorporated but not assimilated, her reflecting likeness remains unacknowledged, just as the information contained in the recovered papers is both included and suppressed.

A similar double sense of liberating openness and hidden design persists in the novel's final moments, as Arthur and Amy complete the destined interweaving of their stories. Their union, long prepared and gradually approached, reads persuasively as the realization of their best possibilities,

[31] Forster, *Life of Dickens,* 2:184–85.

achieved through casting off the burden of the past, but it also forces us to recognize the inescapable element of manipulation required to produce this happy ending. This equivocal force is remarkably condensed in the ritual Amy arranges before they leave the Marshalsea to be married, asking Arthur to burn a folded paper, presumably the suppressed codicil to Gilbert Clennam's will, without reading it. It is a potent "charm" that banishes the haunting family ghosts and confirms their own love. "'Does the charm want any words to be said?' asked Arthur, as he held the paper over the flame. 'You can say (if you don't mind) "I love you!"'" answered Little Dorrit. So he said it and the paper burned away" (893–94). But it also fulfills Amy's pact with Mrs. Clennam, that other woman shut up devouring her own heart, to keep Arthur from knowing what she has done and so renews the rule of secrecy.[32] We can see in this duplicity a reflection of the double force that drives Dickens's fiction, the effort to overcome the haunting past and the need to preserve its secret so that the effort can be renewed from one narrative to the next, but we can also see an acknowledgment of the contrivances that doubleness requires. In its final gesture, as in so many earlier moments where the destinies of characters and the destination of writing are in question, *Little Dorrit* allows us to recognize the artifices and sacrifices necessary to make its narrative cohere.

[32] When she gets control of the recovered papers, Amy thinks of their suppression as affecting only herself. "The secret was safe now! She could keep her own part of it from him; he should never know of her loss [the withheld legacy provided by the codicil]; in time to come he should know all that was of import to himself; but he should never know what concerned her only" (881–82). But if Arthur is destined to learn the truth about his birth and his actual mother's sad fate, that time never comes in *Little Dorrit*.

8

Eliot

A woman who has defied conventional restrictions, who has resented and resisted patriarchal subordination and control, is at last made to submit. In surrendering to forces stronger than her own fierce will, she reveals long-suppressed information about the hero's birth and delivers a container of papers that concern both his parentage and his patrimony, papers whose contents are never actually disclosed. This time, however, the tamed rebel is not the repentant Tattycoram but the Princess Leonora Halm-Eberstein, formerly Alcharisi, the mother of Daniel Deronda.[1] The crossing of their paths when she summons Deronda to meet her in Genoa will have momentous consequences. Revealing his hidden origins, it establishes Deronda's identity as a Jew, the crucial requirement for realizing his destiny both in the private fulfillment of his marriage to Mirah and in his public role of working to establish a Jewish homeland.

Other convergences and fulfillments are also being accomplished here. Most striking is the way bringing Deronda to Genoa sets up a crucial intersection in the double plot structure that repeatedly interweaves his story with Gwedolen Harleth's. Their first encounter at the novel's opening, followed by the long double analepsis that brings both their stories up to that moment, is motivated by its prefigurative function. Disconcerting her with his "measuring" gaze (38) and redeeming her necklace, he is destined to become "a part of her conscience" (468), her confessor and moral guide, a relation that

---

[1] Restoring the hero's identity also reintroduces the question of proper names we have encountered in Dickens. "'Then it is not my real name?' said Deronda. . . . 'Oh, as real as another,' said his mother, indifferently. 'The Jews have always been changing their names.'" George Eliot, *Daniel Deronda* (Harmondsworth: Penguin, 1967), p. 701. Subsequent references are all to this edition.

reaches its climax when they meet again in Genoa at the most desperate moment of her story, the crisis precipitated by Grandcourt's drowning.[2]

The novel's form draws together thematic strands as well as plot lines at this nodal point. The forces that have compelled Leonora to disclose the truth appear to her as haunting emanations of the suppressed past released by her fatal illness: "Shadows are rising round me. Sickness makes them" (691). In the grip of its pain, she reverts to her youthful state of resentful subjection to the father she could not defy in life.

> Then a great horror comes over me: what do I know of life or death? and what my father called "right" may be a power that is laying hold of me— that is clutching me now. . . . Often when I am at ease it all fades away; my whole self comes quite back; but I know it will sink away again, and the other will come—the poor, solitary, forsaken remains of self, that can resist nothing. It was my nature to resist, and to say, "I have a right to resist." Well, I say so still when I have any strength in me. . . . But when my strength goes, some other right forces itself upon me like iron in an inexorable hand; and even when I am at ease, it is beginning to make ghosts upon the daylight. (699)

The same Gothic figure has appeared just thirty pages previously to represent Gwendolen's obsessive thoughts of Grandcourt's death, the only release she can imagine from his domination. "The thought of his dying would not subsist: it turned as with a dream-change into the terror that she should die with his throttling fingers on her neck avenging that thought. Fantasies moved within her like ghosts, making no break in her acknowledged consciousness and finding no obstruction in it: dark rays doing their work invisibly in the broad light" (669). The ghostly force of guilty memories and fantasies, of Gothic figures infiltrating the novel's realism, is in both cases working its way from hidden private experience into the daylight of objectified events and consequences.

Both women's waking nightmares bear out the warning of the novel's epigraph, which advertises it as an internalized tale of terror.

---

[2] Intersecting plot lines also figure earlier in George Eliot's fiction as effects of destiny. As the narrator of *Middlemarch* observes, "Any one watching keenly the stealthy convergence of human lots, sees a slow preparation of effects from one life on another, which tells like a calculated irony on the indifference of the frozen stare with which we look at our unintroduced neighbor. Destiny stands by sarcastic with our *dramatis personae* folded in her hand." George Eliot, *Middlemarch* (Harmondsworth: Penguin, 1994), p. 95. The tension between the stealthy, slow effects required by Eliot's realism and the mythic figure of a sarcastic Destiny is skewed in *Daniel Deronda* toward the more stylized pattern of Gwendolen and Deronda's repeatedly interwoven lots.

Let thy chief terror be of thy own soul:
There, 'mid the throng of hurrying desires
That trample o'er the dead to seize their spoil,
Lurks vengeance, footless, irresistible
As exhalations laden with slow death,
And o'er the fairest troop of captured joys
Breathes pallid pestilence.

The admonition clearly prefigures Gwendolen's spiritual development from the "spoiled child" of the opening to the "guilty woman" Deronda encounters directly after his final interview with Leonora: "Her lips a little apart with the peculiar expression of one accused and helpless, she looked like the ghost of that Gwendolen Harleth whom Deronda had seen turning with firm lips and proud self-possession from her losses at the gaming-table" (753). Her liability to fear, triggered whenever that self-possession is shaken, becomes "a root of conscience" (733) that grows as she comes to see her marriage as a repetition of the wrong Deronda points out in gambling, "to make [her] gain out of another's loss" (500). Lydia Glasher's prophetic words haunt her: "The willing wrong you have done me will be your curse" (406); soon "her confidence in herself and her destiny had turned into remorse and dread" (484). Deronda urges her to cultivate those feelings: "Turn your fear into a safeguard. Keep your dread fixed on the idea of increasing that remorse which is so bitter to you" (509). Fear counters her growing murderous desire for Grandcourt's death, and her mind becomes the scene of a confrontation between opposing Gothic figures. "In Gwendolen's consciousness Temptation and Dread met and stared like two pale phantoms, each seeing itself in the other—each obstructed by its own image; and all the while her fuller self beheld the apparitions and sobbed for deliverance from them" (738).

The apparitions, ghosts, and phantoms that throng together as the narrative of Gwendolen's haunting converges with that of Leonora's are figures pressing toward literalization, fantasies becoming actual, or entering a realm where these oppositions break down. "Events come upon us like evil enchantments," says Leonora in accounting for her broken resistance, "and thoughts, feelings, apparitions in the darkness are events—are they not?" (693). The force of apparitions is likewise traced in a sequence of events and images that spans Gwendolen's development. It begins with the disturbing discovery on her arrival at Offendene of "the picture of an up-turned dead face, from which an obscure figure seemed to be fleeing with outstretched arms" (56). Its reappearance disrupts her later performance in a tableau of Hermione's revival: "She looked like a statue into which a soul of Fear had entered" (91). Established as an image of terror, it returns in her fantasies and fears of murdering Grandcourt. "Her vision of what she had to dread took more decidedly than ever the form of some fiercely impulsive deed, committed as in a dream that she would instantaneously wake from to find the effects real though the images had been false: to find death under her hands, but instead of darkness, daylight; instead of satisfied hatred, the dismay of guilt; instead of freedom, the palsy of a new terror—a white dead face from which she was for ever trying to flee and for ever held back" (737–38). Finally, after Grandcourt has drowned, she tells Deronda, "His face will not be seen above the water again. . . . Not by any one else—only by me—a dead face—I shall never get away from it" (753). In the extremity of her guilt it is impossible for Gwendolen (and for the reader) to determine the extent of her responsibility, to distinguish fact from fantasy: "I know nothing—I only know that I saw my wish outside me" (761).[3]

In the long and carefully plotted course of Gwendolen's development, as in the highly condensed account of Leonora's, Eliot draws heavily on the phantasmal figuration and dream logic of Gothic to construct a genealogy of conscience. Terror of one's own soul, a soul of fear, "a fear which is the shadow of justice" (455): these become increments of a psychology that roots morality in primitive dread. We have seen in Poe and his predecessors that the most radical disturbance with which Gothic confronted nineteenth-century readers was a vision of a world where meaning and value have lost any transcendental or communal support and are determined only by power. The world Gwendolen moves through, from the casino's cosmopolitan "scene of dull, gas-poisoned absorption" (37)[4] to the intensified isolation of Grandcourt's yacht, "as bad as a nightmare" (738), seems just such a realm, the site of a privileged but rootless existence that offers no purpose beyond asserting one's will. The "ghostly army" that quells Gwendolen's resistance (503), like the apparitions in the darkness that overwhelm Leonora's, are spiritual agents that enforce "some other right" than self-assertion, punishing the pursuit of selfish desires. In the absence of su-

[3] Deronda, in trying to relieve Gwendolen of direct responsibility for Grandcourt's death, both reinstates the distinction between inside and outside and confirms their inseparability. "That momentary murderous will cannot, I think, have altered the course of events. Its effect is confined to the motives in your own breast. Within ourselves our evil will is momentous, and sooner or later it works its way outside us—it may be in the vitiation that breeds evil acts, but also it may be in the self-abhorrence that stings us into better striving" (764).

[4] After elaborating on the international and social diversity of the assembled gamblers, the narrator notes their isolating egoistic preoccupation. "But while every single player differed markedly from every other, there was a certain uniform negativeness of expression which had the effect of a mask—as if they had all eaten of some root that for the time compelled the brains of each to the same narrow monotony of action" (37).

pernatural sanctions, these figural remnants of religious belief represent an inner necessity that enforces moral obligations, just as Deronda's saving influence represents the way "our brother may be in the stead of God to us" (833). The terrors of the soul are mustered to ward off the deeper terror of nihilism.[5]

Interlacing Leonora's narrative with the account of Gwendolen's descent into her private nightmare works to generalize the moral psychology of terror, but it also offers an alternative version of their experiences that opens up reflections on their narrative logic. Both narratives are inflected by retributive fatality, the "vengeance, footless, irresistible" that pursues those who have followed their "hurrying desires" and broken pledges to others, but in Leonora those transgressions also appear as legitimate struggles for individual autonomy. The Jewish identity that Deronda gladly embraces as the path of destiny is for her an oppressive fate, the constricting role of "the Jewish woman" as prescribed by her father: "'this you must be,' 'that you must not be'—pressed on me like a frame that got tighter and tighter as I grew" (693). Breaking out of those constrictions into the "large life" she longs for permits the fulfillment of her own destiny, allowing scope for her exceptional gifts as a singer and actress.[6] But just as her success is an escape from patriarchal bondage ("You can never imagine what it is," she tells Deronda, "to have a man's force of genius in you, and yet to suffer the slavery of a girl" [694]), so her eventual submission is to the destiny dictated by anatomy. The narrator's earlier account of Gwendolen's narrow preoccupations also contrasts the small scope of a girl's life with the epic scale of historical movements and conflicts. "Could there be a slenderer, more insignificant thread in human history than this consciousness of a girl, busy with her small inferences of the way in which she could make her life pleasant? . . . What in the midst of that mighty drama are girls and their blind visions? They are the Yea or Nay of that good for which men are en-

---

[5] Nemesis had always been a leading deity in George Eliot's secular pantheon, but in her earlier fiction it figured more as an objective force working through the consequences of her characters' actions. In *Adam Bede* Mr. Irwine warns Arthur of "the inward suffering which is the worst form of Nemesis. Our deeds carry their terrible consequences . . . that are hardly ever confined to ourselves." George Eliot, *Adam Bede* (Harmondsworth: Penguin, 1980), p. 217. Plotting that enforces moral retribution reappears in several subsequent novels, most notably with Bulstrode's fate in *Middlemarch*. In *Daniel Deronda,* however, nemesis becomes almost completely internalized; Leonora's and Gwendolen's isolated inward suffering figures as the principal force, indicating the loss of community that Deronda's Zionist mission aims to restore.

[6] Compare Catherine Arrowpoint's determination to marry Klesmer despite her parents' dismay at his lower status and fortune: "I have always felt my fortune to be a wretched fatality of my life" (292). Here too realizing a more fulfilling destiny is associated with music and art.

during and fighting. In these delicate vessels is borne onward through the ages the treasure of human affections" (159–60). Leonora's story reinterprets this affirmation in more concrete bodily terms. Her father "wished I had been a son; he cared for me as a makeshift link" (694), a vessel for transferring his legacy, and in the end that is the role she is forced to play.[7] In her renewed subordination, and in the larger structural subordination of Gwendolen's story, we can again recognize the sacrifice necessary for achieving narrative coherence. Working out Deronda's happy destiny also requires their much harsher fates.

This interdependence offers another version of the double force we have repeatedly found in narrative form, the tension between a coherence that is desired and one that is feared, between fulfillment and oppression. The fatality that informs the fearful cohesion of Leonora's and Gwendolen's stories, with its recurrent Gothic motifs, is opposed but closely related to the desired destiny that Deronda's story moves toward, which is marked by a different strain of preternatural motifs. A crucial pivot between these discourses is "second-sight," which first appears unobtrusively in the Gwendolen plot, associated with fear. "'Don't let Gwendolen ride after the hounds, Rex' said Anna, whose fears gifted her with second-sight" (98). A little more portentously, Grandcourt's insistence on marrying Gwendolen makes him seem to Lush "like a man who was fey—led on by an ominous fatality. . . . Having protested against the marriage, Lush had a second-sight for its evil consequences" (362). But it is in the Deronda plot, where it is linked with desire, that the notion of preternatural foresight becomes prominent. A passage on Deronda's desire for a confidant ends, "But he had no expectation of meeting the friend he imagined. Deronda's was not one of those quiveringly-poised natures that lend themselves to second-sight" (527). Neither Anna nor Lush seems very quiveringly-poised either, but it soon becomes clear that much more than momentary anticipations of the future is now at stake as the next chapter immediately takes up and expands the term. "'Second-sight' is a flag over disputed ground. But it is matter of knowledge that there are persons whose yearnings, conceptions—nay, travelled conclusions—continually take the form of images which have a foreshadowing power: the deed they would do starts up be-

---

[7] The same values inform Grandcourt's will, in which Gwendolen's inheritance depends on whether she has produced an heir, as well as the responses of Mr. Gascoigne and Sir Hugo, whose first concern after learning of Grandcourt's death is whether Gwendolen is pregnant. Sir Hugo is also pleased that with Grandcourt's death he has become "master of his estates, able to leave them to his daughters, or at least—according to a view of inheritance which had just been strongly impressed on Deronda's imagination—to take makeshift feminine offspring as intermediate to a satisfactory heir in a grandson" (789).

fore them in complete shape, making a coercive type; the event they hunger for or dread rises into vision with a seed-like growth, feeding itself fast on unnumbered impressions" (527). This leads into the first internalized account of Mordecai, whose yearning for someone who will carry on his beliefs and purposes after his own approaching death has taken such a visionary form. "The yearning, which had panted upward from out of overwhelming discouragements, had grown into a hope—the hope into a constant belief, which, instead of being checked by the clear conception he had of his hastening decline, took rather the intensity of expectant faith in a prophecy which has only brief space to get fulfilled in" (528). His second sight focuses on an increasingly distinct image of the one who will become his "expanded, prolonged self," and even of the moment when he will appear: "He habitually thought of the Being answering to his need as one distantly approaching or turning his back toward him, darkly painted against a golden sky," a scene he associates with Blackfriars bridge at sunset (530).

Eliot's sympathetic exposition forms an analepsis that allows us to understand Mordecai's anxious, intense interest in Deronda. "It was Deronda now who was seen in the often painful night-watches, when we are all liable to be held with the clutch of a single thought—whose figure, never with its back turned, was seen in moments of soothed reverie or soothed dozing, painted on that golden sky which was the doubly blessed symbol of advancing day and of advancing rest" (537). Everything in Eliot's account that prompts psychological insight here, however, does not give us the foresight to expect that his vision will be so precisely realized at their next meeting, when Deronda rows from Chelsea to Blackfriars bridge and encounters Mordecai there at sunset. For Mordecai, "feeling in that moment that his inward prophecy was fulfilled," this confirms all his expectations. "Obstacles, incongruities, all melted in the sense of completion with which his soul was flooded by this outward satisfaction of his longing. . . . The prefigured friend had come from the golden background, and had signalled to him: this actually was: the rest was to be" (550). For Deronda, who knows nothing of Mordecai's hopes and "could not but believe that this strangely-disclosed relation was founded on an illusion," it is a critical test of his "receptiveness . . . a rare and massive power" (553).[8] For the reader, however, the corroboration of Mordecai's second sight seems to endow him with preternatural authority. As in the experiences of

---

[8] The notion of receptiveness as a kind of power offers striking reflections of and for the reader. On the one hand, it declares the text's need for our sympathetic response to realize its potential; on the other it dissimulates the text's manipulative designs on us and disarms resistance—precisely at a point where skeptical resistance is likely.

Leonora and Gwendolen, images here become actual as Mordecai too sees his wish outside himself, and it may be that everything that follows will also bear out his prefigurative visions.

As with Miss Wade's prophetic utterance on destiny in *Little Dorrit*, the sense that a character has some privileged knowledge of what is yet to happen poses questions of narrative conventions and form. It suggests a shift between levels in which the character assumes the position of an extra-diegetic narrator or author who knows or determines the course of events. Opening up from the midst of a narrative the possibility of grasping it as a completed whole, such intimations can replace the contingencies and choices through which the story uncertainly advances with the assurance of a predestined pattern it must follow, an irresistible force it must obey. Mordecai seems an unlikely double for the narrator or author, with his marginal position and passionate, idiosyncratic beliefs, but he too is an author and desperately concerned about the destination of his work, as when he tries to get young Jacob Cohen to memorize the words of his poetry. "'The boy will get them engraved within him,' thought Mordecai; 'it is a way of printing. . . . My words may rule him some day. Their meaning may flash out on him. It is so with a nation—after many days'" (533). The desire to rule through the determining force of his thoughts is also at work in the moment when his prophecy is fulfilled by the encounter with Deronda. Eliot attempts to construe his experience in naturalistic terms: "His exultation was not widely different from that of the experimenter, bending over the first stirrings of change that correspond to what in the fervour of concentrated prevision his thought has foreshadowed" (550), but the scene resembles art more than science, figuring within the narrative the intense thought and desire that have created it.[9]

To pursue the reflexive implications of second sight it will help at this point to recall Eliot's earlier and more concentrated fiction of clairvoyance, "The Lifted Veil" (1859). Her only experiment with the Gothic tale (and a *Blackwood's* tale at that, like those Poe had imitated and mocked a generation earlier), it too uses the self-enclosed monologue to scrutinize the logic of narrative. "The time of my end approaches": from its first words Latimer's account of his devastating experience invites reflections on narrative teleology.[10] His affliction with preternatural powers of "foresight" effects

---

[9] On the struggle to reconcile conceptions of science and art by Eliot and several of her contemporaries, see Suzanne Graver, *George Eliot and Community: A Study in Social Theory and Fictional Form* (Berkeley: University of California Press, 1984), pp. 71–79. As Graver notes, Eliot's presentation of Deronda's destiny as a synthesis of the real and the ideal can be seen as an instance of this effort.

[10] George Eliot, *The Lifted Veil* (Penguin: Harmondsworth, 1985), p. 1. If we consider this

the sort of metalepsis we have sensed in Mordecai's prophetic visions, just as his powers of "insight" endow him with the knowledge of others' thoughts that is reserved to authorial narrators in more realistic fictions. Several commentators, in trying to account for Eliot's apparently aberrant departure from her usual realist mode, have proposed her autobiographical implication in the figure of the miserable Latimer,[11] but "The Lifted Veil" can also help us recognize how the disturbance of Gothic extremity works in tension with the narrative continuities of realistic probability to develop far-reaching reflections.

Probability underlies Latimer's opening declaration: "I have lately been subject to attacks of *angina pectoris;* and in the ordinary course of things, my physician tells me, I may fairly hope that my life will not be protracted many months" (1). But this prediction based on ordinary expectations is quickly replaced by an extraordinary claim to "true prevision. For I foresee when I shall die, and everything that will happen in my last moments." He goes on to foretell exactly how his fatal heart attack will take place "just a month from this day, on the 20th of September 1850." The end of his narrative fulfills this prophecy: "It is the 20th of September 1850. I know these figures I have just written, as if they were a long familiar inscription. I have seen them on this page in my desk unnumbered times, when the scene of my dying struggle has opened upon me . . ." (66–67, ellipsis in text). The end of the story, already written at the beginning of the narrative, is left for us to infer.

"Every story is over before it begins," begins Michael Roemer's extended meditation on "the preclusive form of narrative."[12] Concentrating as he does on the fixity of a story's predestined conclusion and disregarding its open discursive destination produces a skewed figuration, but that is clearly the aspect "The Lifted Veil" confronts. Not only its foregone conclusion but every stage of Latimer's story appears in his account as the operation of a mysterious and implacable fatality that makes him its helpless victim. Hypersensitive and sickly, suffering the "dumb passion" of having "the

---

opening declaration as "spoken" not by a homodiegetic narrator but by the tale itself, we get an effect of explicit self-referentiality like that produced by postmodern metanarratives such as John Barth's "Autobiography: A Self-Recorded Fiction" or "Title," which begins, "Beginning: in the middle, past the middle, nearer three-quarters done, waiting for the end." *Lost in the Funhouse* (New York: Doubleday, 1988), p. 105. While "The Lifted Veil" clearly draws on the conventions of the Gothic tale to reflect on narrative force, it also comes closer than most Gothic reflections to such direct self-reference.

[11] The fullest development of this interpretation appears in Sandra M. Gilbert and Susan Gubar, *The Madwoman in the Attic: The Woman Writer and the Nineteenth-Century Literary Imagination* (New Haven: Yale University Press, 1979), pp. 443–77.

[12] Michael Roemer, *Telling Stories* (Lanham, Md.: Rowman and Littlefield, 1995), p. 3.

poet's sensibility without his voice," he is already enclosed in "a fatal solitude of soul" even before being visited by preternatural knowledge (8–9). He mistakes his first vision of the future for a sign of creative imagination until he discovers his lack of control, and when he also begins to sense the thoughts of others they too are experienced as uncontrollable intrusions. "The vagrant, frivolous ideas and emotions of some uninteresting acquaintance . . . would force themselves on my consciousness like an importunate, ill-played musical instrument, or the loud activity of an imprisoned insect" (19). Elsewhere in Eliot's fiction imagining others' thoughts and feelings offers escape from egoistic isolation, just as anticipating probable consequences is a condition of morally responsible action, but the fatal certainty of Latimer's knowledge enforces his self-confinement and passivity. His "superadded consciousness" becomes

> an intense pain and grief when it seemed to be opening to me the souls of those who were in a close relation to me—when the rational talk, the graceful attentions, the wittily-turned phrases, and the kindly deeds, which used to make the web of their characters, were seen as if thrust asunder by a microscopic vision, that showed all the intermediate frivolities, all the suppressed egoism, all the struggling chaos of puerilities, meanness, vague capricious memories, and indolent makeshift thoughts, from which human words and deeds emerge like leaflets covering a fermenting heap. (19–20)[13]

Just as such disillusioning knowledge estranges him further from others, so his repeatedly confirmed visions of a determined future rob him of hope and even prevent him from attempting to escape his misery in suicide. "I was too completely swayed by the sense that I was in the grasp of unknown forces, to believe in my power of self-release. Towards my own destiny I had become entirely passive" (51).

As in many other first-person Gothic tales, the question of control in "The Lifted Veil" also implicates the reader. Instead of accepting Latimer's account, several have tried to replace it with an alternative version that questions his reliability and assigns him moral responsibility for the fate of which he claims to be the helpless victim.[14] While this kind of struggle to

---

[13] Latimer's distress and repulsion at the messy reality of other minds have usually been taken as evidence of his deficient sympathy and failure to show the concern for others' perspectives that Eliot always urges on her readers. They might instead be seen as showing how the ethical effort of recognizing others is a matter not of knowledge but of narrative construction, imagining a different version of a shared story.

[14] See for example Beryl Gray's afterword: "Preternatural though [Latimer's] gifts are, his spir-

regain control over Gothic disturbance always forms a relevant part of the cultural drama staged by such tales, Eliot's presentation of Latimer poses special problems for an ironic reading that seeks to oppose him to an implied author. Not only does his partial knowledge of the future and others' thoughts resemble the "omniscience" of the authorial narrators in Eliot's other fictions, but the generalizations in which he preserves the bitter fruits of his experience also recall their comprehensive formulations.

> Our sweet illusions are half of them conscious illusions, like effects of colour that we know to be made up of tinsel, broken glass, and rags. (45)

> There is no short cut, no patent tram-road to wisdom: after all the centuries of invention, the soul's path lies through the thorny wilderness which must be still trodden in solitude, with bleeding feet, with sobs for help, as it was trodden by them of old time. (31)[15]

Latimer's repeated modulations from estranged singularity to the "we" of moral wisdom make it hard to keep him distinct from his author. Eliot's own effort to clarify her position produces similar uncertainties. The motto she wrote fourteen years after the tale was published and added as its epi-

---

itual predicament is created through his misinterpretation or misapplication of what is revealed to him" (72–73); "Latimer's prescience reveals only the consequences of his actions, not his predetermined fate" (74).

[15] Compare the criticism in *The Mill on the Floss* (on which Eliot was at work when she wrote "The Lifted Veil") of "men of maxims" who believe in "general rules, thinking that these will lead them to justice by a ready-made patent method." George Eliot, *The Mill on the Floss* (Harmondsworth: Penguin, 1979), p. 628. The most remarkable echo occurs not in one of Latimer's moral generalizations but in his description of sensing others' thoughts: "It was like a preternaturally heightened sense of hearing, making audible to one a roar of sound where others find perfect stillness" (26). Many readers have recognized his anticipation of one of Eliot's most striking and thematically charged images: "If we had a keen vision and feeling of all ordinary human life, it would be like hearing the grass grow and the squirrel's heart beat, and we should die of that roar which lies on the other side of silence." *Middlemarch*, p. 194. Less often observed is the way this passage follows the account of "the dream-like strangeness of [Dorothea's] bridal life," her confused and painful apprehension of Rome, which culminates in a disturbing prolepsis. "Our moods are apt to bring with them images which succeed each other like the magic lantern pictures of a doze; and in certain states of dull forlornness Dorothea all her life continued to see the vastness of St Peter's, the huge bronze canopy, the excited intention in the attitudes and garments of the prophets and evangelists in the mosaics above, and the red drapery which was being hung for Christmas spreading itself everywhere like a disease of the retina" (193–94). The conjunction of nightmarish distortion, fatally heightened perception, and narrative foresight reveals the tension exerted by Gothic extremity (compare Poe's use of intensified hearing in "The Tell-Tale Heart" and "The Fall of the House of Usher") within one of the greatest achievements of nineteenth-century realism. I return to this moment in the conclusion.

graph when it was republished for the first time under her name four years later invokes the values of solidarity and the natural.

> Give me no light, great Heaven, but such as turns
> To energy of human fellowship;
> No powers beyond the growing heritage
> That makes completer manhood.[16]

As an authorial secular prayer these lines seem intended to distance their speaker from Latimer's self-absorption, but we could also imagine Latimer himself addressing such a plea to the "unknown forces" that hold him in their grasp and could recall that the light and powers he has instead received were not solicited. Rather than marking his moral failure, the supplementary epigraph can reinforce our sense of his victimization.

Recognizing the way Latimer's preternatural knowledge figures in the story as an arbitrary curse should lead us beyond the familiar moral problem of egoism and its most obvious narratological corollaries. If "his powers express the determinism and solipsism latent in the act of writing fiction,"[17] those problems are not resolved by the move in Eliot's later fiction from single consciousness to multiplicity, as we shall see when we return to *Daniel Deronda*. Rather, both his powers and his impotence reflect persistent structural conditions of narrative, which his tale figures in its shifting relations of knowledge and desire. Since Latimer's insight and foresight push him into passive withdrawal, he would have no role as an agent nor his story any narrative drive were it not for a crucial blind spot. Of all those with whom he comes in touch, only Bertha Grant remains impenetrable to his insight, and only she can provoke his interest and desire. "About Bertha I was always in a state of uncertainty: I could watch the expression on her face, and speculate on its meaning; I could ask for her opinion with the real interest of ignorance; I could listen for her words and watch for her smile with hope and fear: she had for me the fascination of an unravelled destiny" (21).

"Unravelled" would normally describe a destiny already completed or known rather than one still uncertain or not yet (un)ravelled as Latimer

---

[16] Eliot included a slightly different version of these lines in a letter to her publisher refusing to allow "The Lifted Veil" to be republished yet but affirming the importance of the tale to her. "I care for the idea which it embodies and which justifies its painfulness. A motto which I wrote on it yesterday perhaps is a sufficient indication of that idea." *The George Eliot Letters*, ed. Gordon S. Haight (New Haven: Yale University Press, 1955), 5:380.

[17] Gillian Beer, "Myth and the Single Consciousness: *Middlemarch* and *The Lifted Veil*," in *This Particular Web: Essays on Middlemarch*, ed. Ian Adam (Toronto: University of Toronto Press, 1975), pp. 91–115.

presumably means, but both senses are pertinent.[18] As his "oasis of mystery in the dreary desert of knowledge," Bertha returns Latimer to the position of a typical acting and suffering character, provoking "a passion enormously stimulated, if not produced by [his] ignorance" (26) and drawing him into oedipal rivalry with his older brother, to whom she is engaged.[19] But he also experiences their relation through the perspective usually available only to authorial or retrospective narration in an intense vision of a future moment when they are married and hate each other. "It was a moment of hell. I saw into her pitiless soul—saw its barren worldliness, its scorching hate—and felt it clothe me round like an air I was obliged to breathe" (29). Even this foreknowledge, however, is powerless to destroy his passion: "Such is the madness of the human heart under the influence of its immediate desires [that] I felt a wild hell-braving joy that Bertha was to be mine" (30). He manages to discount his foresight in order to sustain his desire, and with it his story, both dependent on a feigned uncertainty. Latimer's "double consciousness" not only presents the psychological conflict of "insight at war with passion" (32) but registers the double force of narrative, in which open possibility and foreclosure coincide.

Most of Latimer's psychological generalizations arise from his efforts to explain his "hell-braving" infatuation; their inclusive plural formulations seek our recognition of kinship between his exceptional case and our own.[20] As they attempt to normalize his perverse desire for Bertha, however, they also probe the general conditions of narrative desire, in which as readers we are necessarily implicated.[21] The fullest account of those con-

[18] J. Hillis Miller discusses the "double antithetical" sense of "ravel" as a term in which the general problem of narrative endings "is neatly tied up." See *Reading Narrative* (Norman: University of Oklahoma Press, 1998), p. 55.

[19] For a reading of "The Lifted Veil" in terms of its oedipal dynamics, see Terry Eagleton, "Power and Knowledge in 'The Lifted Veil,'" *Literature and History* 9 (1983): 52–61.

[20] "Are you unable to give me your sympathy—you who read this? Are you unable to imagine this double consciousness at work within me, flowing on like two parallel streams which never mingle their waters and blend into a common hue? Yet you must have known something of the presentiments that spring from an insight at war with passion; and my visions were only like presentiments intensified to horror" (31–32).

[21] "Many readings are perverse, implying a split, a cleavage. Just as the child knows its mother has no penis and simultaneously believes she has one (an economy whose profitability Freud has demonstrated), so the reader can keep saying: *I know these are only words, but all the same* . . . (I am moved as though these words were uttering a reality). Of all readings, that of tragedy is the most perverse: I take pleasure in hearing a story told to me *whose end I know*: I know and I don't know: I know perfectly well Oedipus will be unmasked, that Danton will be guillotined, *but all the same* . . . " Roland Barthes, *The Pleasure of the Text,* trans. Richard Miller (New York: Hill and Wang, 1975), pp. 47–48. The translation has been corrected according to Armine Kotin Mortimer, *The Gentlest Law: Roland Barthes's The Pleasure of the Text* (New York: Peter Lang, 1989).

ditions comes as Latimer's desire nears fulfillment and he reflects on the happiness of "these last months in which I retained the delicious illusion of loving Bertha" (43). Retrospective knowledge of impending disillusionment redoubles the force of his clairvoyant prevision and makes him realize the crucial value of uncertainty.

> No matter how empty the adytum, so that the veil be thick enough. So absolute is our soul's need of something hidden and uncertain for the maintenance of that doubt and hope and effort which are the breath of its life, that if the whole future were laid bare to us beyond to-day, the interest of mankind would be bent on the hours that lie between. . . . Conceive the situation of the human mind if all propositions whatsoever were to become self-evident except one, which was to become self-evident at the close of the summer's day. . . . Art and philosophy, literature and science, would fasten like bees on that one proposition which had the honey of probability in it. (43–44)

From the honey of probability we fashion the sweet illusions that sustain life. Realism typically opposes the probable to the fanciful or unlikely, and in Eliot's particular version of realism illusions typically appear as figments of desire, egoistic fantasies that must be outgrown. Here, however, probability is opposed to fatal certainty, and in Latimer's claim that our sweet illusions are half of them conscious illusions we can recognize our own participation in the conscious illusion of fiction, which likewise evinces the need to sustain desire.[22]

The grasp of narrative form may depend on its approaching end, but narrative desire is never simply for the end; it prolongs itself precisely by courting what exceeds its grasp.[23] Latimer's story demonstrates this not only in his infatuation with Bertha but in what follows the attainment of his desire. Death leads to both the fulfillment and the extinction of Latimer's passion. His brother's death, which he fails (or refuses) to foresee, clears the way for him to marry Bertha; his father's prepares for his disillusionment by momentarily lifting him out of his own preoccupations: "Perhaps it was the first day since the beginning of my passion for [Bertha], in which that passion was completely neutralised by the presence of an absorbing feeling

---

[22] On the relations between probability and fictional illusion, see Robert Newsom, *A Likely Story: Probability and Play in Fiction* (New Brunswick: Rutgers University Press, 1988).

[23] Compare the teleology of desire postulated by Peter Brooks: "If the motor of narrative is desire, totalizing, building ever-larger units of meaning, the ultimate determinants of meaning lie *at the end,* and narrative desire is ultimately, inexorably, desire *for* the end." *Reading for the Plot: Design and Intention in Narrative* (New York: Knopf, 1984), p. 52.

of another kind" (48). Briefly released from his self-confinement ("In the first moments when we come away from the presence of death, every other relation to the living is merged, to our feeling, in the great relation of a common nature and a common destiny"), he finds Bertha no longer an enticing mystery. "The terrible moment of complete illumination had come to me, and I saw that the darkness had hidden no landscape from me, but only a blank prosaic wall" (49). Once the veil has been lifted Latimer becomes increasingly estranged from Bertha; having "no desires," he withdraws into passive suffering. His story is threatened with losing all momentum, his narrative with lapsing into uneventful summary. "That course of life which I have indicated in a few sentences filled the space of years. So much misery—so slow and hideous a growth of hatred and sin, may be compressed into a sentence!" (51–52).

What follows is a process of narrative reanimation, culminating in a sensational scene of literal revival. Latimer's withdrawal from others leads to decreased awareness of their thoughts, permitting the reintroduction of mystery, a dark secret, of which he is only vaguely and indifferently aware, between Bertha and her maid, Mrs. Archer. This time the veil is lifted not by clairvoyance but by the magical power of "science" represented by Latimer's only friend, Charles Meunier. Watched eagerly by Bertha, who fears exposure, Mrs. Archer dies of peritonitis, then is briefly revived by Meunier's experimental transfusion and in a "gasping eager voice" reveals her mistress's secret: "You meant to poison your husband" (65). As striking as the Gothic melodrama of this scene is its gratuitous contrivance. It makes little contribution to the plot: Latimer can hardly become more disillusioned with Bertha; he merely separates from her and resumes his passive, lonely misery. The hollow artifice of this sequence as the tale's culminating horror rather works to confirm the absoluteness of narrative's need of something hidden and uncertain.

As Latimer's life and tale near their predestined ends, their hidden and uncertain elements shift from the action to its setting and themselves become more absolute, taking on metaphysical overtones. Isolated and so freed from insight into other minds, Latimer is instead possessed by visions of places, "of strange cities, of sandy plains, of gigantic ruins, of midnight skies with strange bright constellations, of mountain-passes, of grassy nooks flecked with the afternoon sunshine through the boughs: I was in the midst of such scenes, and in all of them one presence seemed to weigh on me in all these mighty shapes—the presence of something unknown and pitiless" (55). After he separates from Bertha, he wanders among these scenes, never staying long in one place. "Once or twice, weary of wandering, I rested in a favourite spot, and my heart went out towards the men and women and children whose faces were becoming familiar to me: but I was driven away again in terror at the approach of my old insight—driven to live continually with the one Unknown Presence revealed and yet hidden by the moving curtain of the earth and sky" (66). Latimer does not link these intimations with traditional religious belief. "Continual suffering had annihilated religious faith within me: to the utterly miserable—the unloving and unloved—there is no religion possible, no worship but a worship of devils" (55). Instead of traditional religious significance, we might find in this ultimate sense of an unknown and pitiless presence the tale's deepest insight into the logic of narrative. To stress the preclusive force of narrative, to insist on the sense in which every story is over before it begins, invites us to worship not devils but fate, to dwell on our abject helplessness before the ultimate power of nature or the gods, of forces utterly indifferent to us and our desires.[24] Latimer's overwhelming sense of being in the grasp of unknown forces unveils the situation of all narrative agents: certain knowledge of their fixed fate threatens to deprive them of agency and us of interest.

But along with this demoralizing awareness, "The Lifted Veil" also offers a sense of narrative as a dialogical transaction, as a message with no fixed destination. Latimer may have exhausted all hope and desire as an agent in his story, but as a narrator he tells it in the hope that it "will perhaps win a little more sympathy from strangers when I am dead, than I ever believed it would obtain from my friends while I was living" (4). Like so many previous Gothic first-person narrators, he is drawn into relation with his audience even as he describes his isolation and singularity: "Are you unable to give me your sympathy—you who read this?" (31–32). More strikingly, the sense of the ultimate figured in the pitiless Unknown Presence also appears in Latimer's vision of his death, where instead of final fixity it displays a surprising dynamism. After anticipating the physical agonies of his last moments, Latimer foresees something more. "Darkness—darkness—no pain—nothing but darkness: but I am passing on and on through the darkness: my thought stays in the darkness, but always with a sense of moving onward . . . " (2, ellipsis in text). This survival of consciousness, recalling some of Poe's more speculative fictions, allows us to revise the tale's account of narrative as the language of destiny: not only closed by its predestined conclusion but also open to a future it cannot foresee as it moves onward through an endless series of readings. The time of his end has already come when we read his first words, but it has also not yet arrived

[24] Thus for Michael Roemer the epitome of "traditional narrative" is found in myth and classical tragedy, with their insistent subordination of human agency to the sacred.

when we reach his last, just as his narrative will never reach a final destination. Though Latimer cannot know it, the darkness through which his thought moves has the same force as the light the tale's epigraph asks for, turning to energy of human fellowship. Not only within the story but in the continuing life it receives from its unseen audience, we recognize the necessary persistence of something unknown.

The motif of second sight in *Daniel Deronda* is much less prominent, but as we have already seen it also links impulses of fear and desire with the sense of a determined future that prompts reflections on narrative form. Instead of the closed circle formed by the beginning and end of "The Lifted Veil," Eliot's last novel stresses the imponderable continuities that make those circumscribing limits necessary fictions. "Men can do nothing without the make-believe of a beginning" (36), begins the epigraph to the first chapter, while the conclusions of both Gwendolen's and Deronda's stories forgo retrospective summaries like those of the "Finale" to *Middlemarch* and leave their futures uncertain.[25] But these formal gestures of openness are themselves open to being read otherwise. The arbitrariness of the beginning becomes retroactively motivated by the double analepsis that retraces the paths that have brought Gwendolen and Deronda to their initial encounter at Leubronn, marking it as a crucial moment that, as we have seen, prefigures their destined relationship. Beginning in medias res here holds out the promise of eventually grasping inclusive narrative configurations.

How we understand the working out of those patterns at the conclusion makes a great difference for our comprehension of the whole novel. The final stages of the double plot pose questions about both the main figures' destinies. After the pivotal intersections at Genoa, book 8, "Fruit and Seed," traces their consequences and the new possibilities they open. In Gwendolen's story, the main compositional problem is negotiating her return from the depths of terror and despair without neutralizing the extremity of her Gothic ordeal. The account of her return from Genoa juxtaposes the comfortably practical discussions among Sir Hugo, Mr. Gascoigne, and her mother about living arrangements and politics with her own secret memories. "Gwendolen sat by like one who had visited the spirit-world and was full to the lips of an unutterable experience that threw a strange unreality over all the talk she was hearing of her own and the world's business" (832). The tension persists in her relation to Deronda,

---

[25] Compare Hans Meyrick on his proposed series of paintings representing the story of Berenice, whose end is unknown: "I break off in the Homeric style. The story is chipped off, so to speak and passes with a ragged edge into nothing" (514).

her "outer conscience" (833), on whom she now depends more than ever. "Deronda felt this woman's destiny hanging on his over a precipice of despair" (835), and where he has before urged the moral value of dread he now tries to guide her back toward resuming domestic life and finding purpose in duty to her family. "Other duties will spring from it. . . . There will be unexpected satisfactions—there will be newly-opening needs—continually coming to carry you on from day to day. You will find your life growing like a plant" (839). Here the prospect of an open future is marked by a reassuring sense of sheltered organic growth, perhaps leading to the destiny of a conventional domestic resolution in her union with Rex Gascoigne.[26]

But these developments also prepare for the shock of her last interview with Deronda, where the long accumulation of dramatic irony produced by the narrative of his emerging identity and mission is violently discharged and Gwendolen is at last forced to realize that he has a destiny leading him far from her personal concerns and limited sphere. Earlier, the narrator has remarked that "it was as far from Gwendolen's conception that Deronda's life could be determined by the historical destiny of the Jews, as that he could rise into the air on a brazen horse, and so vanish from her horizon in the form of a twinkling star" (607), but that is in effect what happens. For Gwendolen, Deronda's impending departure to the East is just such an astonishing disappearance, suddenly confronting her with a scale of action that dwarfs her private cares. "The world seemed getting larger round poor Gwendolen, and she more solitary and helpless in the midst" (875). Her fate is (like) that of being overtaken by historical forces.

There comes a terrible moment to many souls when the great movements of the world, the larger destinies of mankind, which have lain aloof in newspapers and other neglected reading, enter like an earthquake into their own lives. . . . That was the sort of crisis which was at this moment beginning in Gwendolen's small life: she was for the first time feeling the

[26] Henry James shrewdly notes the moves signaling this possibility in "Daniel Deronda: A Conversation":
Theodora. Perhaps some day Gwendolen will marry Rex.
Pulcheria. Pray, who is Rex?
Theodora. Why, Pulcheria, how can you forget?
Pulcheria. Nay, how can I remember? But I recall such a name in the dim antiquity of the first or second book. Yes, and then he is pushed to the front again at the last, just in time not to miss the falling curtain. Gwendolen will certainly not have the audacity to marry any one we know so little about.
George Eliot: The Critical Heritage, ed. David Carroll (New York: Barnes and Noble, 1971), pp. 426–27.

pressure of a vast mysterious movement, for the first time being dislodged from her supremacy in her own world, and getting a sense that her horizon was but a dipping onward of an existence with which her own was revolving. (875–76)

The sense of an open future here is linked with threat and disruption, with dismaying blank uncertainty rather than promise. The final, long-prepared effect Deronda exerts on Gwendolen's development is a humiliating shock that displaces her from the center of her world, and while we may consider this humiliation a necessary preparation for her further growth, it also closes her story with a return to the register of extremity. Instead of restoring her to the daylight of domestic duties and affections after the long nightmare of her descent into a private underworld, this version of Gwendolen's destiny engulfs her in the sublimity of collective crisis.

Deronda is clearly the rhetorical beneficiary of this version. His own account of his hopes for "restoring a political existence to my people, making them a nation again" may be modestly qualified: "At the least, I may awaken a movement in other minds, such as has been awakened in my own" (875).[27] But the terms in which the narrator registers its impact on Gwendolen give his project the aura of world-transforming crises, "when the slow urgency of growing generations turns into the tread of an invading army or the dire clash of civil war," historical cataclysms that seem like eruptions of divine force. "Then it is as if the Invisible Power that has been the object of lip-worship and lip-resignation became visible, according to the imagery of the Hebrew poet, making the flames his chariot and riding on the wings of the wind, till the mountains smoke and the plains shudder under the rolling fiery visitation" (875).

These are the sublime, prophetic tones associated with Mordecai, and our understanding of Deronda's destiny depends to a large extent on whether we take it as the fulfillment of Mordecai's vision. Here the grasp of narrative form in the assurance or uncertainty we sense in the novel's conclusion directly relates formal features to ideological implications, just as Deronda's story links personal to political destinies. Mordecai's passionate injunction to "revive the organic centre: let the unity of Israel which has made the growth and form of its religion be an outward reality" (592), his conviction that "the vision is there; it will be fulfilled" (598), and that, as he tells Deronda, "when my long-wandering soul is liberated from this

[27] Barbara Hardy notes that these words "are not in the manuscript, and were presumably added in proof in order to make Daniel's statement and his political destiny sound more tentative and realistic." Note to the Penguin edition, p. 903.

weary body, it will join yours, and its work will be perfected" (600) all project a future beyond the novel's conclusion in which his dream is realized.[28] In this version, prophetic foresight meshes with a narrative teleology that assures political success, as Deronda's life is not only determined by but becomes in turn the means of fulfilling the historical destiny of the Jews.

The perfection of Mordecai's work, Deronda's mission of "restoring or perfecting [the] common life" of the Jews (792), may lie beyond the ending of *Daniel Deronda*, but the ending itself has already granted Deronda "the very best of human possibilities—the blending of a complete personal love with a larger duty" (685). As the motifs of perfection and completion join ideal values with narrative consummation, we can sense the force of desire that makes the conclusion a wish fulfillment not only for Mordecai but for Deronda, "enjoying one of those rare moments when our yearnings and our acts can be completely one, and the real we behold is our ideal good" (817)—and also, as "our" and "we" indicate, for their implied author and reader as well. The terror and guilt of Gwendolen's seeing her wish outside herself is replaced here by the joyful completion of realized dreams in which outward and inward, public and private, collective and individual destinies merge. These dreams are the antithesis of Gothic nightmares, but such rare and privileged moments risk the same kind of reductive reading we found haunting *Little Dorrit*, the collapse of broad social representation into private fantasy, and we can consider Gwendolen, punished for her self-enclosed egoism and overwhelmed by the vast mysterious movement of history, as a sacrifice to Deronda's public mission, a destiny that absorbs him completely in the dream world the novel has prepared for him just as she is emerging from hers.

But even considered as fantasy the conclusion links the personal with the political. The sacrificial figure who most clearly indicates the ideological stakes here is not Gwendolen but the one with which we began, the delinquent mother who is summoned before the bar of history to give her account and make her indispensable contribution to the fulfillment of Deronda's destiny. In the context of that destiny's emerging form and the commentary that invests it with larger significance, Leonora's fate, the haunting apparitions that drive her to confession, become not just private experiences but the effects of an impersonal necessity. She realizes that in spite of all her rebellious efforts to realize her own destiny, "I have after all been the instrument my father wanted" (726), and Deronda, abandoning his usual efforts to enter into others' experience, endorses her forced submission.

---

[28] Concluding with Mordecai's death seems to invite this reading: his soul joins Daniel's, who will now perfect the work Mordecai could envision but not accomplish.

The effects prepared by generations are likely to triumph over a contrivance which would bend them all to the satisfaction of self. Your will was strong, but my grandfather's trust which you accepted and did not fulfill—what you call his yoke—is the expression of something stronger, with deeper, farther-spreading roots, knit into the foundations of sacredness for all men. You renounced me—you still banish me—as a son. . . . But that stronger Something has determined that I shall be all the more the grandson whom you willed to annihilate. (727)

Asserting his identity as grandson confirms his mother's role as makeshift link, while the invocation of a mysterious sanctified agency determining both their lives surrounds the artifice of Eliot's plot with the aura of a providential design.

This pivotal conjunction of fate and destiny, in which the parent's defeat again leads to the child's fulfillment, is also the point of Eliot's deepest autobiographical implication. In Leonora's thwarted apostasy we can recognize a repetition and reversal of the young Mary Ann Evans's "Holy War" with her father that broke out when she refused to accompany him any longer to church (Mary Ann[e] Evans, Marian Evans, Marian Lewes, George Eliot: it is not only the Jews who are always changing their names).[29] Her subsequent intellectual and imaginative life continually renegotiated the truce concluding that war, elaborating forms of secularized spirituality of which Deronda's proto-Zionist mission is the last and most remarkable. Invoking the support of a mystical Something risks abandoning the secular in the effort to restore spirituality, just as appearing to credit Mordecai with powers of second sight risks linking Deronda's political project with organicist notions of racial inheritance and destiny.[30] Eliot

---

[29] See Gordon S. Haight, *George Eliot: A Biography* (Oxford: Oxford University Press, 1968), pp. 39–44.

[30] Deronda, in accounting for the process by which he has been brought to "full consent" to his Jewish identity, proposes a version of his story to Mordecai that draws heavily on the inheritance of acquired characteristics. "It is through your inspiration that I have discerned what may be my life's task. It is you who have given shape to what, I believe, was an inherited yearning—the effect of brooding, passionate thought in many ancestors—thoughts that seem to have been intensely present in my grandfather. Suppose the stolen offspring of some mountain tribe brought up in a city of the plain, or one with an inherited genius for painting, and born blind—the ancestral life would lie within them as a dim longing for unknown objects and sensations, and the spell-bound habit of their inherited frames would be like a cunningly-wrought musical instrument, never played on, but quivering throughout in uneasy mysterious moanings of its intricate structure that, under the right touch, gives music. Something like that, I think, has been my experience" (819). Eliot had already told such a story of recovered racial inheritance in *The Spanish Gypsy* (1868), where the musical figure becomes literal. The heroine Fedalma, ignorant of her Gypsy birth, is stirred by some street music to take up a tam-

clearly runs these risks, but she also stages resistance to the coercive force of her wishful narrative teleology. Leonora refuses to accept her fate: "I don't consent. We only consent to what we love. I obey something tyrannic" (693), and she shrewdly interprets Deronda's glad acceptance of his revealed identity in terms of personal desire: "You are in love with a Jewess" (725). When she learns that Mirah too has not been brought up as a practicing Jew, she observes, "Ah! like you. She is attached to the Judaism she knows nothing of," and when Deronda tells her that though Mirah is also a singer she has no independent ambitions she adds, "Why, she is made for you then" (729). The irony is not just Leonora's but becomes part of the novel's repeated acknowledgment of its biased designs.[31]

If this resistance exists only to be overcome, if its effect is only to confirm the irresistible force of destiny, then Deronda's story remains governed by an assured outcome such as Mordecai foresees. If, however, it serves as a distancing reflection on the make-believe of an ending, then our grasp of the novel's form, and its grasp on us, become much less certain.[32] Such an open relation to ends and origins plays an important part in Deronda's own reflections on his identity and mission. When Joseph Kalonymos delivers the patrimonial chest of papers, he asks, "You will call yourself a Jew and profess the faith of your fathers?"

---

bourine and dance: it's in her blood. The poem anticipates several other features of *Daniel Deronda*, including the project of establishing a Gypsy homeland in Africa, though there racial loyalties and national aspirations lead to tragedy. See Bernard Semmel, *George Eliot and the Politics of National Inheritance* (New York: Oxford University Press, 1994), pp. 108–17.

[31] A much fuller voicing of such irony appears in Hans Meyrick's letter, inserted between Deronda's two interviews with his mother, which, as Cynthia Chase has shown, exposes the double logic by which Deronda's identity is both freely chosen and determined in advance by narrative requirements. See "The Decomposition of the Elephants: Double-Reading *Daniel Deronda*," *PMLA* 93 (1978): 215–25. Eliot even occasionally admits some qualifying irony in her narrator's comments, as in these on Deronda, eager to see Mirah and Mordecai as soon as he returns to London. "The strongest tendencies of his nature were rushing in one current— the fervent affectionateness which made him delight in meeting the wishes of beings near to him, and the imaginative need of some far-reaching relation to make the horizon of his immediate, daily acts. It has to be admitted that in this classical, romantic, world-historic position of his, bringing as it were from its hiding place his hereditary armour, he wore—but so, one must suppose, did the most ancient heroes whether Semitic or Japhetic—the summer costume of his contemporaries" (815).

[32] Uneasiness with the element of arbitrariness in narrative endings goes back to the beginnings of Eliot's career as a writer of fiction. Responding to Blackwood's advice in 1857 about "the danger of huddling up my stories," she observes, "Conclusions are the weak point of most authors, but some of the fault lies in the very nature of a conclusion, which is at best a negation." *Letters,* 2:324. On "the persistence of the narratable even in its closure" in *Middlemarch,* see D. A. Miller, *Narrative and Its Discontents: Problems of Closure in the Traditional Novel* (Princeton: Princeton University Preess, 1981), pp. 107–94.

"I shall call myself a Jew," said Deronda deliberately. . . . "But I will not say that I shall profess to believe exactly as my fathers have believed. Our fathers themselves changed the horizon of their belief and learned of other races. But I think I can maintain my grandfather's notion of separateness with communication. I hold that my first duty is to my own people, and if there is anything to be done towards restoring or perfecting their common life, I shall make that my vocation."

It happened to Deronda at that moment, as it has often happened to others, that the need for speech made an epoch in resolve. His respect for the questioner would not let him decline to answer, and by the necessity to answer he found out the truth for himself. (792)

To call oneself a Jew, in this version, is not to claim an unchanging essential identity but to enter into a dialogue with the past and present while exploring future possibilities, just as to find out the truth is not to discover a preexisting reality but to create one in the process of articulation. In such moments we get a very different version of Deronda's story from the closed circuit of prophecy and fulfillment that Mordecai proclaims.[33]

Like the novel's other oppositions, these alternative versions disclose their own internal differences. The Jewish and English plots, often opposed as romance and realism, both set the extremity of preternatural Gothic or visionary elements against the more commonplace and probable; Mordecai's mystical faith in a predetermined destiny is set against Deronda's sense of the gradual action of ordinary causes.[34] But as we have just seen, Deronda also alternates between a tentative, open exploration of what his discovered identity may mean or lead to and invocations of a stronger Something or racial memories that have shaped his life. We can consider these ideological tensions as effects of Eliot's struggles to conserve values formerly grounded in traditional communities and religious beliefs, as unresolved conflicts in the incomplete (and perhaps uncompletable) work of secularizing spirituality, but we can also recognize how closely these ten-

---

[33] Amanda Anderson makes a strong case for distinguishing Deronda's dialogical sense of separateness with communication from Mordecai's monological convictions, though she also acknowledges the novel's unresolved tensions between a conception of constructed racial or national identities and an impulse to invest them with organicist mystification. See "George Eliot and the Jewish Question," *Yale Journal of Criticism* 10 (1997): 39–61.

[34] For example, as Deronda considers how to respond to Mordecai's conviction that they have been brought together by destiny, he reminds himself, "What I can be to him, or he to me, may not at all depend on his persuasion about the way we came together. To me the way seems made up of plainly discernible links" (573). "To show the gradual action of ordinary causes rather than exceptional" is how Eliot described her realistic "design" in *Middlemarch*. See *Letters*, 5:168.

sions are bound up with the logic of narrative closure. As in Eliot's more concentrated reflections on teleology in "The Lifted Veil," the closed forms of fate and destiny in *Daniel Deronda* take on qualities of the sacred. Whether through the punitive actions that bear so heavily on Leonora and Gwendolen or through the sequences that contrive to reward Deronda, whether through visitations of terror or the fulfillment of desire, the sense of an inevitable or assured ending seems to offer a guarantee of meaning like that provided by religious faith.

It is all the more remarkable that even as it presses toward such assurance the novel invites us to recognize the contrivances it requires and to sense their coercive force. In allowing the possibility of competing versions of its story, *Daniel Deronda* opens itself to the dialogical response of readings it cannot control or foresee, like Daniel Deronda himself in his more open, dialogical relations with others and with the historical destiny of the Jews. Instead of imagining community as a restored organic unity, this version of narrative force enacts it in the ongoing interplay of differences that animates every reading. As in *Little Dorrit,* Eliot's narrative figures its open, discursive dimension in the uncertain destination of writing, the texts of Mordecai and Daniel Charisi. That we learn little of their contents can be taken as a way of leaving undecided the question of what Deronda will make of them and they of him. As the novel ends, these transmitted writings have yet to arrive.

9

James

Near the end of his life, Henry James wrote a note to the painter Sir William Blake Richmond, whose wife had died after being hit by a motorcar in London. "How can I 'write' to you under this cruelest & most unspeakable of calamities, & yet how can I be silent? . . . To have been what she was, with that flawless distinction, all the years, with this black atrocity *waiting*, makes one ask what is the sense of life?" As David Plante observes, "that he should have thought of the accident, 'this black atrocity,' as *waiting* echoed all down his fiction."[1] A little over a year earlier, in a more well-known letter, James had expressed his horror at the outbreak of the First World War in similar terms. "The plunge of civilization into this abyss of blood and darkness . . . is a thing that so gives away the whole long age during which we had supposed the world to be with whatever abatement gradually bettering, that to have to take it all now for what the treacherous years were all the while really making for *meaning* is too tragic for my words."[2] Both the private and the public catastrophes are construed through a dark narrative teleology that retrospectively organizes events and imposes a meaning that threatens the sense of life, the sense of flawless distinction or gradual bettering, now violently displaced by the waiting atrocity, swallowed in the dark abyss. James's imagination of disaster here is a sense of fate as hidden final cause, not the haunting past that pursues Dickens's protagonists or the destiny that summons Eliot's but an unforeseen, devastating revelation of meaning, a story whose form is grasped too late.

[1] David Plante, "The Secret Life of Henry James," *New Yorker,* November 28, 1994, p. 92. James's letter was written November 23, 1915.
[2] Letter to Howard Sturgis, August 4–5, 1914, in *The Letters of Henry James,* ed. Percy Lubbock (New York: Scribner's, 1920), 2:384.

Of course, James's fiction also offers many instances of those other versions, just as summoning destinies figure importantly in Dickens and pursuing fates in Eliot, but focusing on the force of a delayed and devastating grasp of narrative form will allow us to see most readily how James extends the developments we have been following. James draws on and transforms the work of several of his nineteenth-century predecessors with a critical self-consciousness that makes him an appropriate destination for our study of Gothic reflections, just as he provided a point of departure. From its own starting point "The Turn of the Screw" offered an exemplary display of such self-consciousness that allowed us to understand Gothic as a reflection on narrative force, and we could now add to it several other of James's shorter fictions that develop both the reflexive possibilities of the Gothic tale and its role as an alternative to the realist novel. But after our readings of Dickens and Eliot, it will be more revealing to consider how the language of destiny also works more widely in his fiction.

Most of James's novels and tales confine their stories to more realistic social representation, yet the hallmark of his later style is a discourse whose elaborate figuration of his characters' consciousnesses infiltrates the narrative with phantasmal apparitions like those we have found haunting the novels of Dickens and Eliot.[3] At the same time, the figural and syntactic elaborations of James's later style evince a very different relation to his audience than those Dickens and Eliot enjoyed, making demands and offering rewards that enforce a widening separation between popular and high art. In tracing Gothic reflections in Dickens and Eliot we encountered critical points where the perspective shifts, the imaginative movement from isolation to community reverses, and their broad social representations threaten to collapse into solipsistic private dramas. In the later James, that inward turn seems to have already happened, and his characters' subjective adventures all seem destined finally to become reflections of his own imaginative activity. This reflexivity is a familiar aspect of his fiction, foregrounded in the general reflections of his critical prefaces and elaborated in the narrative theory that builds on them in stressing point of view and the compositional role of a central "consciousness . . . subject to fine intensification and wide enlargement."[4] In the tension between this expansive awareness and the fatal enclosure of a waiting doom, between a desired

---

[3] For a survey of James's career that traces the implications of such themes and effects, see T. J. Lustig, *Henry James and the Ghostly* (Cambridge: Cambridge University Press, 1994). Lustig registers the echoes of several precursors that haunt James's texts, though he is more concerned with Hawthorne than with Dickens and Eliot.

[4] Preface to *The Princess Casamassima*, in *The Art of the Novel: Critical Prefaces*, ed. R. P. Blackmur (New York: Scribner's, 1934), p. 67.

and a feared coherence, we can find the strongest links between James and earlier nineteenth-century Gothic.

To trace those links as far as possible, and to show how James's drama of consciousness is illuminated by characteristically Gothic reflections on narrative force, I want to focus on two texts that prominently thematize the dynamics of fate and destiny. "The Beast in the Jungle" and *The Ambassadors,* a naturalistic but uncanny tale and a realist novel of manners published in the same year, both reflect on narrative teleology through stories whose form is grasped too late.[5] Without introducing the preternatural, and while, like *The Ambassadors,* keeping to a tightly focalized third- rather than first-person narration, "The Beast in the Jungle" manages to produce the disturbing claustrophobic effect of Gothic self-enclosure. John Marcher lives with the hidden sense that he is marked for some extraordinary fate, whose anticipation makes him "a haunted man."[6] As his sole confidante, May Bartram, reminds him, "You said you had from your earliest time, as the deepest thing within you, the sense of being kept for something rare and strange, possibly prodigious and terrible, that was sooner or later to happen to you, that you had in your bones the foreboding and the conviction of, and that would perhaps overwhelm you" (503). By emptying this version of fate of any specific content, the tale pushes its logic toward formal abstraction: in place of the preternatural knowledge that forecloses "The Lifted Veil," we have only Marcher's obsessive sense of something awaiting him that will "suddenly break out in my life; possibly destroying all further consciousness, possibly annihilating me; possibly, on the other hand only altering everything, striking at the root of all my world and leaving me to the consequences, however they shape themselves" (503–4). As a result, his story becomes an extreme demonstration of the teleological imagination at work, with its sense of an inevitable awaiting ending whose force determines the meaning of everything that precedes it.

The force of that extreme emphasis also puts pressure on the notions of narrative beginnings and middles, of event and agency. May's initial account of Marcher's secret foreboding and conviction recalls his unique disclosure to her ten years earlier: the tale and their relation can begin only by already having begun through this recovered memory whose loss or re-

---

[5] Although *The Ambassadors* was written earlier (1901–2), it was published in 1903, the same year as "The Beast in the Jungle," written in 1902.

[6] Henry James, "The Beast in the Jungle," in *Complete Stories 1898–1910* (New York: Library of America, 1996), p. 508. Marcher's anticipation also makes him, like so many previous obsessive Gothic protagonists, an isolated figure who hides what he takes to be his true self. "He wore a mask painted with the social simper, out of which there looked eyes of an expression not in the least matching the other features" (510–11).

pression by Marcher is quite as remarkable as its abstraction.[7] As the make-believe of a beginning, this recollection fulfills his wish for a reason to consider her as "an old friend. . . . He would have liked to invent something, get her to make-believe with him that some passage of a romantic or a critical kind *had* originally occurred" (500). Offering a revised version of the past, it also already exerts the effect of retrospectively "altering everything" to be produced by his waiting fate. "He had thought of himself so long as abominably alone, and lo he wasn't alone a bit. He hadn't been, it appeared, for an hour—since those moments on the Sorrento boat. It was *she* who had been . . . she who had been made so by the graceless fact of his lapse of fidelity" (503). The basic elements that will compose the story are already in place at the outset: the absence, suppression, or deferral of "a romantic or a critical passage" between them and the make-believe sustained by her unreciprocated fidelity as they wait together for whatever is to come.

The development of those elements can hardly take the form of a sequence of actions: Marcher's fate, he explains, "isn't something I'm to *do*" but "to wait for—to have to meet, to face" (503). As the singular, decisive event of his life, it strips him of agency and leaves him nothing to do except speculate with May about the form it may take. Their long vigil is given theatrically dramatic form by a series of scenes that typically close with May delivering an emphatic curtain line: "I'll watch with you" (505), "You'll never find out" (515), "What *was* to" (527). As these lines suggest, the tensions that animate the drama arise from asymmetries of understanding: the narrative remains confined to Marcher's baffled point of view while May, who has begun by remembering what he has forgotten, seems to discover and withhold knowledge of his fate. In their last scene together, she speaks from the edge of the grave of "the thing that we began in our youth to watch for" as already past: "You've nothing to wait for more. It *has* come" (529), once again dislocating the temporality of the narrative by placing its anticipated end somewhere in the middle. "This . . . is the *other* side," she declares. "Before, you see, it was always to *come*. That kept it present" (530–31). After her death, Marcher is left to try to understand what has happened, "to win back by an effort of thought the lost stuff of consciousness" (534), but it is only the shock of an accidental encounter at her grave with a grief-ravaged stranger that at last makes him grasp the horrifyingly empty form of his life. "The fate he had been marked for he had

[7] The memory is recovered for the narrative but not, apparently, for Marcher, who requires May to report what he told her and who even then gives no sign of actually remembering his earlier confidence. As a simulacrum, a repetition of a lost origin, the opening offers another version of the necessary make-believe of a beginning, stressing not its arbitrariness but its undecidable location.

met with a vengeance—he had emptied the cup to the lees; he had been the man of his time, *the* man, to whom nothing on earth was to have happened" (540).

Marcher's belated recognition is doubled by the reader's, giving a sharp new sense to the tale as a story in which "nothing happens."[8] In both the ethical and the narratological registers, the equivocation has been at work throughout: the uneventfulness of the story that culminates in Marcher's self-condemnation for his failure to act, to commit himself in love, is registered in a narrative whose most striking events are discursive. When, for example, Marcher is obsessively, fruitlessly trying to "win back" awareness of what has happened, "the lost stuff of consciousness became thus for him as a strayed or stolen child to an unappeasable father; he hunted it up and down very much as if he were knocking at doors and enquiring of the police" (534). The figure represents him as much more actively and purposefully engaged than he ever is in the literal action of the story, and the comparison, poignant in itself, becomes excruciating in its incongruity between the torment of an anguished parent and his actual deficient feeling for May in both life and death.

The most elaborate figurative transformation of "nothing" into event develops the imagery of the title, which first enters the narrative in the account of Marcher's rationalizations for not committing himself to May in marriage. "Something or other lay in wait for him, amid the twists and the turns of the months and the years, like a crouching beast in the jungle. It signified little whether the crouching beast were destined to slay him or to be slain. The definite point was the inevitable spring of the creature; and the definite lesson from that was that a man of feeling didn't cause himself to be accompanied by a lady on a tiger-hunt. Such was the image under which he had ended by figuring his life" (508–9). The image of the tiger hunt, with its self-dramatizing aura of imperial adventure, allows Marcher to figure his selfish, passive existence as a heroic quest. After May's death, the figure is extended to his desolate sense of loss, not of her but of the "distinction" conferred by the fate that, as she has told him, no longer lies in wait, "now that the Jungle had been threshed to vacancy and the Beast had stolen away. . . . What it presently came to in truth was that poor Marcher waded through his beaten grass, where no life stirred, where no breath sounded, where no evil eye seemed to gleam from a possible lair, very much

[8] This equivocal sense of nothingness also figures in earlier exchanges between May and Marcher. "You know something I don't," Marcher says. "You've shown me that before." "I've shown you, my dear, nothing" (524). "Don't you know—now?" she asks. "I know nothing" (527).

as if vaguely looking for the Beast, and still more as if acutely missing it" (533–34). What Marcher and the narrative have come to "in truth" is a point where the figurative and the literal converge.[9] At the end, when he finally realizes the full horror of his failure, he struggles to hold onto the pain of his long-delayed knowledge.

> That, at least, belated and bitter, had something of the taste of life. But the bitterness suddenly sickened him, and it was as if, horribly, he saw, in the truth, in the cruelty of his image, what had been appointed and done. He saw the Jungle of his life and saw the lurking Beast; then, while he looked, perceived it, as by a stir of the air, rise, huge and hideous, for the leap that was to settle him. His eyes darkened—it was close; and, instinctively turning, in his hallucination, to avoid it, he flung himself, face down, on the tomb. (541)

The hallucination is shared. In the most Gothic moment of this phantasmal tale of terror, the figure, index of imaginative transformation and the constitutive power of language, becomes the climactic event.

Yet the hallucinatory power of the conclusion is at odds with its import. As a narratological fable, "The Beast in the Jungle" appears to show the vitiating effect of imagining one's life as a story whose meaning will be determined by its outcome, of conceiving the meaning of stories as determined by their endings: waiting for some extraordinary fate to befall him, Marcher fails to live. But to read the tale this way we have to credit the authority of Marcher's final revelation, which is to accept the determining power of the end. And indeed we have been drawn into such a reading whenever we sense the irony that exposes Marcher's self-deceptions. When he tells himself that "a man of feeling didn't cause himself to be accompanied by a lady on a tiger-hunt," we can easily recognize that in drawing on her sympathetic interest while giving nothing in return he is indeed taking May along on his trip to nowhere, and that considering himself as a man of feeling, like reassuring himself that because he remembers her birthday "he hadn't sunk into real selfishness" (512), is an act of bad faith whose transparency anticipates the harsh light of the narrative's ultimate exposure. Marcher's final realization that "she had loved him for himself; whereas he had never thought of her (ah how it hugely glared at him!) but

---

[9] Compare the earlier figure for Marcher and May's renewed relationship after they have recovered the memory of their previous encounter. "That recovery . . . had served its purpose well, had given them quite enough; so they were, to Marcher's sense, no longer hovering about the headwaters of their stream but had felt their boat pushed sharply off and down the current. They were *literally* afloat together" (506, emphasis added).

in the chill of his egotism and the light of her use" (540) is the goal toward which all those ironic perceptions have been pointing, the truth that lies in wait at the end.

Reading "The Beast in the Jungle" this way is to treat it as a kind of mystery story, following the linear logic of Barthes's hermeneutic code in which enigmas are posed, elaborated, and ultimately solved so that everything fits together. But James's tale does not cohere so completely, and its mysteries continue to resist solution by the pat formulations offered at the end. The trick answer to the riddle of Marcher's life, "he had been the man of his time, *the* man, to whom nothing on earth was to have happened," has the cleverness of the ironic fulfillment of an oracle, but it hardly answers all the questions raised by his story. What it means for something or nothing to happen is, as we have already seen, a problem that this striking phrase brings clearly into focus but cannot solve. Marcher's sense of a missed alternative to his fate is even more problematic: "The escape would have been to love her, *then* he would have lived" (540). To consider loving May as an act he has failed to perform, a choice he might have made, is quite as mystifying as any of Marcher's earlier rationalizations. It makes sense only if we suppose that desire is voluntary, replacing the fatalism of a predetermined end with a fantastically exaggerated conception of agency. It may be Marcher's fate—and hers as well—that he cannot love May, but it can hardly be his fault.[10]

The tension between the extremes of an inevitable disastrous fate and the freedom that makes Marcher responsible for his empty life is dramatized in the tale's central scene. Fearing that May believes he has been mistaken, Marcher asks for reassurance.

> "I *haven't* lived with a vain imagination, in the most besotted illusion? I haven't waited but to see the door shut in my face?"
>
> She shook her head again. "However the case stands *that* isn't the truth. Whatever the reality, it *is* a reality. The door isn't shut. The door's open," said May Bartram.
>
> "Then something's to come?"
>
> She waited once again, always with her cold sweet eyes on him. "It's

---

[10] The problem of imposing affective norms is brought out quite sharply by Eve Kosofsky Sedgwick's "The Beast in the Closet: James and the Writing of Homosexual Panic," in *Sex, Politics, and Science in the Nineteenth-Century Novel*, ed. Ruth Bernard Yeazell (Baltimore: Johns Hopkins University Press, 1986), pp. 148–86. Arguing that "to the extent that Marcher's secret has *a* content, that content is homosexual" (169), Sedgwick can expose in the claim that Marcher should have loved May the premise of "compulsory heterosexuality" and its attempt to regulate desire.

never too late." She had, with her gliding step, diminished the distance between them, and she stood nearer to him, close to him, a minute, as if still full of the unspoken. (526)

At the end, as Marcher condemns himself for his failure to respond to her in time, he remembers this moment.

> Her spoken words came back to him—the chain stretched and stretched. The Beast had lurked indeed, and the Beast, at its hour, had sprung; it had sprung in that twilight of the cold April when, pale, ill, wasted, but all beautiful, and perhaps even then recoverable, she had risen from her chair to stand before him and let him imaginably guess. It had sprung as he didn't guess; it had sprung as she hopelessly turned from him, and the mark, by the time he left her, had fallen where it *was* to fall. He had justified his fear and achieved his fate; he had failed, with the last exactitude, of all he was to fail of. (540)

Between "never too late" and "too late" falls the spring of the beast, making it a punctual event. That is also how May represents it when Marcher questions her in their last interview. "'You mean that it has come as a positive definite occurrence, with a name and a date?' 'Positive. Definite. I don't know about the "name," but oh with a date!'" (529). Yet the beast also springs, or is about to spring, in the tale's final lines, and if it is Marcher's fate to be the man to whom nothing was to have happened, that can hardly take the form of a singular event. The "nothing" that "happens" consists in a lack, a continuing refusal of passion and its risks that never happens consciously and of which Marcher's apprehension of an extraordinary fate is both the fearful symptom and the defense. James presents this case as a stylized sequence of scenes without dramatic incident, an elaborately figured narrative of inner life without awareness, so that the final shattering recognition comes not as a culmination but as a violent intervention. The end reveals the truth, the meaning of the whole, yet it also rings hollow. Like the more extended investigations of fate and destiny in *Little Dorrit* and *Daniel Deronda,* "The Beast in the Jungle" offers a demonstration of both the compelling force and the arbitrary artifice of narrative form.

In its displacement of action from story to discourse, however, it also offers more. At the end of the essay in which he exposes the "confusion" or "fallacy" that enables narrative to function as the language of destiny, Barthes presents an alternative to considering it as the representation of a causally connected series of events. "'What takes place' in a narrative is from the referential (reality) point of view literally *nothing;* 'what happens' is language alone, the adventure of language, the unceasing celebration of its coming."[11] Whatever the general merits of this claim, it does help to explain the uncanny effects we have observed in "The Beast in the Jungle." Barthes sets up a strong evaluative opposition between the deceptive and constraining forces of narrative consequence and closure and the open processes, the unceasing celebration of language. The tension between these aspects in James's tale is more complex and unstable: "The Beast in the Jungle" depends on the drive of a narrative teleology whose power it ultimately questions; it invests its verbal energies in figuring an inner drama of consciousness that repeatedly fails. (Even the devastating recognition of the closing lines cannot be sustained, as Marcher turns to avoid it and flings himself on the tomb.) Yet even (Barthes might say especially) in this ironic mode where "nothing happens," subjective adventures reflected in the adventure of language offer an alternative to the enclosing language of destiny. Instead of Barthes's generalized opposition between "language" and narrative representation, however, we can recognize here a version of the recurrent nineteenth-century opposition between the extremity and reflexivity of the Gothic tale and the more realistic mode of the novel.

It would not be difficult to add other examples of the Gothic in James, uncanny tales like "The Altar of the Dead" or "The Jolly Corner" where haunting obsessions project alternative versions of the past and future that all reflect back on the imaginative activity that produced them.[12] But it is much more revealing to see how many of the themes and effects that find heightened expression in such tales reappear in the highly nuanced social and psychological representation of his novels, how phantasmal or monstrous figures move from Gothic darkness into the light of common day. The narrative forces of *Little Dorrit* and *Daniel Deronda*—secrecy and the return of the repressed past, prophecy and the convergence of separate destinies—have readily recognizable Gothic sources. *The Ambassadors,* with its cosmopolitan scene, stylized comedy, and unassuming, sociable, middle-aged protagonist, seems far removed from the Gothic, yet it shares with Dickens's and Eliot's novels the organizing themes and dynamics of fate and destiny, and like "The Beast in the Jungle" it is shaped by knowledge that comes too late and haunted by an anxious sense of failure to live fully. *The Ambassadors* may well carry us at last far beyond the boundaries of the Gothic, but in recognizing not only the Gothic affinities of these elements

---

[11] Roland Barthes, "Introduction to the Structural Analysis of Narratives," in *Image, Music, Text,* trans. Stephen Heath (New York: Hill and Wang, 1977), p. 124.

[12] "The Jolly Corner" (1908), in which Spencer Brydon confronts the spectral double who figures the self he might have become, is self-consciously *about* alternative versions.

but their characteristic role in producing narrative reflections we have a further opportunity to see how their distinctive effects can work within and be reworked by realism.

Unlike its companion tale, where recognition is entirely deferred to a violent conclusion, *The Ambassadors* takes a moment of recognition as its compositional starting point and deploys a long series of perceptions to advance and retard its development, but the sense of belatedness haunts them all. "It's too late," Strether tells Bilham, in the outburst that, as we know from James's preface, was the original "germ" from which the novel grew and that is strategically planted in its middle.

> And it's as if the train had fairly waited at the station for me without my having had the gumption to know it was there. Now I hear its faint receding whistle miles and miles down the line. What one loses one loses; make no mistake about that. The affair—I mean the affair of life—couldn't, no doubt, have been different for me; for it's at the best a tin mould, either fluted and embossed, with ornamental excrescences, or else smooth and dreadfully plain, into which, a helpless jelly, one's consciousness is poured—so that one "takes" the form, as the great cook says, and is more or less compactly held by it: one lives as one can. Still, one has the illusion of freedom; therefore don't be, like me, without the memory of that illusion.[13]

Strether's sense of fate as a constraining form imposed on the passive helpless jelly of consciousness makes freedom an illusion. The aesthetically enriched life would seem as completely determined as the dreadfully plain, yet he also urges his young friend to profit by his mistake and "live all you can." A possible destiny that escapes the mold of circumstance remains open here, not just for Bilham but for Strether as well.

Contemplating the empty expanse of his past, Strether feels his "acceptance of fate was all he had to show at fifty-five" (115), yet he also wonders whether all his losses—his dead wife and son, his various failed enterprises—may not have left him open to new possibilities, "whether, since there had been fundamentally so little question of his keeping anything, the fate after all decreed for him hadn't been only to *be* kept. Kept for something, in that event, that he didn't pretend, didn't possibly dare as yet to divine" (116). The retrospective vantage offered by James's account of working out the implications of his germinal anecdote allows us to recognize more clearly that the scene at Gloriani's garden party forms the des-

[13] Henry James, *The Ambassadors* (Harmondsworth: Penguin, 1986), p. 215.

tination for all the preceding narrative through the first five books. From the moment of his arrival as Mrs. Newsome's ambassador, charged with bringing her prodigal son Chad back to Woollett, Strether's experience of Europe has been calculated to make him sense how much his life has lacked, and as he comes to feel he has failed to live fully, the question for both him and his author is whether it is too late. "*Would* there yet perhaps be time for reparation?—reparation, that is, for the injury done his character . . . ? The answer to which is that he now at all events *sees;* so that the business of my tale and the march of my action, not to say the precious moral of everything, is just my demonstration of this process of vision."[14]

Strether's vision depends, of course, on "the light of Paris," in which, as Miss Barrace says, "one sees what things resemble," but he anxiously wonders whether it also shows them "for what they really are" (207). His intensely appreciative response to its sensory appeal and refinement, like his subsequent appreciation of Chad's newly acquired polish and Madame de Vionnet's charm that disturbs the simplistic moral sense he brings from Woollett, is repeatedly figured in visual terms that join attraction with confusion. "It hung before him this morning, the vast bright Babylon, like some huge iridescent object, a jewel brilliant and hard, in which parts were not to be discriminated nor differences comfortably marked. It twinkled and trembled and melted together, and what seemed all surface one moment seemed all depth the next" (118).

As Strether's process of vision unfolds through all its moments of perplexity and enlightenment, the question of its possible destination sometimes yields to a sense that the process itself may be the reparation for which he believes it is too late.[15] Such a shift of perspective would replot Strether's story. Determined neither by the fate of his past deprivation nor by the destiny of where he may eventually "come out," its meaning and value would lie in the richness of his impressions, the intensity of his moments of vision: not the fruit of his experience but the experience itself would be the end.[16]

---

[14] *Art of the Novel,* p. 308.

[15] "Didn't you adjure me," Little Bilham asks Strether, "to see, while I've a chance, everything I can?" (262). The substitution of "see" for "live" suggests that Strether's imaginative perceptions enable him to live intensely. The suggestion is weakened, however, by the way this altered recollection helps Bilham to evade Strether's questions about Chad's relation with Madame de Vionnet, so that Strether again feels "the brush of his sense of moving in a maze of mystic closed allusions" (262).

[16] "Every moment some form grows perfect in hand or face; some tone on the hills or on the sea is choicer than the rest; some mood of passion or insight or intellectual excitement is irresistibly real and attractive to us,—for that moment only. Not the fruit of experience, but experience itself is the end." Walter Pater, "Conclusion," *The Renaissance* (Cleveland: Meridian, 1961), p. 222. For a discussion of the relation of *The Ambassadors* to Pater's aestheticism,

The novel clearly invites us to entertain this view, to recognize with Strether "that a man might have—at all events such a man as he—an amount of experience out of any proportion to his adventures" (222), but though an exemplary Jamesian man of imagination he is hardly a Paterian aesthete.[17] His aesthetic receptivity is in continually renewed tension with his need to see things as they really are, a need that drives the narrative forward, generating a momentum that denies perfection to any of its moments and gives a distinctive turn to the question of belated vision. The tension we found in "The Beast in the Jungle" between the thrust of narrative teleology and the arresting interest of discursive figuration, between moment and movement, reappears here within the representation of Strether's process of vision.

Strether's main perceptual problem, of course, is determining the nature of Chad's relation to Madame de Vionnet, understanding the sense in which it is a "virtuous attachment" and why if Chad is now so "good" he is not "free."[18] From the standpoint of narrative reflections, it is notable how the moments in this effort when Strether experiences an immediate and compelling perception of what he takes to be the truth are repeatedly marked with signs of illusion and self-deception, while his more complex and lasting perceptions are never punctual events but distributed over time.

Immediately after Strether's exhortation to Bilham, for instance, he turns toward the figure of the celebrated sculptor Gloriani, who represents "the 'great world.'" Watching him in conversation with the equally worldly Duchess, Strether senses "something in the great world covertly tigerish, which came to him across the lawn and in the charming air as a waft from the jungle" (216). He can for a moment admire and envy "the glossy male tiger, magnificently marked," but the imaginative attraction of such amoral sexual power conflicts directly with the morality of Woollett, preparing him to turn the next moment toward an image of innocence.

---

and a reading of the novel in terms of its intense moments of vision, see Leon Chai, *Aestheticism: The Religion of Art in Post-Romantic Literature* (New York: Columbia University Press, 1990), pp. 111–39.

[17] James's preface recalls how Strether gave him the welcome "opportunity to 'do' a man of imagination." *Art of the Novel*, p. 310. On the issue of imagination in relation to the general Jamesian opposition of "the romantic" and "the real," see Charles Feidelson, "James and 'The Man of Imagination,'" in *Literary Theory and Structure,* ed. Frank Brady, John Palmer, and Martin Price (New Haven: Yale University Press, 1973), pp. 331–52.

[18] See especially Strether's bafflement when Little Bilham explains that Chad "wants to be free. He isn't used, you see . . . to being so good." "Why isn't he free if he's good?" Strether asks, to which Bilham responds with an ingenious evasion, later classified as "a technical lie": "Because it's a virtuous attachment" (186–87). James's comedy of manners often plays on the ambiguity produced in exchanges between Strether and Chad, Bilham, or Maria Gostrey by the overlap of incompatible cultural codes in such deceptively simple shared terms.

A young girl in a white dress and a softly plumed white hat had suddenly come into view, and what was presently clear was that her course was toward them. What was clearer still was that the handsome young man at her side was Chad Newsome, and what was clearest of all was that she was therefore Mademoiselle de Vionnet, that she was unmistakeably pretty— bright gentle shy happy wonderful—and that Chad now, with a consummate calculation of effect, was about to present her to his old friend's vision. What was clearest of all indeed was something much more than this, something at the single stroke of which—and wasn't it simply juxtaposition?—all vagueness vanished. It was the click of a spring—he saw the truth. (217)

The subjectivized visual effect of this image coming into focus, as if seen through Strether's pince-nez, and the tactful irony of James's indirect discourse make it clear enough to the reader that instead of suddenly seeing the truth Strether is grasping at an interpretation that will reconcile the conflict between his aesthetic appreciation and his moral qualms: Chad's attachment must be to the daughter rather than the mother and its virtuousness thus unambiguous. A parallel to this misrecognition occurs four chapters later when Strether encounters Madame de Vionnet in Notre Dame. Again, she appears first as an anonymous figure seated in a chapel; again she becomes a romanticized image. "She reminded our friend—since it was the way of nine tenths of his current impressions to act as recalls of things imagined—of some fine firm concentrated heroine of an old story" (273). And again, once identified, she becomes the beneficiary of a sanguine interpretation. "Unassailably innocent was a relation that could make one of the parties to it so carry herself. If it wasn't innocent why did she haunt the churches?—into which, given the woman he could believe he made out, she would never have come to flaunt an insolence of guilt" (276).

Unlike these hasty, wishful narrative constructions, formed in response to appealing visual impressions, Strether's deeper, more unsettling perceptions take time to develop. The process is repeatedly noted in the account of his response to Chad's first appearance. So changed that Strether fails to recognize him, Chad bewilders him with his civilized ease and maturity, presenting "a case of transformation unsurpassed" (154). The narrative stresses the way Strether returns to this moment in his reflections. "Our friend was to go over it afterwards again and again . . ." (153). "He was to know afterwards, in the watches of the night . . ." (155). The stylistic signature of these passages, like several more that follow, is the note of anticipated recall. The full import of Strether's impressions is not immediately present but develops only in his subsequent reflections, yet the narrative registers those recollections within the account of his initial experience as their subjective destination. Significance is marked by, and depends on, the way "he was to know afterwards"; the scene dilates to include Strether's deferred interpretations, presented as only a sampling, which also work to defer narrating the first moment of direct exchange with Chad. "If we should go into all that occupied our friend in the watches of the night we should have to mend our pen; but an instance or two may mark for us the vividness with which he could remember" (156). When he and Chad are at last alone and he has the chance to perform his embassy ("I've come, you know, to make you break with everything, neither more nor less, and take you straight home" [163]), Chad's response is contained in a tellingly convoluted piece of Jamesian syntax. "'Do I strike you as improved?' Strether was to recall that Chad had at this point inquired" (164). Direct speech and experience are embedded in their foreseen memory.

The "*anticipation of retrospection,*" Peter Brooks proposes, is "the master trope" of narrative logic. Such anticipation is usually tacit: whether or not we envision how a narrative sequence will turn out, "we read in a spirit of confidence, and also a state of dependence, that what remains to be read will restructure the provisional meanings of the already read."[19] By making this anticipation explicit, inscribing the logic of narrative in the turns of his syntax, James opens a perspective in which belated vision sheds the pathos of "too late," in which subsequent reflections coincide with the events that prompt them. In Gothic terms, these moments are haunted by the ghost of the future. Impossible in actual experience, such effects seem to offer a promise of aesthetic autonomy and fulfillment that would repair the failures and losses that have previously defined the meaning of Strether's life. Just as the first half of the novel builds up to Strether's aria of loss at Gloriani's garden party in book 5, the second moves toward a series of charged moments in book 11 where the possibility of reparation emerges most powerfully.

The series begins with a recapitulation of the theme of loss as Strether waits alone late at night for Chad to return, in a scene marked in advance with the sign of anticipated retrospection. "Strether spent an hour in waiting for him—an hour full of strange suggestions, persuasions, recognitions; one of those that he was to recall, at the end of his adventures, as the particular handful that most had counted" (425). He recalls the earlier stages of his Parisian experience, trying and failing to recover the impression that Chad's apartment first made on him, and realizing thereby how he has

[19] Peter Brooks, *Reading for the Plot: Design and Intention in Narrative* (New York: Knopf, 1984), p. 23.

changed in the past three months. The relation of this moment to the recent past is indicated by the formal parallels in which the novel abounds, explicitly noted here through Strether's reflections. "He spent a long time on the balcony; he hung over it as he had seen little Bilham hang the day of his first approach, as he had seen Mamie hang over her own the day little Bilham himself might have seen her from below" (426). But the memorably "strange suggestions, persuasions, recognitions" he ponders in this hour concern a more remote past that becomes a haunting compound of presence and absence.

> He felt, strangely, as sad as if he had come for some wrong, and yet as excited as if he had come for some freedom. But the freedom was what was most in the place and the hour; it was the freedom that most brought him round again to the youth of his own that he had long ago missed. He could have explained little enough to-day either why he had missed it or why, after years and years, he should care that he had; the main truth of the actual appeal of everything was none the less that everything represented the substance of his loss, put it within reach, within touch, made it to a degree it had never been, an affair of the senses. That was what it became for him at this singular time, the youth he had long ago missed—a queer concrete presence, full of mystery, yet full of reality, which he could handle, taste, smell, the deep breathing of which he could positively hear. (426)

It is not some past experience that returns with hallucinatory vividness but something that never existed, "the youth he had long ago missed" that becomes an immediate concrete presence. It can appear only as an imaginary object, yet it carries no sense of delusion like his earlier wishful perceptions of "truth." The result of all he has experienced since he arrived, Strether's reverie represents an intense awareness of loss in utterly private terms, unlike his earlier public exhortation, and instead of voicing a sense of the hard, constraining mold of fate, it flowers from an exciting sense of freedom. This passage is the point where *The Ambassadors* is most palpably touched by uncanny effects like those of the Gothic, but the mysterious apparition it renders is not an alien intruder but a strangely familiar ghost and produces a thrill not of dread but of wonder. Like the hallucinatory presence of the beast as it prepares to spring, it figures the constitutive power of imagination to summon an alternative version, a power shared here by James and his protagonist.[20]

---

[20] Compare the invocations and apparitions of his "good angel," "blest Genius," or "demon of patience" in James's notebooks. "I sit here, after long weeks, at any rate, in front of my ar-

The questions of loss and reparation, belatedness and imagination, aesthetic appreciation and the recognition of truth all culminate in the novel's most famous episode, Strether's day in the country. Released from the strain of his failed embassy, he can pursue a small quest of his own, seeking "the chance of seeing something somewhere that would remind him of a certain small Lambinet that had charmed him, long years before" (452). The picture in the Boston dealer's in Tremont Street that he had been unable to afford clearly represents his past deprivation, and finding or recreating it in the French countryside offers an imaginative recompense that Strether savors fully. "The oblong gilt frame disposed its enclosing lines; the poplars and willows, the reeds and river—a river of which he didn't know, and didn't want to know, the name—fell into a composition, full of felicity, within them; the sky was silver and turquoise and varnish; the village on the left was white and the church on the left was grey; it was all there, in short—it was what he wanted: it was France, it was Tremont Street, it was Lambinet. Moreover he was freely walking about in it" (453). Like cinematic special effects that allow characters to cross the ontological threshold between life and art, Strether's excursion takes him into the painting as his aesthetic appreciation transforms past lack into fulfilled presence. "He really continued in the picture—that being for himself his situation—all the rest of this rambling day," and by the time he reaches the village he has chosen as his destination, "a village that affected him as a thing of whiteness, blueness and crookedness, set in coppery green" (457), his process of vision has intensified to painterly impressionism and active composition: "One had to make one's account with what one lighted on" (458).

This is the point where Strether's imaginative development most closely approaches the artist's power to reshape experience. No longer a passive, helpless jelly formed by the mold of circumstance, his consciousness seems to allow him to recoup his former losses as he freely walks about in the picture he is himself composing. In place of the inevitable belatedness of narrative understanding, his experience is figured not only through the immediacy of visual art but through that of drama. "For this had been all day at bottom the spell of the picture—that it was essentially more than anything else a scene and a stage" (458). Yet there is something missing in this picture, and the stage will soon become the scene of "a sharp fantastic

rears, with an inward accumulation of material of which I feel the wealth, and as to which I can only invoke my familiar demon of patience, who always comes, doesn't he?, when I call. He is here with me in front of this green Pacific—he sits close and I feel his soft breath, which cools and steadies and inspires, on my neck." *The Complete Notebooks of Henry James,* ed. Leon Edel and Lyall H. Powers (New York: Oxford Univeristy Press, 1987), p. 237. For a survey of other instances, see Edel's introduction, pp. xiii–xiv.

crisis" that bursts the enclosing gilt frame. As Strether gazes out at the river from the garden of the inn, "the view had an emptiness" that prepares him to seize on the chance element that completes the composition. "What he saw was exactly the right thing—a boat advancing around the bend and containing a man who held the paddles and a lady, at the stern, with a pink parasol. It was suddenly as if these figures, or something like them, had been wanted in the picture, had been wanted more or less all day, and had now drifted into sight, with the slow current, on purpose to fill up the measure" (461).[21] In a precisely counterpointed repetition and reversal of the pattern of earlier encounters, these figures again appear first as anonymous objects of imaginative appreciation, but the truth that emerges once they are identified is not another piece of wishful self-deception but the reality of Chad and Madame de Vionnet's affair that Strether has been trying to avoid acknowledging. Revealing in its moment of apparent fulfillment the exclusions on which his composition has depended, this recognition forces a shift of perspective in which aesthetic terms become marks of falsity. As all three strive to keep up appearances, "fiction and fable *were,* inevitably, in the air"; Madame de Vionnet's manner seems to him "a performance" that fails to disguise "that there had been simply a *lie* in the charming affair" (465–66), and "it was the quantity of make-believe involved . . . that most disagreed with his spiritual stomach" (468).

These critical perceptions are the product of Strether's later reflections, for after the story has taken this turn James's narrative once again calls, and more extensively than at any other point, on the trope of anticipated retrospection. "He was to reflect later on and in private" (463); "Strether indeed was afterwards to remember"; "Strether was to remember afterwards further" (464). The awkwardness of the encounter permits little immediate reflection. "Why indeed—apart from oddity—the situation should have been really stiff was a question naturally not practical at the moment, and in fact, so far as we are concerned, a question tackled later on and in private, only by Strether himself" (463). As a result, Strether's foreseen reflections become the narrative frame for the rest of the episode. "Since we have spoken of what he was, after his return, to recall and interpret, it may as well immediately be said that his real experience of these few hours put on in that belated vision—for he scarce went to bed till morning—the aspect that is most to our purpose" (465). In the story's sequence of events,

---

[21] Between the sense of suggestive emptiness in the view and the advancing boat that fills it falls a masterfully placed chapter break, marking the boundary of self-contained imaginative pleasure as the action overflows its aesthetic frame. James's adroit disposition of formal features here both demonstrates and questions the power of art to shape experience.

Strether's "real experience" is distinct from "what he was, after his return, to recall and interpret," but in James's narrative discourse they appear together. The significance of what has happened is not immediate, but here it can "immediately be said," so that we get both "his impression" and "the impression, destined only to deepen, to complete itself" (465). Completion here, however, can only be relative. Strether's "belated vision" is "most to our purpose," most closely aligned with the aims and interests of the implied author and reader, because it enacts the open process of revision inherent in narrative, in which meaning is destined to continual change.[22]

As the novel nears its end, that sense of change becomes stronger, producing an increasing tension with the need for completion and closure. Anticipated retrospection can become a figure of reparation, the discursive coincidence of events and their subsequent interpretation making up for what has been missed, but its revisionary logic also works against any final fulfillment. The possibility of continuing reinterpretation becomes clear as Strether ponders the implications of his encounter with Chad and Madame de Vionnet and their pretense that they too have only come out for the day. Set against his sense of how much "the quantity of make-believe involved" has "disagreed with his spiritual stomach" is the fuller understanding of their relationship he derives from their quick coordinated response to the crisis. "He moved, however, from the consideration of that quantity—to say nothing of the consciousness of that organ—back to the other feature of the show, the deep, deep truth of the intimacy revealed." Appreciation of this truth makes him realize how he has avoided acknowledging the reality of their clandestine affair, "the way he had dressed the possibility in vagueness," and as he anticipates discussing it with Maria he imagines her exasperated question, "'What on earth . . . had you then supposed?' He recognized at last that he had really all along been trying to suppose nothing. Verily, verily, his labour had been lost. He found himself supposing innumerable and wonderful things" (468).

Those suppositions lead to revised views of each of the lovers. In his last interview with Madame de Vionnet he recognizes her vulnerability as he contemplates "the passion, mature, abysmal, pitiful she represented, and the possibilities she betrayed. She was older for him to-night, visibly less exempt from the touch of time; but she was as much as ever the finest and

[22] Strether's "belated vision" is also disjoined from literal seeing: as James specifies, it takes place in the dark. Thinking about how they had all "blinked" the truth of the situation, "Strether didn't quite see what else they could have done. Strether didn't quite see *that* even at an hour or two past midnight, even when he had, at his hotel, for a long time, without a light and without undressing, sat back on his bedroom sofa and stared straight before him" (465–66).

subtlest creature, the happiest apparition, it had been given him, in all his years, to meet; and yet he could see her there as vulgarly troubled, in very truth, as a maidservant crying for her young man" (483). As for Chad, whose miraculous transformation had been the strongest reason for Strether's withdrawing his allegiance from Woollett and supporting Madame de Vionnet, "she had made him better, she had made him best, she had made him anything one would; but it came to our friend with supreme queerness that he was none the less only Chad" (482). These revisions, abandoning the romance of his most idealized appreciations and recognizing the compromised realities of passion, prepare for Strether's departure and the novel's conclusion. We can consider his latest perceptions as his arrival at the real after a long romantic detour, but there is no need to consider them as the final destination for Strether's process of vision.[23] His own anticipations of retrospection point further, as when, approaching his last meeting with Madame de Vionnet, "he knew in advance he should look back on the perception actually sharpest with him as on the view of something old, old, old, the oldest thing he had ever personally touched; and he also knew, even while he took his companion in as the feature among features, that memory and fancy couldn't help being enlisted for her" (476). Similarly, when Strether is "to recall, at the end of his adventure," the handful of moments "that most had counted" (425), it must be at some point beyond the diegetic boundaries of the story, and there is no telling just how they will then count. His destination, the end of his adventure, merges with our own ongoing interpretations.[24]

The open, unfinished aspect of narrative implicit in the trope of anticipated retrospection is linked with the possibilities of both release from the determining force of the past and compensation for what it has lacked. As in Barthes's narrative reflections, resistance to social constraints is figured

---

[23] "The real represents to my perception the things we cannot possibly *not* know, sooner or later, in one way or another; it being but one of the accidents of our hampered state, and one of the incidents of their quantity and number, that particular instances have not yet come our way. The romantic stands, on the other hand, for the things that, with all the facilities in the world, all the wealth and all the courage and all the wit and all the adventure, we never *can* directly know; the things that can reach us only through the beautiful circuit and subterfuge of our thought and our desire." James's preface to *The American*, in *Art of the Novel*, pp. 31–32.

[24] The open, affirmative quality of Strether's anticipated retrospections appears in clear contrast to James's use of this trope in "The Beast in the Jungle," where it reinforces the closed fatality of Marcher's belated vision by framing the chance encounter that precipitates his final recognition. "It was a thing of the merest chance—the turn, as he afterwards felt, of a hair, though he was indeed to live to believe that if light hadn't come to him in this particular fashion it would still have come in another. He was to live to believe this, I say, though he was not to live, I may no less definitely mention, to do much else" (364).

in James through undoing irreversible linearity and closure, but here the opposing desire for a formally satisfying conclusion is far more insistent. Much of the novel's last book aims at fulfilling that desire by stressing symmetries between beginning and end. Strether's final interviews with Madame de Vionnet, Chad, and Maria repeat his initial encounters in reverse order, and each invokes the earlier moment. Thus, as Strether and Chad near the end of their last conversation, "they were face to face under the street lamp as they had been on the first night" (504), and Chad justifies his reverting to the financial arguments for his return, which Strether originally advanced and now opposes, "only because it was part of our original discussion. To wind up where we began" (505). The shifting positions of Strether and Chad describe the symmetrical chiasmic pattern that led Forster to call *The Ambassadors* "a book the shape of an hour-glass," an example of rigid stylized form that sacrifices "most of human life . . . in the interests of the pattern," achieving a Pyrrhic victory of the aesthetic. "Beauty has arrived, but in too tyrannous a guise."[25]

Forster's spatial figure invites us too to wind up where we began our discussion of the novel, with Strether's figure of the affair of life as a rigid mold imposed on the helpless jelly of consciousness, its fearful symmetry now figuring the enclosure of narrative form as an implacable fate. In finishing off its symmetrical form, even with all its ornamental excrescences, does *The Ambassadors* return us to that fatalism after all? "What one loses one loses; make no mistake about that" (215): Strether's admonition may serve to recall us from the error of hoping that reparation for past losses was ever really possible, that the aesthetic play of imagination could regain what was missed in the passing moment. The last moments of his story, however, are devoted to reprising just this issue of loss and gain, and as they bring the novel to its conclusion they also pose the question of aesthetic value in new and troubling terms.[26]

Having lost any hope or desire for a reconciliation with Mrs. Newsome and preparing to return to only "a great difference," Strether is presented at the last moment with Maria's offer of herself as recompense.

[25] E. M. Forster, *Aspects of the Novel* (New York: Harcourt, Brace and World, 1927), pp. 153–64.

[26] We can also recognize that the syntax of anticipated retrospection always contains a fatalistic potential: from the vantage of narrative hindsight, the anticipated event may appear to have been predetermined. As might be expected, this aspect is foregrounded in "The Beast in the Jungle," most explicitly at the point where Marcher realizes that May believes what they have waited for has already taken place. "What then has happened?" he asks. "What *was* to" (354).

"There's nothing, you know, I wouldn't do for you."

"Oh yes—I know."

"There's nothing," she repeated, "in all the world."

"I know. I know. But all the same I must go." He had got it at last. "To be right."

"To be right?"

She had echoed it in vague deprecation, but he felt it already clear for her. "That, you see, is my only logic. Not, out of the whole affair, to have got anything for myself."

She thought. "But with your wonderful impressions you'll have got a great deal."

"A great deal"—he agreed. "But nothing like *you*. It's you who would make me wrong!" (512)

Strether's final renunciation transposes the ideal of disinterestedness from the aesthetic to the ethical register, linking the tightness of formal completion with the rightness of not gaining anything for himself. He may retain his "wonderful impressions," the enrichments of consciousness that allow him to take back "a handful of gold-pieces for imagination and memory," but his integrity requires giving up the worldly security that marrying Maria would bring.[27] As material loss becomes the condition for spiritual gain, aesthetic responsiveness, with its dangers of deceptive illusion, gives way to ascetic rectitude.

Reading the novel's final moment this way helps to make clear how James carries on the work of secularizing spirituality we have observed in Dickens and Eliot, and it also makes all the more remarkable the way James himself reads this scene in his preface. There he describes it as "an artful expedient for mere consistency of form," the final and finest instance of his skill in disguising the purely functional role played by Maria Gostrey.[28] James's method of narrative focalization requires the use of confidants; hence, he explains, the opening move of establishing the relation between Strether and Maria "without even the pretext, either, of *her* being [like Waymarsh] Strether's friend. She is the reader's friend much rather . . . and she acts in that capacity, and *really* in that capacity alone, with exemplary

---

[27] In his "Project" for *The Ambassadors*, James describes Strether's situation after reconciliation with Mrs. Newsome has become impossible: "He is out of pocket by it, clearly, materially; but he has a handful of gold-pieces for imagination and memory." *Complete Notebooks*, p. 568. The stress on Strether's material losses marks the opposition between his departure and that of Chad, who seems sure to return before long to take up the lucrative work of advertising the nameless little object manufactured in Woollett.

[28] *Art of the Novel*, p. 324.

devotion, from beginning to end of the book. She is an enrolled, a direct aid to lucidity; she is in fine, to tear off her mask, the most unmitigated and abandoned of *ficelles*" (322). James exposes Maria's mere functionality by playfully substituting an item of French dramaturgical vocabulary in a phrase that would conventionally end with a term of sexual censure. Instead of a respectable appearance masking sexual impropriety, sexuality is the disguise here, with Maria's attraction and devotion to Strether working to keep her formal motivation "artfully dissimulated" through the whole narrative. The last scene, carrying this strategy to completion, becomes in James's account an exemplary instance of "the refinements and ecstasies of method. . . . To project imaginatively, for my hero, a relation that has nothing to do with the matter (the matter of my subject) but has everything to do with the manner (the manner of my presentation of the same) and yet to treat it, at close quarters and for fully economic expression's possible sake, as if it were important and essential—to do that sort of thing and yet muddle nothing may easily become, as one goes, a signally attaching proposition" (324). Accepting James's invitation to share in the pleasure of these refinements, taking up the position of "the form-lover" and assenting to the disjunction of form and content it presupposes, would seem to yield a very different reading from one that dwells on the moral quality of Strether's renunciation, which now becomes an empty appearance serving only "to make Miss Gostrey's false connexion carry itself . . . as a real one" (324). Yet while it is hardly possible to entertain both readings at once, they both offer a sense of vicarious distinction gained by rising above commonplace concerns, whether for material security or for representational content, and both moral and formal integrity are gained at a woman's expense. Whether Maria is Strether's friend or the reader's, she ends up used and discarded.

Thinking of Maria as in another sense the most abandoned of *ficelles*, we might recall the forlorn May Bartram, also considered only in the light of her use, and recall as well the figures of Dickens's Miss Wade and Eliot's Leonora.[29] If Maria seems to confirm Forster's charge that James sacrifices "life" for the sake of patterned form, considering her together with those earlier cases can help us to recognize more specifically narrative issues here, as well as to bring our study of fate and destiny to a provisional conclu-

---

[29] James's figures of abandoned women offer points where we might locate his autobiographical implication, particularly in the case of "The Beast in the Jungle," which is often glossed by reference to his relationship with Constance Fenimore Woolson. See, for example, Leon Edel, *Henry James: The Master* (Philadelphia: Lippincott, 1972), pp. 133–41. As our readings of both that tale and *The Ambassadors* have indicated, however, he is more deeply implicated as the author whose narrative art demands such sacrifices.

sion. Using those terms once more, we could say that it is the fate of each of these characters to be the means for fulfilling another's destiny, whether their subordination is marked by the mix of self-torment and defiance we find in Miss Wade and Leonora or by Maria's self-sacrificing devotion. All embody a certain excess as figures each narrative can neither accommodate nor do without, registering the coercive power of the formal requirements imposed on them and exposing the arbitrariness and limitations of those constraints.[30]

As these narratives reach their destinations, whether with the weddings that conclude *Little Dorrit* and *Daniel Deronda* or the final separation that Maria sighs "all comically, all tragically away" in *The Ambassadors,* these excessive auxiliaries can invite us to question the way each novel achieves its resolution. Like Maria, Miss Wade and Leonora may be the reader's friends in their subjection to the grasp of form, but unlike her they also serve us by voicing the dissidence that sustains reading in its continually re-newed movement beyond any fixed destination. Maria's gracious, wistful acquiescence may mark the distance that separates *The Ambassadors* from the Gothic, like its benign ghosts of the past and future, but it cannot completely dissimulate the sense that not only her fate but Strether's is a necessary acceptance of individual isolation, that the gains of an enriched consciousness cannot really compensate for the loss of human connection and community. In this ghostly echo of a narrative of Gothic confinement, *The Ambassadors* too admits an alternative version that confronts the im-pulse toward formal closure with the endlessly renewable resources of di-alogical exchange.

[30] The problem of a figure that exceeds its function appears clearly in James's comments on Henrietta Stackpole in his preface to *The Portrait of a Lady,* which are linked with those on Maria Gostrey: both are supposedly part of "the form" rather than "the essence. . . . Each of these persons is but wheels to the coach; neither belongs to the body of that vehicle, or is for a moment accommodated with a seat inside." In the earlier case, however, James feels the need to explain "why . . . I have suffered Henrietta (of whom we have indubitably too much) so officiously, so strangely, so almost inexplicably, to pervade." *Art of the Novel,* pp. 53–55.

Conclusion

In spite of all the ways Gothic fiction sets itself against the norms of realism, against the familiar, the natural, or the probable, the complexity and constraints of common personal experience and social life, it is a mistake to think of it as "a horrible wonder apart."[1] As we have seen in Poe and his predecessors as well as in the great nineteenth-century monster stories, Gothic narratives of extreme situations and exceptional figures not only confront those norms, they include and depend on them in exerting their distinctive force. The novels of Dickens, Eliot, and James develop similar tensions by introducing Gothic motifs and effects into their more realistic social and psychological representations. All of them stage dialogues between narrative perspectives, posing in many different ways alternative versions of their stories, and it is those alternatives, arising in early Gothic from the problematic of the preternatural and heightened by the use in nineteenth-century Gothic of first-person narrators, that enable the reflections on narrative force we have traced in writers from Walpole to James.

Reading Gothic fiction reflexively allows us to realize that even as it tells stories of isolated and often aberrant individuals, it repeatedly presents narrative as a social transaction, disclosing the dialogical basis of both narrative and the self. This realization significantly changes our understanding of Gothic, allowing us to locate it within the larger literary and cultural field by recognizing how its interplay of disturbance and control reflects a

---

[1] Compare Dickens on "the criminal intellect, which its own professed students perpetually misread, because they persist in trying to reconcile it with the average intellect of average men, instead of identifying it as a horrible wonder apart." Charles Dickens, *The Mystery of Edwin Drood* (London: Oxford University Press, 1956), p. 225.

concern with the relation of self and society that, even with all their differences, it shares with realism. Such a rapprochement should also change our understanding of realism, and to conclude I want to consider some directions that change might take.

The first would be to reassess the oppositions of norms and extremes or moderation and excess with which nineteenth-century realist fiction repeatedly establishes its truth claims as it "defines itself against the excesses, both stylistic and narrative, of various kinds of romantic, exotic, or sensational literatures."[2] We encountered an instance of this oppositional self-definition near the outset in *Northanger Abbey*.[3] When Catherine Morland is awakened from "the visions of romance," disavows her dark suspicions of General Tilney, and realizes that Radcliffe's fiction may not be a reliable guide to "human nature, at least in the midland counties of England," the effect is to enforce the authority of Austen's realism. The effect changes, however, when, having learned of his deluded mercenary motives for first courting her favor and then angrily sending her away, Catherine feels "that in suspecting General Tilney of either murdering or shutting up his wife, she had scarcely sinned against his character, or magnified his cruelty."[4] Here Gothic extremity is not just dismissed but appropriated: the humor of Catherine's overstated response invites a moderated restatement, through which the General can be recognized as a version of villainy all too probable in the midland counties of England.

This kind of appropriation and moderation is a common realist tactic, enhancing verisimilitude by scaling down the exaggerations of sensational modes like Gothic, but it also produces a perceptible tension. In seeing General Tilney as a middling version of Radcliffe's Montoni, we grant Gothic some validity as we shift our emphasis from disparities to affinities between its lurid nightmares and the waking "anxieties of common life."[5] Such possibilities of shifting stress are already enough to show that internal opposi-

---

[2] George Levine, *The Realistic Imagination: English Fiction from Frankenstein to Lady Chatterley* (Chicago: University of Chicago Press, 1981), p. 5. Levine's choice of *Frankenstein* as his point of departure and his use of it as a metaphorical pattern to describe the realist project make it clear that he does not accept an exclusive opposition between realism and the "excesses" of Gothic. His concern with realism as a representational effort "to use language to get beyond language" (6), however, takes him in a different direction from the questions of narrative form and force I have been pursuing.

[3] See the discussion in the introduction.

[4] Jane Austen, *Northanger Abbey* (Harmondsworth: Penguin, 1972), p. 243. The preceding quoted phrases are on pages 201 and 202.

[5] Austen, *Northanger Abbey*, p. 203. For an account that heavily stresses Gothic affinities not only in Austen but also in Eliot, see Judith Wilt, *Ghosts of the Gothic: Austen, Eliot, and Lawrence* (Princeton: Princeton University Press, 1980).

tions between normality and extremity are as important to the effects of realism as to those of the Gothic. But as long as they simply extend the representational range of realism without challenging its premises, as long as they simply cite the conventions of Gothic setting, characterization, or plotting while attenuating their disturbing force, these shifts do not bring into play the kind of alternative versions and narrative reflections we have traced in nineteenth-century Gothic. To show not only that those effects are possible but that they can play a crucial role in the reflexive articulation of realism, I want to return to an example briefly noted earlier that can represent nineteenth-century realism in its highest ambitions and achievements.[6]

The point where *Middlemarch* returns to Dorothea's story in chapter 20 after an interval of several chapters and six weeks of story time is critical in Eliot's multiple narrative. As Miss Brooke she had been the focus of the opening sequence showing how her naïve idealism and limited opportunities led to her engagement to Casaubon, but since then Eliot has introduced several other characters and centers of narrative interest, including Lydgate and Rosamond, Fred and Mary, Bulstrode, Featherstone, and Farebrother. Now Dorothea has become Mrs. Casaubon, and Eliot's concern is not only to resume her protagonist's story but to give a sense of her experience since her marriage and reestablish the reader's interest and sympathy. Eliot's tactics for accomplishing these aims are remarkably oblique. Dorothea first reappears in chapter 19 only as a figure briefly observed by Will Ladislaw and his friend Naumann, who sees her as a symbolic image and potential subject for his painting, "a sort of Christian Antigone—sensuous force controlled by spiritual passion."[7] The next chapter finds her alone, "sobbing bitterly" (192), but explaining this intense, solitary emotion requires the further indirection of an analeptic review of her experience in Rome that concludes with the scene of her first quarrel with Casaubon earlier that morning.

It is not the scene of domestic conflict that conveys the intensity of Dorothea's subjective state, however, but the preceding synopsis of her confused response to Rome, whose "stupendous fragmentariness heightened the dream-like strangeness of her bridal life" (192). Eliot recalls the reasons why "the weight of unintelligible Rome" should bear so heavily on

---

[6] See chapter 8, n. 15.

[7] George Eliot, *Middlemarch* (Harmondsworth: Penguin, 1994), p. 190. This indirect observation matches the last glimpse we get of Dorothea before her marriage in chapter 10, where she is the object of less aesthetically elevated appreciation by Mr. Standish and Mr. Chichely.

Dorothea, but the stress falls on rendering the quality of her "inward amazement" and its lasting effects.[8]

> Forms both pale and glowing took possession of her young sense, and fixed themselves in her memory even when she was not thinking about them, preparing strange associations which remained through her after-years. Our moods are apt to bring with them images which succeed each other like the magic lantern pictures of a doze; and in certain states of dull forlornness Dorothea all her life continued to see the vastness of St Peter's, the huge bronze canopy, the excited intention in the attitudes and garments of the prophets and evangelists in the mosaics above, and the red drapery which was being hung for Christmas spreading itself everywhere like a disease of the retina. (193–94)

The final image is powerfully disturbing not only in its surreal extremity but in its erasure of the boundary between inside and outside: we cannot tell whether the whole dome of St. Peter's has become a vast diseased eye or whether the spreading red stains arise from the morbid state of the perceiver. Here dreamlike strangeness becomes a nightmare of alienation, producing a Gothic effect without invoking specific Gothic conventions.[9] The more readily recognizable Gothic affinities in *Middlemarch* emerge in the later stages of Bulstrode's story with the return of his repressed past. Eliot's plot contrivances in this sequence have seemed to some readers, like James, inconsistent with her usual realism. "It has a slightly artificial cast, a melodramatic tinge, unfriendly to the richly natural coloring of the

---

[8] Prominent among those reasons is the desire for historical intelligibility that is a recurrent theme in Dorothea's relations with Casaubon. Earlier she has believed his learning would lead her beyond "that toy-box history of the world adapted to young ladies which had made the chief part of her education," opening the prospect of "a binding theory which could bring her own life and doctrine into strict connection with that amazing past, and give the remotest sources of knowledge some bearing on her actions" (86). Their quarrel is also concerned with integrating historical knowledge: it is precipitated when she urges him to "begin to write the book which will make your vast knowledge useful to the world" (200). Unlike Poe (or Auden's version of Poe), Eliot includes "historical existence" in her concern with intense "states of being" (see chapter 1).

[9] We might, however, compare this scenic image with early Gothic uses of setting. Rome and Catholicism may not be as exotic and sinister in Eliot as in Radcliffe, but the impact of "the gigantic broken revelations of that Imperial and Papal city thrust abruptly on the notions of a girl who had been brought up in English and Swiss Puritanism, fed on meagre Protestant histories" (193) plays a large part in Dorothea's painful disorientation. The vastness of St. Peter's contrasts with the usual claustrophobic enclosure of Gothic settings, but it can be seen as a revision of them in which the oppressive ancient structure threatens the self with helpless exposure and loss rather than with suffocating confinement.

whole."[10] But it also shares several features with Dorothea's Roman ordeal, including similes of bodily damage ("memory set smarting like a reopened wound") and an estranging conflation of inside and outside, also rendered in a vivid synopsis.

> Night and day, without interruption save of brief sleep which only wove retrospect and fear into a fantastic present, he felt the scenes of his earlier life coming between him and everything else, as obstinately as when we look through the window from a lighted room, the objects we turn our backs on are still before us, instead of the grass and the trees. The successive events inward and outward were there in one view; though each might be dwelt on in turn, the rest still kept their hold on the consciousness. (615)[11]

There is a wide difference between Bulstrode's guilty fear and Dorothea's depression, but they are alike in the nightmarish intensity that cuts both of them off from others, as well as in the force of an oppressive temporality, the pursuing fate that overtakes Bulstrode or the destined recurrence of "certain states of dull forlornness" that will haunt Dorothea "all her life."

Most notable is the way Eliot takes up Dorothea's isolated state as an occasion for reflecting on the opposition between norms and extremes so important to the conception of realism.

> Not that this inward amazement of Dorothea's was anything very exceptional: many souls in their young nudity are tumbled out among incongruities and left to "find their feet" among them, while their elders go about their business. Nor can I suppose that when Mrs. Casaubon is discovered in a fit of weeping six weeks after her wedding, the situation will be regarded as tragic. Some discouragement, some faintness of heart at the new real future which replaces the imaginary, is not unusual, and we do not expect people to be deeply moved by what is not unusual. That element of tragedy which lies in the very fact of frequency, has not yet wrought itself into the coarse emotion of mankind; and perhaps our frames could hardly bear much of it. If we had a keen vision and feeling of all ordinary human life, it would be like hearing the grass grow and the squirrel's heart beat, and we should die of that roar which lies on the other side

[10] Henry James, unsigned review (1873), in *George Eliot: The Critical Heritage*, ed. David Carroll (New York: Barnes and Noble, 1971), p. 358.

[11] Compare the account of Gwendolen's haunted state in *Daniel Deronda*: "Fantasies moved within her like ghosts, making no break in her acknowledged consciousness and finding no obstruction in it: dark rays doing their work invisibly in the broad light." George Eliot, *Daniel Deronda* (Harmondsworth: Penguin, 1967), p. 669.

of silence. As it is, the quickest of us walk about well wadded with stupidity. (194)

The well-known concluding lines both disparage and reaffirm an aesthetics of extremity. It is only because of our coarse sensibilities, our moral stupidity, that we require the strong stimulation of the exceptional or sensational to be moved. The more discerning, sensitive perception of ordinary human life that realism offers discloses a deeper and more inclusive truth, and yet its disclosure becomes in its own way as extreme and threatening as the darkest Gothic vision.[12] The force of Eliot's rhetoric here reaches beyond her immediate aim of soliciting sympathy for her protagonist to revise the general opposition between the commonplace and the extraordinary, as the clarity of waking consciousness intensifies into the distortions of nightmare. Considering a little further how these tensions work and are worked out in *Middlemarch* will also allow us to reach a tentative conclusion about the more general relation between Gothic and realist modes.

Here, as we have seen in so many previous examples, Gothic is the preferred nineteenth-century mode for dramatizing solitary subjectivity under stress, and here too the dynamics of narrative open up alternative perspectives on the relationship between an isolated consciousness and the social group. The rest of Dorothea's story can be read as a process of bringing her out of the painful isolation she experiences in Rome into communion and effective interaction with others. Part of this plotting is the deferred romance of her relationship with Will Ladislaw, blocked first by her mistaken marriage to Casaubon and then by the injunction of his codicil. Another is the inward struggle of her imaginative development, emerging from the "moral stupidity" in which we all begin, partly through coming to recognize Casaubon's "equivalent centre of self" (211). As Eliot marks the stages of this development, she refers back at one point to Dorothea's experience in Rome, noting how the "scene of old Featherstone's funeral . . . always came back to her at the touch of certain sensitive points in memory, just as the vision of St Peter's at Rome was inwoven with moods of despondency. . . . The dream-like association of something alien and ill-understood with the deepest secrets of her experience seemed to mirror that sense of loneliness which was due to the very ardour of Dorothea's nature." Released for a moment from being "shut up in the library" (a faint echo of a

---

[12] As we saw earlier, the Gothic affinities of this passage are marked by its echo of Latimer's devastating experience in "The Lifted Veil," both in the motif of fatally heightened perception and in its association with a disturbing vision of the future.

Gothic heroine's captivity), she can express her imaginative interest in others. "I am fond of knowing something about the people I live among. . . . One is constantly wondering what sort of lives other people lead, and how they take things" (326).[13] The climax of this development, leading to a more lasting release, comes through a more concentrated, deliberate expression of her concern with how others take things that allows her to resolve her solitary crisis of jealous anger and despair following her discovery of Will and Rosamond together. "Was she alone in that scene? Was it her event only?" (787). Turning from her private pain, struggling to think of those others, she again looks out, feels "the largeness of the world," and realizes that "she was a part of that involuntary, palpitating life, and could neither look out on it from her luxurious shelter as a mere spectator, nor hide her eyes in selfish complaining" (788). Her crucial decision to return to Rosamond not only enacts her moral involvement with others but leads to the personal fulfillment of her union with Will.

In reviewing this sequence, we are tracing part of a well-marked path whose whole course runs from the opening "Prelude" to the closing "Finale" of *Middlemarch*. Like realist appropriations and moderations of Gothic, it reduces heroic aspirations to a domestic scale, replacing the "epic life" demanded by Saint Theresa's "passionate, ideal nature" (3) with "the home epic" (832). The segment we are concerned with, starting from the nightmarish vision of St. Peter's, seems not just to diminish but eventually to reverse the intense isolation and estrangement condensed in that scenic image. But just as the realist dream of achieving a keen vision and feeling of all ordinary human life is inseparable from the threatening fatal roar on the other side of silence, the fulfillment of Dorothea's happy life as a wife and mother is shadowed by regret for her being "absorbed into the life of another" (836). The muted tone of that regret can be seen as another instance of scaling down, and Dorothea's lingering feeling "that there was always something better which she might have done, if she had only been better and known better" (835), is certainly far removed from the misery of her first marriage. Yet in the destiny of being absorbed into the life of another we might also catch a hint of vampirism, a sacrifice that is confirmed by comparison with "the far sadder sacrifice" of those "many Dorotheas" whose lives are evoked as the novel ends (838). These closing qualifications hold open an alternative, darker version of "the Dorothea whose story we know," and the persistence not only of the sense of thwarted desire but of

[13] For a detailed discussion of the interpenetration of the personal and the socio-historical in this scene, see Harry E. Shaw, *Narrating Reality: Austen, Scott, Eliot* (Ithaca: Cornell University Press, 1999), pp. 231–36.

the resulting states of dull forlornness that are foretold in her vision of St. Peter's can suggest a more general understanding of how and why Gothic traces persist in realism.

If Gothic reflections on narrative as a social transaction offset its stories of isolated figures with an insistent awareness of how the self is always constituted in dialogical relations with others, within realist social representations they can remind us of what remains hidden and incommunicable. The dreamlike association of something alien and ill understood with the deepest secrets of Dorothea's experience, like the fantastic mingling of retrospect and fear woven by Bulstrode's guilty secrets, is not just a problem for the narrative to solve, a temporary opacity yielding to its advancing light. We may understand that Dorothea's loneliness is due to the ardor of her nature, that Bulstrode's estrangement is due to his deceptions of himself as well as others, but for the characters their secrets remain untold, untellable, and in their solitary centers of self Eliot's narrative encounters and acknowledges a necessary resistance to its encompassing integration of stories and perspectives. In our earlier readings of Dickens and James, as well as Eliot, we found a comparable tension produced by shifts of perspective in which their inclusive social representations appear as projections of private fantasies. Here it is the privacy of the characters' experience that stands apart from the general narrative movement of disclosure and assimilation, but again we find Gothic elements and effects working to offer alternative versions.[14]

Such Gothic reflections offer one way, though only one among many, of recognizing the unresolved tensions that persist in these novels and qualify the effect of multiple perspectives converging on a shared social reality.[15] As a closing thought, I want to suggest a more distinctive role for Gothic, returning once more to that salient moment in chapter 20 of *Middlemarch*. The whole passage recounting Dorothea's experience of Rome is structured by a rhythm that rises to moments of exceptional intensity ("like a disease of the retina," "that roar which lies on the other side of silence") and then drops back to the quotidian ("Not that this inward amazement of

[14] Compare Gwendolen returning from her Gothic ordeal in *Daniel Deronda* "like one who had visited the spirit-world and was full to the lips of an unutterable experience" (832), a more extreme version of untellable secrets, as well as the secrets in *Little Dorrit* that are still untold at the end.

[15] See my earlier discussion of dialogical tensions between individual and collective perspectives in *The Victorian Multiplot Novel* (New Haven: Yale University Press, 1980). For a contrary view, in which "differences in realism are always concordable, never irreducible," see Elizabeth Ermarth, *Realism and Consensus in the English Novel* (Princeton: Princeton University Press, 1983).

Dorothea's was anything very exceptional," "However, Dorothea was crying"). This alternation between extremity and the ordinary, between dreamlike strangeness and the commonplace, enacts the tensions we have found in both realism and Gothic as it frames Eliot's remarkable reflections on realist representation, tracing a movement that also recalls recurrent Gothic accounts of narrative origins and elaboration. Stories of how *The Castle of Otranto, Frankenstein,* or *Dr. Jekyll and Mr. Hyde* began in dreams are echoed within these and several other Gothic narratives by accounts of dreams and other episodes like the hypnotic sessions in *Dracula* that both evoke the private, unconscious origins of fiction and engage in the social transaction that makes narrative possible. Eliot's efforts to convey her protagonist's disturbing experience can also be seen as one more Gothic reflection on the force that impels narrative and the force it seeks to exert on its readers.

Index

225